Self-Objectification in Women

Self-Objectification in Women

Causes, Consequences, and Counteractions

Edited by Rachel M. Calogero,
Stacey Tantleff-Dunn, and J. Kevin Thompson

American Psychological Association • Washington, DC

Published by
American Psychological Association
750 First Street, NE
Washington, DC 20002
www.apa.org

To order
APA Order Department
P.O. Box 92984
Washington, DC 20090-2984
Tel: (800) 374-2721; Direct: (202) 336-5510
Fax: (202) 336-5502; TDD/TTY: (202) 336-6123
Online: www.apa.org/pubs/books
E-mail: order@apa.org

In the U.K., Europe, Africa, and the Middle East, copies may be ordered from
American Psychological Association
3 Henrietta Street
Covent Garden, London
WC2E 8LU England

Typeset in Goudy by Circle Graphics, Inc., Columbia, MD

Printer: Maple-Vail Books, York, PA
Cover Designer: Mercury Publishing Services, Rockville, MD

The opinions and statements published are the responsibility of the authors, and such opinions and statements do not necessarily represent the policies of the American Psychological Association.

Library of Congress Cataloging-in-Publication Data

Self-objectification in women : causes, consequences, and counteractions / edited by Rachel M. Calogero, Stacey Tantleff-Dunn, and J. Kevin Thompson. — 1st ed.
    p. cm.
  Includes bibliographical references and index.
  ISBN-13: 978-1-4338-0798-5
  ISBN-10: 1-4338-0798-X
  1. Body image in women. 2. Body image disturbance. 3. Self-perception in women.
I. Calogero, Rachel M. II. Tantleff-Dunn, Stacey. III. Thompson, J. Kevin.

  BF697.5.B63S45 2011
  155.3'33—dc22

                                    2010017432

British Library Cataloguing-in-Publication Data

A CIP record is available from the British Library.

Printed in the United States of America
First Edition

For all the women and men working toward the
empowerment of girls and women everywhere.

CONTENTS

CONTRIBUTORS

Casey L. Augustus-Horvath, PhD, Laureate Psychiatric Clinic and Hospital, Tulsa, OK

Rachel M. Calogero, PhD, Virginia Wesleyan College, Norfolk

Stephenie R. Chaudoir, PhD, Bradley University, Peoria, IL

Jamie L. Goldenberg, PhD, University of South Florida, Tampa

Rachel W. Kallen, PhD, University of Cincinnati, Cincinnati, OH

Michael P. Levine, PhD, Kenyon College, Gambier, OH

Nita Mary McKinley, PhD, University of Washington, Tacoma

Jessie E. Menzel, MA, University of South Florida, Tampa

Sarah K. Murnen, PhD, Kenyon College, Gambier, OH

Diane M. Quinn, PhD, University of Connecticut, Storrs

Tomi-Ann Roberts, PhD, Colorado College, Colorado Springs

Linda Smolak, PhD, Kenyon College, Gambier, OH

Stacey Tantleff-Dunn, PhD, University of Central Florida, Orlando

J. Kevin Thompson, PhD, University of South Florida, Tampa

Marika Tiggemann, PhD, Flinders University, Adelaide, South Australia, Australia

Tracy L. Tylka, PhD, The Ohio State University, Columbus

ACKNOWLEDGMENTS

We are very grateful to the contributing authors of this book for investing their time and energy in the preparation of the excellent chapters set out in this volume. Their expertise and insight will surely be instrumental in advancing knowledge in the area of women's objectification. We also thank the American Psychological Association for its interest in showcasing this important area of women's psychology, especially Beth Hatch for her patience, support, and scrutiny of the manuscript—and the two independent reviewers for their constructive and thoughtful feedback. We acknowledge the support of the Economic and Social Research Council Postdoctoral Research Fellowship to Rachel Calogero during the preparation of this volume.

We would also like to extend our thanks to people who were inspirational and supportive to us. Rachel would like to thank her University of Kent colleagues, especially Afroditi Pina, Robbie Sutton, Karen Douglas, Alison Benbow, Tirza Leader, Diane Houston, and Dominic Abrams, for their encouragement and stimulating discussions on the objectification of women. She is appreciative of all her family and friends who supported her throughout the process of preparing this book as she traveled between the United States and the United Kingdom. She is also grateful to Saverio Stranges, for reading parts of the manuscript and for believing in her and the importance of this book.

She gives special thanks to her sister Mary Kay Calogero, mother Mary Calogero, and grandmother Agnes Meyers—three generations of women who have provided the motivation and inspiration for tackling these complex issues that affect so many girls and women.

Stacey would like to thank her family and friends for their never-ending support. She would like to thank her graduate students Sharon Hayes and Danielle Lindner and undergraduate research assistants Danielle Shields and Annie Pierre for their encouragement and participation in spontaneous and lively explorations of the topic of sexual objectification in the context of the empirical literature as well as everyday life. Stacey wishes to give special thanks to her two daughters, Nickie and Cassidy, whose joyful spirits and love provide all the inspiration anyone could ever need. Stacey can only hope that this book contributes in some small way to a better tomorrow for her girls and women everywhere.

Kevin would like to thank his wife Veronica, daughter Carly, and son Jared for their encouragement and support. He also thanks former and current members of the Body Image Research Group for their inspirational work ethic and important contributions to the field of body image. He also thanks the American Psychological Association for its support of this book and other projects. In particular, he would like to offer great thanks to Susan Reynolds, whose initial interest and support of the concept of this book made its eventual publication possible.

I

INTRODUCTION AND ASSESSMENT

1

OBJECTIFICATION THEORY:
AN INTRODUCTION

RACHEL M. CALOGERO, STACEY TANTLEFF-DUNN,
AND J. KEVIN THOMPSON

Taught from infancy that beauty is women's sceptre, the mind shapes itself to the body, and roaming round its gilt cage, only seeks to adorn its prison.

—Mary Wollstonecraft (1792, p. 90)

Men act and women appear. Men look at women. Women watch themselves being looked at. This determines not only most relations between men and women but also the relation of women to themselves. The surveyor of woman in herself is male: the surveyed female. Thus she turns herself into an object—and most particularly an object of vision: a sight.

—John Berger (1972, p. 41)

It is a fine spring day, and with an utter lack of self-consciousness, I am bouncing down the street. Suddenly I hear men's voices. Catcalls and whistles fill the air. These noises are clearly sexual in intent and they are meant for me; they come from across the street. I freeze. As Sartre would say, I have been petrified by the gaze of the Other. My face flushes and my motions become stiff and self-conscious. The body which only a moment before I inhabited with such ease now floods my consciousness. I have been made into an object. While it is true that for these men I am nothing but, let us say, a "nice piece of ass," there is more involved in this encounter than their mere fragmented perception of me. They could, after all, have enjoyed me in silence . . . I could have passed by without having been turned to stone. But I must be *made* to know that I am a "nice piece of ass": I must be made to see myself as they see me.

—Sandra Lee Bartky (1990, p. 27)

Westernized societies tend to objectify people in general, often treating people as if they are things or commodities. Yet, because Westernized societies are saturated with heterosexuality, whereby gender acts as a pervasive organizer of culture, objectification is most often apparent within heterosexual relations (Henley, 1977; Horney, 1937; Lerner, 1983). Women are defined, evaluated, and treated more often as objects than men are. In particular, it is the viewing of women as *sex objects*, as instruments for the sexual servicing and pleasure of men, that is perhaps the phenomenon most familiar to scholars and laypersons alike. Although observations on the sexual objectification, or *sexualization*, of women are hardly new (Bartky, 1990; de Beauvoir, 1952/1989; Gardner, 1980; Henley, 1977; Jeffreys, 2005; Mulvey, 1975; Orbach, 1993), the development of a formal theoretical framework and measurement tools has stimulated more systematic empirical study on the objectification of women over the past decade. This book integrates recent developments and current knowledge on the objectification of women from the perspective of objectification theory (Fredrickson & Roberts, 1997) and makes a call to action for future scholars to help guide theory, research, and social practice in this critical area.

Specifically, we focus on *self-objectification* in women. We clarify concepts and propositions, delineate open questions, and summarize current knowledge for scholars and students interested in the topic of self-objectification and in the psychology of women more broadly. Although the coverage of the topic in this volume is wide, we recognize that it is still a limited treatment of such a complex phenomenon. Much remains to be illuminated about why and how self-objectification in women persists and the implications for individual women, men, and society. We hope that this book will foster lively and constructive exchange among scholars across disciplines about the causes and consequences of self-objectification for girls' and women's daily lives, and the imperative for developing counteractions.

This introductory chapter provides an overview of the key conceptual phenomena that frame the study of self-objectification. We begin by defining and describing the sexual objectification of women, a widespread cultural practice that is generally regarded as the primary environmental antecedent driving self-objectification. Drawing heavily from prior scholarship on women's self-objectification, we then offer a broad conceptualization of what it means to self-objectify and how it structures women's self-body relations. An overview of Fredrickson and Roberts's (1997) objectification theory framework follows, which summarizes the main theoretical propositions and implications of self-objectification for women's lived experiences. Relying on empirical research, we submit that self-objectification meets the criteria for a harmful cultural practice that inhibits the full development of individual girls and women, underscoring the urgency for more scholarship in this area. We close with an overview of how the rest of the book is organized.

SEXUAL OBJECTIFICATION

To *objectify* is to make into and treat something that is not an object as an object or as having an objective reality (Merriam-Webster Dictionary OnLine; http://www.merriam-webster.com). According to Jean Baker Miller (1986), "When one is an object, not a subject, all of one's own physical and sexual impulses and interests are presumed not to exist independently. They are to be brought into existence only by and for others—controlled, defined, and used" (p. 60). Philosopher Martha Nussbaum (1995) proposed that objectification involves at least seven ways of treating the other person:

1. as a tool for one's own purposes (instrumentality),
2. as lacking in autonomy and self-determination (denial of autonomy),
3. as lacking in agency and activity (inertness),
4. as interchangeable with others of the same or different types (fungibility),
5. as permissible to break, smash, or break into (violability),
6. as something that is owned by another (ownership), and/or
7. as something whose experience and feelings do not need to be considered (denial of subjectivity).

These qualities represent common attitudes toward the treatment of objects or things. Whether any one of these qualities is sufficient to represent the objectification of a person remains an open question for scholars to answer. What is agreed from a feminist account of objectification is that to treat human beings in any of these seven ways is to objectify them. Thus, to be objectified means to be made into and treated as an object that can be used, manipulated, controlled, and known through its physical properties.

Women are targeted for sexually objectifying treatment in their day-to-day lives more often than men (Argyle & Williams, 1969; Bartky, 1990; Eck, 2003; Gardner, 1980; Goffman, 1979; Henley, 1977; Koss, Gidycz, & Wisniewski, 1987; Krassas, Blauwkamp, & Wesselink, 2003; Macmillan, Nierobisz, & Welsh, 2000; McKinley & Hyde, 1996; Piran & Cormier, 2005; Plous & Neptune, 1997; Puwar, 2004; Reichert, 2003; Swim, Hyers, Cohen, & Ferguson, 2001; Thompson, Heinberg, Altabe, & Tantleff-Dunn, 1999). Although the notion of sexual objectification is complex, Bartky (1990) offered some clarification with the following characterization:

> A person is sexually objectified when her sexual parts or sexual functions are separated out from the rest of her personality and reduced to the status of mere instruments or else regarded as if they were capable of representing her. (p. 26)

This fragmentation of women into a collection of sexual parts manifests in different ways, ranging in degrees of force from sexual violence to sexualized gazing and visual inspection, largely not under women's control and in such a way as to reinforce the subordinate status of women in relation to men (Brownmiller, 1975; Henley, 1977; Kaschak, 1992; Rudman & Borgida, 1995; Saguy, Quinn, Dovidio, & Pratto, 2010; World Health Organization, 2005).

Sexual objectification plays out most obviously in two areas: actual interpersonal or social encounters (e.g., catcalls, "checking out" or gazing at women's bodies, sexual comments, harassment) and exposure to visual media that spotlight women's bodies and body parts, depicting them as the target of a nonreciprocated male gaze. Interpersonal encounters of sexual objectification can include interactions with familiar others (e.g., family, friends, colleagues, employers, acquaintances) or with strangers and begin at a very young age. Samples of American youth have indicated that elementary and middle school age girls are more frequently targets and suffer more devastating effects of sexual harassment than boys (Bryant, 1993; Murnen & Smolak, 2000; Murnen, Smolak, Mills, & Good, 2003). According to research supported by the American Association of University Women, adolescent girls were nearly 5 times more likely than boys to be afraid at school and 3 times less confident after experiences of sexual harassment (Bryant, 1993). Moreover, one third of the girls did not want to attend school, and nearly one third did not want to speak up in class because of the sexual harassment. In adult samples, women report significantly more explicit sexual objectification than men, including sexually degrading jokes, being sexually harassed, being called sexual names, having body parts leered at or ogled, and being the victim of unwanted sexual advances (Gardner, 1980; Hill & Fischer, 2008; Klonoff & Landrine, 1995; Kozee, Tylka, Augustus-Horvath, & Denchik, 2007; Macmillan et al., 2000; Moradi, Dirks, & Matteson, 2005; Swim et al., 2001).

Encounters with media that depict sexually objectified images of women are virtually impossible to avoid or ignore (American Psychological Association, 2007; Busby & Leichty, 1993; Grogan & Wainwright, 1996; Harper & Tiggemann, 2008; Peter & Valkenburg, 2007; Reichert & Carpenter, 2004; Ward & Friedman, 2006). As evident from the endless variety of ways in which women's bodies are sexually objectified in mainstream media, it is not merely sexual gazing but actual violence against women that is also eroticized and rendered normative in these portrayals—as Wolf (1991) described it, "beauty sadomasochism." Images of scantily clad and partially nude women commonly appear in contorted positions, bent over or positioned on all fours, physically bound, or physically threatened and/or restrained by men (or groups of men) to sell everything from belts and bracelets to cell phones and credit unions (see Lukas, 2002).

Research has revealed the wide availability of depictions of women in the role of sex object across virtually every medium, including prime-time television programs (e.g., Grauerholz & King, 1997; Ward, 1995), television commercials (e.g., Lin, 1997), music videos (e.g., Gow, 1996; Vincent 1989), and magazines (e.g., Krassas et al., 2003; Plous & Neptune, 1997). Such sexually objectifying images of women have been increasing over time (e.g., Busby & Leichty, 1993; Reichert & Carpenter, 2004): One report indicates a 60% increase in the portrayal of women in "decorative" roles from 1970 to the mid-1980s (Sullivan & O'Connor, 1988). Moreover, the sexual objectification of women in the media affects men's beliefs about women's bodies. Ward, Merriwether, and Caruthers (2006) demonstrated that heavier media usage by men is linked to greater acceptance of traditional gender ideologies that construct women as sex objects and to viewing women's bodies and body parts positively when they serve a sexual function but not when they serve a reproductive function. Consequently, what girls and boys come to learn about women's bodies from sociocultural agents and gender socialization is that it is normative for women's bodies to be looked at, commented on, evaluated, and sexually harassed—to be sexually objectified.

SELF-OBJECTIFICATION

Because the practice of sexually objectifying women is so pervasive, it appears normative in Westernized societies, and its potential negative consequences are often minimized or dismissed. Indeed, "women are encouraged to . . . feel pleasure through their own bodily objectification, especially being looked at and identified as objects of male desire" (Lee, 2003, p. 88). Yet, the role of sexual objectification in the lives of girls and women is hardly innocuous. Feminist theorists have argued that the sexually objectifying experiences encountered by girls and women in their day-to-day environments lead them to internalize this objectifying gaze and to turn it on themselves. Girls and women come to view themselves from the vantage point of an external observer and engage in chronic self-policing: "In contemporary patriarchal culture, a panoptical male connoisseur resides within the consciousness of most women: They stand perpetually before his gaze and under his judgment. Woman lives her body as seen by another, by an anonymous patriarchal Other" (Bartky, 1990, p. 72).

In this way, the accumulation of sexually objectifying experiences serves to shift and shape self–body relations, such that women come to view and treat themselves not as whole persons but as objects, to be looked at and evaluated from the outside (de Beauvoir, 1952/1989). Drawing from Henley's (1977) work on power, Roberts (2002) conceptualized self-objectification as a form of internalized control: "That is, socialization of subordinates in a dominant culture achieves a kind of colonization of the mind that ensures self-imposed powerlessness. So too socialization of girls and women in a sexually objectifying culture achieves self-objectification" (p. 326). Thus, coming to view and value oneself as a sexual object, or self-objectification, is regarded as the principal psychological consequence of regular exposure to sexually objectifying experiences.

Most feminist accounts of the objectification of women consider self-objectification to be a form of social control in that women learn to restrict their physical and social movement, investing their energy and resources in creating a feminized appearance in anticipation of this evaluative sexualized gaze (Bartky, 1990; Dworkin, 1974; Jeffreys, 2005; Young, 1990). It is important for women to monitor their every movement and attire to portray the right amount of femininity:

> Women in short, low-cut dresses are told to avoid bending over at all, but if they must, great care must be taken to avoid an unseemly display of breasts or rump . . . fashion magazines offer quite precise instructions on the proper way of getting in and out of cars. . . . A woman must not allow her arms and legs to flail about in all directions; she must try to manage her movements with the appearance of grace—no small accomplishment when one is climbing out of the back seat of a Fiat—and she is well advised to use the opportunity for a certain display of leg. (Bartky, 1990, p. 69)

A further restriction imposed on women is that the female body that is considered most sexually attractive is a combination of virtually unattainable and physically incompatible body attributes. Most women's bodies have always been, and will continue to be, discrepant from the contemporary ideals of female beauty. Between the 19th and 21st centuries, women have tried to have no waist but large hips, to be full-figured but thin, to have no breasts but lower body curves, and today, to have sizable breasts and muscle but no body fat (for a review, see Calogero, Boroughs, & Thompson, 2007). Indeed, the current feminine beauty ideal may represent the ultimate in unrealistic and unnatural attributes for women's natural bodies (Orbach, 2010). That is, while the current Western ideal for feminine beauty continues to glorify thinness, this ultra lean figure also includes a flat stomach, thin waist, boyish hips, long legs, well-developed breasts, well-defined muscles, and flawless skin (Groesz, Levine, & Murnen, 2002; Harrison, 2003). As most women's bodies will not match this "curvaceously thin ideal" (Harrison, 2003), most women's bodies will be rendered deficient and in constant need of alteration—"objects to be honed and worked on" (Orbach, 2010, p. 2).

Because current feminine beauty ideals are virtually impossible to achieve without some form of surgical modification and further invoke chronic self-surveillance to monitor and minimize discrepancies across these multiple domains of beauty, they represent the ultimate physical constriction of women's bodies. According to Dworkin (1974), these standards of feminine beauty "prescribe her mobility, spontaneity, posture, gait, the uses to which she can put her body. *They define precisely the dimensions of her physical freedom*" (p. 112). In these ways, self-objectification disrupts and usurps cognitive, physical, and financial resources (e.g., time, physical energy, cognitive capacity, health, money) that could be used for achievement and competence-based activities, thereby becoming increasingly disempowering over time (Saguy et al., 2010; Tiggemann & Rothblum, 1997; Wolf, 1991; Zones, 2000).

OBJECTIFICATION THEORY

Consistent with Mary Wollstonecraft's observation over 2 centuries ago, contemporary scholars from a variety of disciplines (e.g., sociology, anthropology, philosophy, psychology) have considered how women's bodies are constructed and controlled through a variety of sociocultural practices (Bartky, 1990; Berger, 1972; de Beauvoir, 1952/1989; Dworkin, 1991; Jeffreys, 2005; MacKinnon, 1989; Martin, 1987; McKinley & Hyde, 1996; Mulvey, 1975; Spitzack, 1990). Objectification theory, developed by Fredrickson and Roberts (1997), is essentially a synthesis and formalization of the many disparate lines of theorizing and research on the sexual objectification of women, offering a focused and formal framework for investigating the consequences of living in such a sexually objectifying cultural milieu that socializes girls and women to view and treat themselves as objects to be evaluated on the basis of their appearance: "We posit that in a culture that objectifies the female body, whatever girls and women do, the potential always exists for their thoughts and actions to be interrupted by images of how their bodies appear" (p. 180). Fredrickson and Roberts also argued that despite the heterogeneity among women with regard to ethnicity, class, sexuality, age, and physical and personal attributes, "having a reproductively mature body may create a shared social experience, a vulnerability to sexual objectification, which in turn may create a shared set of psychological experiences" (p. 175). By elucidating the range of intraindividual psychological outcomes that result from being sexually objectified and the potential mechanisms by which this chain of events occurs, objectification theory has transformed scientific inquiry in the area of women's sexual and self-objectification.

Objectification theory takes as the starting point that cultural practices of sexual objectification (delineated earlier) create multiple opportunities for women to view themselves through the lens of an external observer. In particular, it is the subtle and day-to-day practice of sexualized gazing that women encounter as they move in and out of a variety of social contexts that coaxes girls and women into adopting this evaluative gaze on themselves, or to self-objectify. Most women experience transient states of self-objectification in situations in which attention has been called to their bodies, such as receiving catcalls or catching someone staring at their breasts, or where their gender is a salient feature of the proximal context. For some women this objectified lens becomes internalized, and they come to take a view of themselves as objects virtually all of the time, whether they find themselves in public or private settings. Such women are said to have the persistent *trait* of self-objectification, in contrast to women who at times are in a *state* of self-objectification.

Whether engaged as a state or trait, taking this external vantage point of the self is accompanied by a form of self-consciousness characterized by habitual monitoring of the body's outward appearance:

> A woman must continually watch herself . . . continually accompanied by her own image of herself. Whilst she is walking across a room or whilst she is weeping at the death of her father, she can scarcely avoid envisaging herself walking or weeping. (Berger, 1972, p. 40)

That women adopt a self-objectified view of themselves is not an indication of narcissism or vanity but more accurately reflects a psychological strategy that allows women to anticipate, and thus exert some control over, how they will be viewed and treated by others. Although this self-perspective is unlikely to be consciously chosen, it does reflect a sort of agency in the highly oppressive context of sexual objectification. As Berger (1972) explained,

> She has to survey everything she is and everything she does because how she appears to others, and ultimately how she appears to men, is of crucial importance for what is normally thought of as the success of her life. . . . Men survey women before treating them. Consequently how a woman appears to a man can determine how she will be treated. To acquire some control over this process, women must contain it and interiorize it. (p. 40)

This self-perspective does not merely reflect social comparison with others, or the fact that women simply do not like the size or shape of their bodies, but actually reflects a view of the body as belonging "less to them and more to others" (Fredrickson & Roberts, 1997, p. 193). Given that physical attractiveness serves as a form of currency for women by earning them myriad social and economic rewards for their appearance (Dellinger & Williams, 1997; Eagly, Ashmore, Makhijani, & Longo, 1991; Unger, 1979)—and in an effort to cope with incessant external pressures to meet beauty ideals—self-objectification appears to be a normative, yet nontrivial, view of the self for many women (Costanzo, 1992).

In the objectification theory framework, self-objectification is the primary psychological mechanism that accounts for the link between experiences of sexual objectification at the cultural level and the health and well-being of girls and women at the individual level (see Figure 1.1). Self-objectification is proposed to lead directly to several psychological or experiential consequences that are known to occur at a disproportionately higher rate among girls and women (Fredrickson & Roberts, 1997): body shame, appearance and safety anxiety, reduced concentration or flow experiences on mental and physical tasks, and decreased awareness of internal bodily states (e.g., satiety, hunger, fatigue, emotions).

In turn, this collection of negative psychological consequences is proposed to accumulate and lead directly to a subset of mental health risks that occur at a disproportionately higher rate among girls and women (Fredrickson & Roberts, 1997): unipolar depression, sexual dysfunctions, and eating disorders. That is, by generating recurrent shame and anxiety, consuming mental energy that could be used for more pleasurable and rewarding activities, and reducing sensitivity to internal bodily cues, self-objectification is proposed to indirectly contribute to greater depression, sexual dysfunction, and eating disorders in girls and women. Over a decade of research on objectification theory has provided considerable evidence for many of these propositions, thereby empirically linking self-objectification to more negative subjective experiences and greater mental health risk in girls and women (Moradi & Huang, 2008).

SELF-OBJECTIFICATION AS A HARMFUL CULTURAL PRACTICE

According to the United Nations (1995), a cultural practice is considered harmful to women if the practice (a) is harmful to the health of women and girls, (b) arises from material power differences between the sexes, (c) is for the benefit of men, (d) creates stereotypes that thwart the opportunities of girls and women, and (e) is justified by tradition. Self-objectification would appear to meet these criteria: (a) Plenty of empirical evidence has substantiated that self-objectification is harmful to the health of girls and women (American Psychological Association, 2007; for a review, see Moradi & Huang, 2008); (b) the economic, political, and social power imbalance

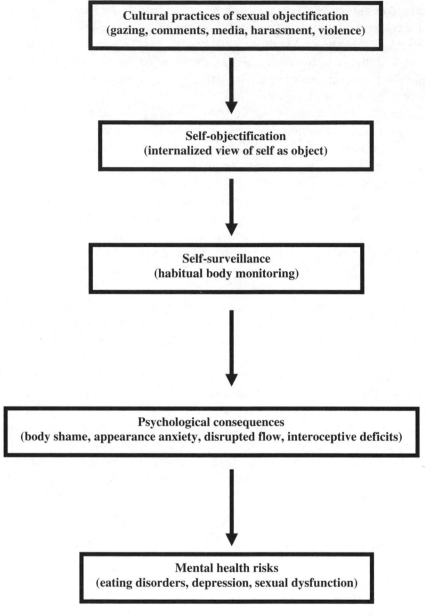

Figure 1.1. A model of objectification theory as proposed by Fredrickson and Roberts (1997).

that favors men over women reinforces and perpetuates women's sexual and self-objectification (Henley, 1977; Horney, 1937; Keltner, Gruenfeld, & Anderson, 2003; Pratto & Walker, 2004; Wolf, 1991); (c) men reap sexual, social, and economic benefits from women's disproportionate investment in their appearance (Bartky, 1990; Fredrickson, Roberts, Noll, Quinn, & Twenge, 1998; Henley, 1977; Jeffreys, 2005; Lerner, 1983; Wolf, 1991); (d) women's view of themselves as a sexual object that exists for the pleasure of men legitimizes and perpetuates traditional gender stereotypes about women's roles and abilities, reinforcing self- and others' perceptions of women *as bodies* (Calogero & Jost, 2010; Leibold & McConnell, 2004; Rudman & Borgida, 1995; Saguy et al., 2010; Ward et al., 2006); and (e) the sexual objectification of women—and resultant self-objectification—may be seen as manifestations of broader sexist ideologies within patriarchal societies that reinforce women's disadvantaged status at both the cultural and the individual level (Bartky, 1990; Calogero & Jost, 2010; Henley, 1977; Jackman, 1994; Maass, Cadinu, Guarnieri, & Grasselli, 2003; see also Jost, 1995; Jost, Banaji, & Nosek, 2004; Nussbaum, 1999).

As Jeffreys (2005) argued,

> the beauty practices that women engage in, and which men find so exciting, are those of political subordinates. . . . The fact that some women say that they take pleasure in the practices is not inconsistent with their role in the subordination of women. (pp. 26–27)

On the basis of these criteria, and the material laid out in the following chapters, we propose that the objectification of women prohibits the full development of individual girls and women and constitutes a harmful cultural practice against them. The wide-reaching implications of self-objectification in girls' and women's lives call for a more exacting treatment of the topic.

THIS BOOK

This book offers timely and integrative coverage of the empirical evidence on objectification theory to help guide future work in the area of self-objectification in women. The central themes represented include

- the evaluation of assessment tools used in the study of self-objectification,
- the cultural and environmental practices that promote sexual and self-objectification,
- the prevalence of self-objectification across the life span,
- an existential analysis of why women are objectified,

- the role of self-objectification in the domains of women's mental health and performance,
- the potential for embodiment versus objectification in the context of athletics, and
- the use of prevention and intervention strategies to reduce sexual and self-objectification.

A broad range of chapters are presented by scholars who bring a variety of viewpoints and expertise to the examination of self-objectification. This book is for professionals and students who have research, clinical, or applied interests in a wider analysis of the objectification of women. The chapters are empirically based, and the authors provide a clear discussion of current knowledge as well as avenues for future research.

The chapters of this book have been organized into five parts. Part I, Introduction and Assessment, provides an overview of the theoretical framework and the assessment tools used in objectification research. Rachel M. Calogero, Stacey Tantleff-Dunn, and J. Kevin Thompson (Chapter 1) review the history and interpretation of the objectification of women and present a fuller description of objectification theory, highlighting its assumptions, propositions, and predictions for girls' and women's experiences. Calogero (Chapter 2) examines the most frequently used measurement tools and approaches to testing the role of self-objectification in objectification theory. The measurement of self-objectification receives the most attention because it forms the crux of objectification theory. Calogero considers the utility of both trait and state measures of self-objectification, offers recommendations for the use and labeling of specific measures, and reviews recent advances in the assessment of objectification theory variables.

Part II, Sexual and Self-Objectification, considers how and why sexual and self-objectification occurs over the course of girls' and women's lives. Linda Smolak and Sarah K. Murnen (Chapter 3) provide an overview of the social developmental context for understanding the sexual objectification of girls and women in Westernized societies. This chapter points to the myriad sexualization practices embedded in social discourse—along with the social role conflicts that these practices create—to explain the inevitable sexual objectification and subsequent self-objectification among girls and women. By offering a social developmental analysis of sexualization, this chapter is particularly adept at articulating how girls and women learn to negotiate social pressures about their bodies in the form of self-objectification.

Jamie L. Goldenberg and Tomi-Ann Roberts (Chapter 4) address a fundamental question: Why are women so often the targets of objectification? This chapter outlines an existential account of the objectification of women, arguing that it provides a psychic defense against the threat associated with women's natural bodies and their life-giving role. Drawing from a terror management framework, the authors offer a wealth of research (much of it conducted by Goldenberg and her colleagues) in support of the view that sexual and self-objectification imbue women's bodies with cultural meaning that serves to distance their bodies from nature, and thereby distances men and women from reminders of their own mortality, making them feel safer. This new and promising perspective sheds a different light on the psychology of objectification.

Nita Mary McKinley (Chapter 5) covers women's experience of objectified body consciousness across the life span. Her chapter describes how self-objectification may vary as a function of the developmental, biological, and cultural context in which girls and women find themselves at different life stages. Although there is a dearth of research that examines self-objectification across the life span (much of it conducted by McKinley), this chapter offers an analysis of critical life stages, developmental tasks, and cohort differences that may inform our understanding of when girls and women may be most at risk for or most protected from sexual and self-objectification.

Part III, Consequences of Self-Objectification, summarizes the literature on the performance deficits and mental health risks associated with self-objectification. Diane M. Quinn, Stephenie R. Chaudoir, and Rachel W. Kallen (Chapter 6) summarize the empirical evidence linking self-objectification to decrements in performance, particularly disrupted concentration or flow states and diminished cognitive and physical performance. By integrating self-regulation theory into our understanding of self-objectification, this chapter provides a new framework for understanding how self-objectification may usurp women's cognitive resources and disrupt cognitive functioning. A particular strength of the self-regulation framework proposed in this chapter is that it identifies how specific psychological processes may be harnessed to hinder or help women in the performance domain.

Marika Tiggemann (Chapter 7) provides an overview of the empirical evidence linking self-objectification to higher levels of disordered eating, depression, and sexual dysfunction in women. Covering a wealth of research (much of it conducted by Tiggemann and her colleagues), this chapter highlights which of the proposed pathways linking self-objectification to mental health risks have been well supported by the evidence and which pathways need further investigation. Tiggemann offers an interpretation of the findings for the role of self-objectification in women's mental health and critically evaluates the gaps and limitations in this area of objectification research.

Part IV, Prevention and Disruption of Sexual and Self-Objectification, considers individual, social, and clinical contexts in which sexual and self-objectification may be disrupted and reduced. Jessie E. Menzel and Michael P. Levine (Chapter 8) consider sexual and self-objectification within the largely neglected context of athletic participation. This chapter provides an in-depth review of the research on positive body image, calling on a multidimensional theory of embodiment to explain how embodied experiences through sport might come to protect girls and women against sexual and self-objectification.

Tracy L. Tylka and Casey L. Augustus-Horvath (Chapter 9) identify key individual and environmental targets for the prevention and disruption of self-objectification in community and clinical contexts. This chapter offers a variety of techniques and strategies to challenge the sexual objectification of women's bodies via interpersonal and media encounters, as well as practical approaches for strengthening individual resilience to these encounters. This chapter is far reaching in that it also considers the management of self-objectification within more severe clinical settings, acknowledging the imperative to develop and implement corresponding interventions for boys and men.

Part V, Concluding Remarks, considers several open questions on self-objectification in women. Calogero, Tantleff-Dunn, and Thompson (Chapter 10) offer several directions for future research that focus on conceptual and empirical gaps in the literature and that stretch our thinking about the role of self-objectification in gender equality. In conjunction with the many recommendations highlighted in the preceding chapters, this chapter serves as a call to action for new and continued scholarship on the psychology of objectification.

It is clear from the chapters in this book that psychologists and other professionals are invested in theoretical, methodological, analytical, and practical issues related to the study of the objectification of women. Objectification theory continues to garner attention and popularity as an explanatory framework for women's lived experiences within the wider sexually objectifying cultural milieu. The primary impetus for this book is to synthesize the empirical support for objectification theory—especially the causes and consequences of self-objectification—and to shed new light on why self-objectification persists and what we can do about it. We hope that this book will not only convey current knowledge but also provide a framework and stimulus for future investigations. We strongly believe that a greater understanding of self-objectification will provide an enhanced awareness of women's lived experiences. Our hope is that research in this area will ultimately lead to changes—societal, interpersonal, and intrapersonal—that will create an environment in which girls and women will feel *subjectified,* and thus emboldened to develop their full self, not just their physical appearance.

REFERENCES

American Psychological Association. (2007). *Report of the APA Task Force on the Sexualization of Girls.* Washington, DC: Author. Retrieved from http://www.apa.org/pi/wpo/sexualization_report_summary.pdf

Argyle, M., & Williams, M. (1969). Observer or observed: A reversible perspective in person perception. *Sociometry, 32,* 396–412. doi:10.2307/2786543

Baker Miller, J. (1986). *Toward a new psychology of women* (2nd ed.). Boston, MA: Beacon Press.

Bartky, S. (1990). *Femininity and domination: Studies in the phenomenology of oppression.* New York, NY: Routledge.

Berger, J. (1972). *Ways of seeing.* London, England: Penguin.

Brownmiller, S. (1975). *Against our will: Men, women, and rape.* New York, NY: Simon & Schuster.

Bryant, A. (1993). Hostile hallways: The AAUW survey on sexual harassment in America's schools. *Journal of School Health, 63,* 355–357. doi:10.1111/j.1746-1561.1993.tb07153.x

Busby, L., & Leichty, G. (1993). Feminism and advertising in traditional and nontraditional women's magazines, 1950s–1980s. *Journalism Quarterly, 70,* 247–264.

Calogero, R. M., Boroughs, M., & Thompson, J. K. (2007). The impact of Western beauty ideals on the lives of women and men: A sociocultural perspective. In V. Swami & A. Furnham (Eds.), *Body beautiful: Evolutionary and sociocultural perspectives* (pp. 259–298). New York, NY: Palgrave Macmillan.

Calogero, R. M., & Jost, J. T. (2010). *Self-subjugation among women: Exposure to sexist ideology, self-objectification, and the protective function of the need to avoid closure.* Manuscript submitted for publication.

Costanzo, P. R. (1992). External socialization and the development of adaptive individuation and social connection. In D. N. Ruble, P. R. Costanzo, & M. E. Olivieri (Eds.), *The social psychology of mental health* (pp. 55–80). New York, NY: Guilford Press.

de Beauvoir, S. (1989). *The second sex* (H. M. Parshley, Trans.). New York, NY: Vintage Books. (Original work published 1952)

Dellinger, K., & Williams, C. L. (1997). Makeup at work: Negotiating appearance rules in the workplace. *Gender & Society, 11,* 151–177. doi:10.1177/089124397011002002

Dworkin, A. (1974). *Woman hating.* New York, NY: Plume.

Dworkin, A. (1991). *Pornography: Men possessing women.* New York, NY: Plume.

Eagly, A. H., Ashmore, R. D., Makhijani, M. G., & Longo, L. C. (1991). What is beautiful is good, but . . . : A meta-analytic review of research on the physical attractiveness stereotype. *Psychological Bulletin, 110,* 109–128. doi:10.1037/0033-2909.110.1.109

Eck, B. A. (2003). Men are much harder: Gendered viewing of nude images. *Gender and Society, 17,* 691–710. doi:10.1177/0891243203255604

Fredrickson, B. L., & Roberts, T. A. (1997). Objectification theory: Toward understanding women's lived experience and mental health risks. *Psychology of Women Quarterly, 21,* 173–206. doi:10.1111/j.1471-6402.1997.tb00108.x

Fredrickson, B. L., Roberts, T. A., Noll, S. M., Quinn, D. M., & Twenge, J. M. (1998). That swimsuit becomes you: Sex differences in self-objectification, restrained eating, and math performance. *Journal of Personality and Social Psychology, 75,* 269–284. doi:10.1037/0022-3514.75.1.269

Gardner, C. B. (1980). Passing by: Street remarks, address rights, and the urban female. *Sociological Inquiry, 50,* 328–356. doi:10.1111/j.1475-682X.1980.tb00026.x

Goffman, E. (1979). *Gender advertisements.* Cambridge, MA: Harvard University Press.

Gow, J. (1996). Reconsidering gender roles on MTV: Depictions in the most popular music videos in the early 1990s. *Communication Reports, 9,* 151–161.

Grauerholz, E., & King, A. (1997). Primetime sexual harassment. *Violence Against Women, 3,* 129–148. doi:10.1177/1077801297003002003

Groesz, L. M., Levine, M. P., & Murnen, S. K. (2002). The effect of experimental presentation of thin media images on body satisfaction: A meta-analytic review. *International Journal of Eating Disorders, 31,* 1–16. doi:10.1002/eat.10005

Grogan, S., & Wainwright, N. (1996). Growing up in the culture of slenderness: Girls' experiences of body dissatisfaction. *Women's Studies International Forum, 19,* 665–673. doi:10.1016/S0277-5395(96)00076-3

Harper, B., & Tiggemann, M. (2008). The effect of thin ideal images on women's self-objectification, mood, and body image. *Sex Roles, 58,* 649–657. doi:10.1007/s11199-007-9379-x

Harrison, K. (2003). Television viewers' ideal body proportions: The case of the curvaceously thin woman. *Sex Roles, 48,* 255–264. doi:10.1023/A:1022825421647

Henley, N. M. (1977). *Body politics: Power, sex, and nonverbal communication.* Englewood Cliffs, NJ: Prentice-Hall.

Hill, M. S., & Fischer, A. R. (2008). Examining objectification theory: Lesbian and heterosexual women's experiences with sexual and self-objectification. *The Counseling Psychologist, 36,* 745–776. doi:10.1177/0011000007301669

Horney, K. (1937). *The neurotic personality of our time.* New York, NY: Norton.

Jackman, M. R. (1994). *The velvet glove: Paternalism and conflict in gender, class, and race relations.* Berkeley, CA: University of California Press.

Jeffreys, S. (2005). *Beauty and misogyny: Harmful cultural practices in the West.* New York, NY: Routledge.

Jost, J. T. (1995). Negative illusions: Conceptual clarification and psychological evidence concerning false consciousness. *Political Psychology, 16,* 397–424. doi:10.2307/3791837

Jost, J. T., Banaji, M., & Nosek, B. A. (2004). A decade of system justification theory: Accumulated evidence of conscious and nonconscious bolstering of the status quo. *Political Psychology, 25,* 881–919. doi:10.1111/j.1467-9221.2004.00402.x

Kaschak, E. (1992). *Engendered lives: A new psychology of women's experience.* New York, NY: Basic Books.

Keltner, D., Gruenfeld, D. H., & Anderson, C. (2003). Power, approach, and inhibition. *Psychological Review, 110,* 265–284. doi:10.1037/0033-295X.110.2.265

Klonoff, E. A., & Landrine, H. (1995). The Schedule of Sexist Events: A measure of lifetime and recent sexist discrimination in women's lives. *Psychology of Women Quarterly, 19*, 439–472. doi:10.1111/j.1471-6402.1995.tb00086.x

Koss, M. P., Gidycz, C. A., & Wisniewski, N. (1987). The scope of rape: Incidence and prevalence of sexual aggression and victimization in a national sample of higher education students. *Journal of Consulting and Clinical Psychology, 55*, 162–170. doi:10.1037/0022-006X.55.2.162

Kozee, H. B., Tylka, T. L., Augustus-Horvath, C. L., & Denchik, A. (2007). Development and psychometric evaluation of the interpersonal sexual objectification scale. *Psychology of Women Quarterly, 31*, 176–189. doi:10.1111/j.1471-6402.2007.00351.x

Krassas, N. R., Blauwkamp, J. M., & Wesselink, P. (2003). "Master your Johnson": Sexual rhetoric in *Maxim* and *Stuff* magazines. *Sexuality & Culture, 7*, 98–119. doi:10.1007/s12119-003-1005-7

Lee, J. (2003). Menarche and the (hetero)sexualization of the female body. In R. Weitz (Ed.), *The politics of female bodies: Sexuality, appearance, and behavior* (pp. 82–99). New York, NY: Oxford University Press.

Leibold, J. M., & McConnell, A. R. (2004). Women, sex, hostility, power, and suspicion: Sexually aggressive men's cognitive associations. *Journal of Experimental Social Psychology, 40*, 256–263. doi:10.1016/S0022-1031(03)00095-7

Lerner, H. E. (1983). Female dependency in context: Some theoretical and technical considerations. *American Journal of Orthopsychiatry, 53*, 697–705.

Lin, C. (1997). Beefcake versus cheesecake in the 1990s: Sexist portrayals of both genders in television commercials. *Howard Journal of Communications, 8*, 237–249. doi:10.1080/10646179709361757

Lukas, S. A. (2002). *The Gender Ads project.* Retrieved from http://www.genderads.com

MacKinnon, C. (1989). *Towards a feminist theory of the state.* Cambridge, MA: Harvard University Press.

Macmillan, R., Nierobisz, A., & Welsh, S. (2000). Experiencing the streets: Harassment and perceptions of safety among women. *Journal of Research in Crime and Delinquency, 37*, 306–322. doi:10.1177/0022427800037003003

Martin, E. (1987). *The woman in the body: A cultural analysis of reproduction.* Boston, MA: Beacon Press.

Maass, A., Cadinu, M., Guarnieri, G., & Grasselli, A. (2003). Sexual harassment under social identity threat: The computer harassment paradigm. *Journal of Personality and Social Psychology, 85*, 853–870. doi:10.1037/0022-3514.85.5.853

McKinley, N. M., & Hyde, J. S. (1996). The Objectified Body Consciousness Scale: Development and validation. *Psychology of Women Quarterly, 20*, 181–215. doi:10.1111/j.1471-6402.1996.tb00467.x

Moradi, B., Dirks, D., & Matteson, A. (2005). Roles of sexual objectification experiences and internalization of standards of beauty in eating disorder symptomatology: A test and extension of objectification theory. *Journal of Counseling Psychology, 52*, 420–428. doi:10.1037/0022-0167.52.3.420

Moradi, B., & Huang, Y.-P. (2008). Objectification theory and psychology of women: A decade of advances and future directions. *Psychology of Women Quarterly, 32,* 377–398. doi:10.1111/j.1471-6402.2008.00452.x

Mulvey, L. (1975). Visual pleasure and narrative cinema. *Screen, 16,* 6–18.

Murnen, S. K., & Smolak, L. (2000). The experience of sexual harassment among grade-school students: Early socialization of female subordination? *Sex Roles, 43,* 1–17. doi:10.1023/A:1007007727370

Murnen, S. K., Smolak, L., Mills, J. A., & Good, L. (2003). Thin, sexy women and strong, muscular men: Grade-school responses to objectified images of women and men. *Sex Roles, 49,* 427–437. doi:10.1023/A:1025868320206

Nussbaum, M. C. (1995). Objectification. *Philosophy & Public Affairs, 24,* 249–291. doi:10.1111/j.1088-4963.1995.tb00032.x

Nussbaum, M. C. (1999). *Sex and social justice.* Oxford, England: Oxford University Press.

Orbach, S. (1993). *Hunger strike: The anorectics struggle as a metaphor for our age.* London, England: Penguin.

Orbach, S. (2010). *Bodies.* London, England: Profile Books.

Peter, J., & Valkenburg, P. M. (2007). Adolescents' exposure to a sexualized media environment and their notions of women as sex objects. *Sex Roles, 56,* 381–395. doi:10.1007/s11199-006-9176-y

Piran, N., & Cormier, H. (2005). The social construction of women and disordered eating patterns. *Journal of Counseling Psychology, 52,* 549–558. doi:10.1037/0022-0167.52.4.549

Plous, S., & Neptune, D. (1997). Racial and gender biases in magazine advertising: A content analytic study. *Psychology of Women Quarterly, 21,* 627–644. doi:10.1111/j.1471-6402.1997.tb00135.x

Pratto, F., & Walker, A. (2004). The bases of gendered power. In A. H. Eagly, A. E. Beall, & R. J. Sternberg (Eds.), *The psychology of gender* (pp. 242–268). New York, NY: Guilford Press.

Puwar, N. (2004). Thinking about making a difference. *British Journal of Politics and International Relations, 6,* 65–80. doi:10.1111/j.1467-856X.2004.00127.x

Reichert, T. (2003). The prevalence of sexual imagery in ads targeted to young adults. *Journal of Consumer Affairs, 37,* 403–412.

Reichert, T., & Carpenter, C. (2004). An update on sex in magazine advertising: 1983 to 2003. *Journalism & Mass Communication Quarterly, 81,* 823–837.

Roberts, T.-A. (2002). The woman in the body. *Feminism & Psychology, 12,* 324–329. doi:10.1177/0959353502012003004

Rudman, L. A., & Borgida, E. (1995). The afterglow of construct accessibility: The behavioral consequences of priming men to view women as sexual objects. *Journal of Experimental Social Psychology, 31,* 493–517.

Saguy, T., Quinn, D. M., Dovidio, J. F., & Pratto, F. (2010). Interacting like a body: Objectification can lead women to narrow their presence in social interactions. *Psychological Science.* doi:10.1177/0956797609357751.

Spitzack, C. (1990). *Confessing excess: Women and the politics of body reduction.* Albany, NY: State University of New York Press.

Sullivan, G., & O'Connor, P. (1988). Women's role portrayals in magazine advertising: 1958–1983. *Sex Roles, 18,* 181–188. doi:10.1007/BF00287788

Swim, J. K., Hyers, L. L., Cohen, L. L., & Ferguson, M. J. (2001). Everyday sexism: Evidence for its incidence, nature, and psychological impact from three daily diary studies. *Journal of Social Issues, 57,* 31–53. doi:10.1111/0022-4537.00200

Thompson, J. K., Heinberg, L. J., Altabe, M. N., & Tantleff-Dunn, S. (1999). *Exacting beauty: Theory, assessment, and treatment of body image disturbance.* Washington, DC: American Psychological Association. doi:10.1037/10312-000

Tiggemann, M., & Rothblum, E. D. (1997). Gender differences in internal beliefs about weight and negative attitudes towards self and others. *Psychology of Women Quarterly, 21,* 581–593. doi:10.1111/j.1471-6402.1997.tb00132.x

Unger, R. K. (1979). *Female and male.* New York, NY: Harper & Row.

United Nations. (1995). *Harmful traditional practices affecting the health and women of children: Fact Sheet No. 23.* Geneva, Switzerland: Author.

Vincent, R. (1989). Clio's consciousness raised? Portrayal of women in rock videos, re-examined. *Journalism Quarterly, 66,* 155–160.

Ward, L. M. (1995). Talking about sex: Common themes about sexuality in prime-time television programs children and adolescents view most. *Journal of Youth and Adolescence, 24,* 595–615. doi:10.1007/BF01537058

Ward, L. M., & Friedman, K. (2006). Using TV as a guide: Associations between television viewing and adolescents' sexual attitudes and behavior. *Journal of Research on Adolescence, 16,* 133–156. doi:10.1111/j.1532-7795.2006.00125.x

Ward, L. M., Merriwether, A., & Caruthers, A. (2006). Breasts are for men: Media, masculinity ideologies, and men's beliefs about women's bodies. *Sex Roles, 55,* 703–714.

Wolf, N. (1991). *The beauty myth.* New York, NY: Morrow.

Wollstonecraft, M. (1792). *A vindication of the rights of woman: With strictures on political and moral subjects.* Boston, MA: Peter Edes.

World Health Organization. (2005). *WHO multi-country study on women's health and domestic violence against women: Summary report of initial results on prevalence, health outcomes and women's responses.* Geneva, Switzerland: WHO Press.

Young, I. M. (1990). *Throwing like a girl and other essays in feminist philosophy and social theory.* Bloomington, IN: Indiana University Press.

Zones, J. S. (2000). Beauty myths and realities and their impacts on women's health. In M. B. Zinn, P. Hondagneu-Sotelo, & M. Messner (Eds.), *Gender through the prism of difference* (2nd ed., pp. 87–103). Boston, MA: Allyn and Bacon.

2

OPERATIONALIZING SELF-OBJECTIFICATION: ASSESSMENT AND RELATED METHODOLOGICAL ISSUES

RACHEL M. CALOGERO

Good research and effective practice are built on a strong foundation of measurement methods. Given that objectification theory has already been subjected to frequent and rigorous empirical testing, the need to identify the most valid assessment methods is clear. Indeed, in just over a decade, between 1996 and 2008, there was a stunning 1,920% increase in the number of peer-reviewed articles with a focus on *self-objectification* or *objectified body consciousness* (on the basis of a PsycINFO search of these keywords). Such a dramatic increase in research and interest in this area warrants careful consideration of the measurement methods that most accurately and reliably assess the constructs critical to objectification theory.

To date, there has not been a systematic evaluation of the measurement methods used in self-objectification research; yet multiple scales and experimental inductions of self-objectification are being used in research, clinical practice, and prevention and intervention contexts. The real-world implications of the findings from this research for girls' and women's lives further underscore the necessity of using the highest quality assessment tools to measure self-objectification and related constructs. The aims of this chapter are to cover the most widely used measures and methods in self-objectification research, outline important methodological issues and caveats, and discuss recent innovations. Throughout this chapter, recommendations are offered for selecting the most appropriate measures of self-objectification across different contexts and populations.

MEASURES OF SELF-OBJECTIFICATION

In 1997, the publication of objectification theory by Fredrickson and Roberts in the journal *Psychology of Women Quarterly* provided a formal framework to systematically study the multiple ways in which women's lives are affected by living in a culture that sexually objectifies the female body. Just prior to the publication of this formal theory, in 1996 McKinley and Hyde published a new scale also in *Psychology of Women Quarterly* to assess the multiple components of women's bodily experiences based on their theory of objectified body consciousness, referred to as the Objectified Body Consciousness Scale (OBCS). In 1998, Noll and Fredrickson published a new scale to measure the construct of self-objectification described by objectification theory, referred to as the Self-Objectification Questionnaire (SOQ). Although published independently, the theoretical underpinnings and rationale for these conceptual frameworks and assessment tools were the same in that they both articulated the toxicity of a culture that sexually objectifies the female body. Because the SOQ and OBCS are the most widely used measures of self-objectification, a large portion of this chapter focuses on the validity and utility of these scales.

Self-Objectification Questionnaire

The SOQ assesses the degree to which respondents' value *observable* physical appearance attributes, but without a judgmental or evaluative component (Noll & Fredrickson, 1998). This is an important distinction because self-objectification, and its negative consequences, can occur in women who are satisfied or dissatisfied with their bodies. Specifically, the SOQ measures the extent to which individuals consider five observable appearance-based body attributes (i.e., weight, sex appeal, physical attractiveness, firm/sculpted muscles, measurements) to be more important than five *nonobservable* competence-based body attributes (i.e., physical coordination, health, strength, energy level, physical fitness level). Respondents are instructed to rank all 10 body attributes in the order of their impact on the physical self-concept, from 0 = *least impact on my physical self-concept* to 9 = *greatest impact on my physical self-concept*. To obtain a scale score, one subtracts the sum of the ranks given to the five competence-based attribute scores from the sum of the ranks given to the five appearance-based attributes. This difference score represents the relative emphasis given to these two dimensions: More positive scores indicate a greater emphasis on physical appearance, whereas more negative scores indicate a greater emphasis on physical competence.

Satisfactory construct validity for the SOQ was demonstrated in Stephanie Noll's doctoral dissertation with predominantly White college-age women and subsequently reported by Noll and Fredrickson (1998). Specifically, the SOQ was shown to be positively correlated with appearance anxiety ($r = .52$) and body-size dissatisfaction ($r = .46$), indicating that self-objectification and negative body image variables are not overlapping constructs but are related in a meaningful way. In addition, the SOQ is consistently unrelated to body mass index ($r = -.02$, Fredrickson, Roberts, Noll, Quinn, & Twenge, 1998; $r = -.10$, Tiggemann & Lynch, 2001). The absence of a significant relationship between self-objectification and body mass index is critical because (a) it supports the theoretical proposition that self-objectification occurs among girls and women across the entire spectrum of weight and shape, and (b) it further discriminates the unique role of self-objectification from body size in girls' and women's body image.

Several issues with the SOQ warrant special mention. First, the words *observable* and *nonobservable* were italicized because this difference between the two sets of attributes seems less well appreciated in the operational definition, yet is critical to using and labeling the SOQ as a measure of self-objectification. Both sets of attributes represent respondents' physicality—thus, the quality of the attributes is held constant. The task then is for respondents to choose between physical attributes that can be readily observed by others (e.g., weight) and those physical attributes that cannot be readily observed by others (e.g., physical coordination) with regard to which attributes are most important to how they see their physical selves: Do women value more those attributes that represent them as a physical object or those that represent them as a physical subject? One reason that this distinction between observable and nonobservable physical attributes might get lost is that the two sets of attributes also carry the labels of appearance or competence, respectively. Referring to the nonobservable attributes as competence-based may not sufficiently qualify that the attributes refer to physical competence and may even suggest a comparison with an entirely different domain altogether, as competence could be easily construed as academic performance or intelligence or other specific types of self-efficacy—nothing at all to do with appearance. For future work, it is recommended that the qualifiers observable and nonobservable be used consistently in the description and interpretation of the SOQ.

Second, the instructions for completing the SOQ deserve more consideration. In brief, respondents are instructed to consider the 10 attributes, and then consider the 10 ranks (0 to 9), and then assign one rank to each attribute in the order that represents which attributes have the greatest to least impact, such that the rank of 0 represents the very least impact, 1 represents the next to least impact, and so forth up to 9, which represents the greatest impact. In my own research, as well as that of others, respondents (typically students) misunderstand these instructions and do not complete the SOQ correctly. The common mistake seems to be that respondents assign the same rank to more than one attribute. Solutions for this issue could take many forms, including reformatting the instructions and items on the page or rewriting the instructions altogether. The take-home message here is that if researchers use the SOQ, they should anticipate mistakes in how respondents complete it and expect to provide additional instruction to ensure proper completion.

Third, as highlighted by Hill and Fischer (2008), the rank-order format and the scoring system of the SOQ do not allow for standard estimates of internal consistency. Consequently, the internal reliability of the SOQ has not been well established in the empirical literature. Hill and Fischer proposed that an estimate of internal consistency for the SOQ could be determined from the correlation between the sum of the appearance-based attributes and the sum of the competence-based attributes. If respondents rank the appearance-based attributes most important, then the competence-based attributes must be ranked less important; therefore, a negative correlation would be expected between the appearance-based attributes and the competence-based attributes. Hill and Fischer reported a highly significant negative correlation between the rankings of the two sets of attributes ($r = -.81$). Given that the ranks of the individual attributes are summed for appearance and for competence, the negative direction of the relationship may not be too surprising, but it still confirms an inverse relationship. Moreover, it is useful to examine the magnitude of the correlation to get a sense of the dispersion of ranks across the two sets of attributes. Thus, it is recommended that future work using the SOQ report the correlation between the rankings of the two sets of attributes as an estimate of the reliability of the respondents' rankings.

It should also be noted that Noll and Fredrickson (1998) originally used a version of the SOQ that required ranking 12 attributes. However, this version was soon reduced to 10 items (see Fredrickson et al., 1998), and the 10-item SOQ is the most frequently used version of the SOQ. Yet, it is worth considering the two deleted attributes: coloring (appearance based) and stamina (competence based), especially coloring. Research has confirmed that skin tone is an important component of body image and appearance concerns (Cafri, Thompson, & Jacobsen, 2006; Cafri, Thompson, Roehrig, et al., 2006; Jackson & Aiken, 2000). Moreover, in an extension of objectification theory to African American women, researchers demonstrated that habitual body monitoring of skin tone was a significant predictor of skin tone dissatisfaction and more general body shame (Buchanan, Fischer, Tokar, & Yoder,

2008). Thus, skin color and skin tone may be additional appearance attributes associated with women's self-objectification, and further refinement of objectification measures that incorporate these components and others is warranted.

The SOQ has been used to measure self-objectification in men, and several studies have demonstrated variability in men's self-objectification as measured by the SOQ (Moradi & Huang, 2008). Because the gay men's subculture contains a high level of sexual objectification (Siever, 1994), it is perhaps not surprising that researchers have documented higher levels of self-objectification in gay men compared with heterosexual men (Martins, Tiggemann, & Kirkbride, 2007), and gay men's SOQ scores more closely approximate women's SOQ scores. Yet, a consistent pattern of findings has emerged that highlights the critical difference between men and women's SOQ scores: Men's scores are largely negative across samples, whereas women's scores are largely positive across samples (e.g., Calogero, 2009; Fredrickson et al., 1998; Hallsworth, Wade, & Tiggemann, 2005; Tiggemann & Kuring, 2004). Negative scores reflect a greater value placed on physical competence attributes. As pointed out by Tiggemann and Kuring (2004), the SOQ was designed for use with women and requires respondents to rank order a set of physical attributes that differ in how observable they are to others (e.g., weight, measurements vs. strength, physical coordination). The increased focus on a muscular appearance ideal for men (Pope et al., 2000; Thompson & Cafri, 2007) may render *strength* an important and observable attribute in men's minds. In this instance, then, highly valuing the attribute of strength would produce a more negative score but would be an indicator of higher (not lower) self-objectification in men. To advance the study of objectification in men, it would seem imperative to develop appropriate assessment tools that represent men's bodily experiences. Importantly, though, these findings for men provide more construct validity for the SOQ, particularly known-groups validity: The SOQ consistently distinguishes between groups that would be expected to differ on this construct (men and women; gay men and heterosexual men).

The SOQ has also been adapted to assess the degree to which women and men objectify other women and men. For example, in Strelan and Hargreaves (2005), after completing the SOQ as a measure of self-objectification, respondents were provided with the same 10 body attributes but with different instructions. For the measure of *other*-objectification, respondents ranked the attributes in order from what is most important to what is least important when they think about or look at others, specifically other women or other men. Scores for other women-objectification and other men–objectification can be calculated in the same way as scores for self-objectification. The use of this adapted measure yielded several interesting findings in support of objectification theory. Specifically, men objectify women more than they objectify other men, and men objectify women more than women objectify other women or men. In short, men are the primary perpetrators of objectification and women are the primary targets. In addition, these researchers demonstrated that the more men and women self-objectify, the more likely they are to objectify others. Thus, there is evidence to suggest that the SOQ can be used to assess the objectification of others as well as self-objectification.

Evidence has accumulated for the SOQ as a useful and valid measure of self-objectification in a variety of samples: American women (adolescent: Harrison & Fredrickson, 2003; college-aged: Aubrey, 2006; middle-aged and older: Grippo & Hill, 2008), Australian women (adolescent: Slater & Tiggemann, 2002; college-aged: Tiggemann & Kuring, 2004; middle-aged and older women: Tiggemann & Lynch, 2001), British women (college-aged: Calogero, 2009), Canadian women (college-aged: Morry & Staska, 2001), women of color (Mitchell & Mazzeo, 2009), heterosexual and lesbian women (Hill & Fischer, 2008), pregnant women (Johnston-Robledo & Fred, 2008), women in eating disorders treatment (Calogero, Davis, & Thompson, 2005), aerobic instructors and aerobic participants (Prichard & Tiggemann, 2005), yoga participants (Daubenmier, 2005), former ballet dancers (Tiggemann & Slater, 2001), exotic dancers (Downs, James, & Cowan, 2006), and heterosexual and gay men (Calogero, 2009; Fredrickson et al., 1998; Hallsworth et al., 2005; Martins et al., 2007). Although this coverage of studies is not exhaustive, it does provide an overview of the range of samples in which the SOQ was used to measure and interpret self-objectification.

Objectified Body Consciousness Scale and Self-Surveillance Subscale

The OBCS is a 24-item measure with a 7-point response format (ranging from 1 = *strongly disagree* to 7 = *strongly agree*) that assesses the degree to which women take the perspective of an external observer on their own bodies (McKinley & Hyde, 1996). The OBCS comprises three subscales that are intended to measure three different components of women's objectified relationships with their bodies: self-surveillance, body shame, and control beliefs. Self-surveillance is measured with the Surveillance subscale, which includes eight items that assess the degree to which women view their bodies as an outside observer, and it is often taken to be an indicator of habitual or chronic body monitoring (example item: "I often worry about whether the clothes I am wearing make me look good"). Body shame is measured with the Body Shame subscale, which includes eight items that assess the degree to which women feel that they are bad people when they view themselves as not meeting cultural appearance standards, particularly for thinness (example item: "When I'm not the size I think I should be, I feel ashamed"). Control beliefs are measured with the Control Beliefs subscale, which includes eight items that assess the degree to which women believe that they are responsible for their appearance and that they can control their appearance with enough effort (example item: "I think a person can look pretty much how they want to if they are willing to work at it"). This last component of objectified body consciousness is commonly referred to as *control beliefs*, but this label can be misleading because, like the use of the label *competence* in the SOQ described above, control beliefs could refer to any number of psychological or life domains. Thus, in keeping with McKinley and Hyde's (1996) conceptualization of this component as women's internalized beliefs about their responsibility (or lack thereof) for their appearance, from this point forward in the chapter the important qualifier *appearance* is used when referring to appearance control beliefs.

In addition to the 7-point response format, respondents may also circle N/A ("not applicable") if an item does not apply to them. Unanswered items or those marked as N/A are considered missing responses. Scale scores are not calculated if more than 25% of a subscale's scores are missing. Satisfactory construct validity was originally demonstrated by McKinley and Hyde (1996). Moderate to high internal consistency was shown for the Surveillance subscale (α = .76–.89), Body Shame subscale (α = .70–.75), and Control Beliefs subscale (α = .68–.76) with predominantly White, undergraduate, and middle-aged women. Good test–retest reliability was demonstrated over a 2-week period. A series of zero-order correlations across two studies found that self-surveillance and body shame were significantly and highly correlated with each other, whereas appearance control beliefs correlated only weakly or were unrelated to self-surveillance and body shame. The potential problems with the measure of appearance control beliefs are elaborated later in this section.

McKinley and Hyde (1996) also demonstrated that self-surveillance and body shame were negatively correlated with body esteem and positively correlated with the fear of fat and disordered eating, whereas appearance control beliefs were unrelated to body esteem and fear of fat but also positively correlated with disordered eating and appearance management behaviors (e.g., cosmetic use). In addition, self-surveillance was positively correlated with public self-consciousness, public body consciousness, and appearance orientation, whereas it was unrelated to private self-consciousness, private body consciousness, and body competence. These tests of construct validity confirm the distinctive components of the OBCS: (a) The assessment of self-surveillance captures vigilance about how one appears or "looks" to others as opposed to how one feels, (b) the assessment of body shame taps into the importance of weight as the cultural standard for comparison, and (c) the assessment of appearance control beliefs taps into behavioral intentions and actions that may be undertaken to manage one's appearance.

Since its introduction in 1996, the OBCS has been used in a variety of ways in studies of objectification. Based on the recommendations of McKinley and Hyde (1996), the OBCS can be used to measure the overall experience of objectified body consciousness by summing responses across the 24 items to create a total score, or it can be used to measure the specific components of objectified body consciousness by summing responses to each subscale separately. Most often the subscales of the OBCS have been used to measure the underlying components separately as opposed to the total score. It should be noted here that although McKinley and Hyde proposed objectified body consciousness as a unitary construct that may be quantified by summing all of the items to create a total score, the use of an OBCS total score is potentially problematic for interpretation and model testing.

First, in the original validation of the OBCS, the three subscales were validated primarily as separate scales. Although the three scales collectively capture a more comprehensive picture of women's bodily experiences, the individual components predict different outcomes. Moreover, as described below, the Surveillance subscale is often used to predict the Body Shame subscale when testing different models proposed by objectification theory. Second, appearance control beliefs do not seem to fit as well within the objectification framework compared with self-surveillance and body shame (Basow, Foran, & Bookwala, 2007; McKinley, 2006) and in some cases demonstrate the opposite relationship (i.e., protective), with measures of health and well-being compared with self-surveillance and body shame (John & Ebbeck, 2008; Sinclair & Myers, 2004). A third related point is that the measure of appearance control beliefs does not consistently correlate with self-surveillance and body shame across studies (McKinley & Hyde, 1996) and thus would seem to undermine the latent objectified body consciousness construct if included as part of a total score. Thus, although the OBCS has been used occasionally as a summed total score, this would only be appropriate when the summing of two (e.g., self-surveillance and body shame) or all three scales is based on a theoretically derived justification (e.g., Fairchild & Rudman, 2008; Muehlenkamp & Saris-Baglama, 2002; Piran & Cormier, 2005). In the absence of a theoretical basis for a total score, it is recommended that the scales of the OBCS be used as independent measures of self-surveillance, body shame, and appearance control beliefs.

The most frequently used subscale of the OBCS as a measure of self-objectification is the Surveillance subscale. Self-surveillance has become conceptualized as the manifestation of self-objectification because it captures the habitual monitoring of external appearance that often occurs among women who have adopted an external observational standpoint on their own bodies. Marika Tiggemann and colleagues were the first to test and demonstrate that self-objectification (as measured by the SOQ) and its corollary self-surveillance (as measured by the Surveillance subscale) are conceptually and empirically distinguishable constructs. In these studies, the SOQ is set to predict self-surveillance, which, in turn, leads to other negative outcomes predicted by objectification theory (e.g., Steer & Tiggemann, 2008; Tiggemann & Kuring, 2004; Tiggemann & Slater, 2001). In other studies, however, the Surveillance subscale and the SOQ have been used to represent the same underlying construct, and both scales have been labeled as self-objectification, which suggests that they are equivalent measures. In some studies the Surveillance subscale has been used as the single measure of self-objectification, whereas in other studies it has been used in conjunction with the SOQ.

The idea that self-objectification leads to habitual self-surveillance is consistent with the propositions of objectification theory whereby the internalization of an objectifying gaze positions women to become their own first surveyors and engage in habitual body monitoring. Conceptually, there is a distinction between the valuing of physical appearance over physical competence (as measured by the SOQ) and engagement in chronic body monitoring (as measured by the Surveillance subscale). It is possible that women may come to highly value physical appearance as a result of living in Westernized societies, where physical attractiveness is so highly socially valued, but these women may engage in different levels of behavioral investment in appearance (Calogero, Herbozo, & Thompson, 2009). Thus, valuing the body as a physical object and behaviorally investing in the body as a physical object are not the same phenomenon. This reasoning is consistent with the low to moderate intercorrelations between these two measures reported in most studies. In addition, recent work on self-objectification that compared the responses of heterosexual and lesbian women underscores the importance of distinguishing between self-objectification and self-surveillance. For example, Hill and Fischer (2008) found no significant differences between heterosexual and lesbian women on the SOQ, but lesbian women reported significantly lower self-surveillance (as measured by the Surveillance subscale) compared with heterosexual women. Kozee and Tylka (2006) demonstrated a more comprehensive model of objectification experiences among lesbian women compared with heterosexual women, whereby experiences of sexual objectification and self-surveillance (as measured by the Surveillance subscale) directly predicted disordered eating among the lesbian women but not the heterosexual women. Replacing the Surveillance subscale with the SOQ in this study would have produced markedly different models and led to different conclusions about the role of objectification in the lives of lesbian and heterosexual women.

However, despite the evidence for distinguishing between self-objectification and self-surveillance, it is not clear that the operationalization of these constructs allows for a straightforward interpretation of these patterns between the SOQ and the Surveillance subscale. The SOQ does not measure the internalization of an objectifying observers' gaze directly, but rather this is implied by the respondents' valuing of physical appearance attributes over physical competence attributes. In addition, the rank-order response format of the SOQ introduces more measurement error, which weakens the relationship between the SOQ and other measures, including the Surveillance subscale. It is possible that the SOQ and the Surveillance subscale would be more strongly related if measurement error in the SOQ was reduced or if the response formats were the same. Because of these open issues, it cannot be concluded at this stage whether the SOQ and the Surveillance subscale represent the same or distinct underlying constructs. If they are distinguishable conceptually, the operationalizations of these constructs need to be refined such that they measure them in a way that addresses these issues of measurement error. Thus, it is recommended in future work that the SOQ and the Surveillance subscale be used judiciously, and labeled distinctively, on the basis of the conceptual and empirical considerations underlying the intended research and sample.

It is important to note that the actual items on the Surveillance subscale have been modified for some samples of girls and women. More recently, researchers created a modified version of the OBCS to make the measure more accessible to preadolescent and adolescent youths (OBC-Youth Scale; Lindberg, Hyde, & McKinley, 2006). The OBC-Youth Scale includes 14 of the original 24 items from the OBCS and represents the same three underlying components, with some of the items rewritten in simpler language. Internal consistency was high for the Surveillance subscale ($\alpha = .88$) and Body Shame subscale ($\alpha = .79$) but low for the Control Beliefs subscale ($\alpha = .56$), and thus these researchers cautioned against using this measure of appearance control beliefs in preadolescent samples. Good test–retest reliability over a 2-week period and satisfactory construct validity support the use of the two-factor OBC-Youth Scale (self-surveillance and body shame) to examine objectified body consciousness in preadolescents. Also, Moradi and Rottenstein (2007) demonstrated lower internal consistency for the Surveillance subscale with a sample of deaf women compared with reliability estimates reported in prior research. These researchers suggested that some body monitoring among deaf women may be associated with their use of the body to serve communication needs rather than self-objectification. Further refinement of this measure for use with deaf women may be warranted.

The Surveillance subscale has also been used to measure self-surveillance in men. McKinley (1998) reported adequate construct validity and reliability for the OBCS among a sample of predominantly White American undergraduate men; however, two items from the Control Beliefs subscale did not load on the relevant factor, and thus caution is recommended when using this subscale with men. The general pattern of findings in this research indicated that men's self-surveillance scores were significantly lower than women's self-surveillance scores, and men's self-surveillance was not linked as strongly to negative outcomes as women's self-surveillance (McKinley, 1998). This pattern of findings has been demonstrated in other samples (Calogero, 2009; Calogero & Watson, 2009; Grabe, Hyde, & Lindberg, 2007), although, in contrast, particularly strong relationships between self-surveillance and negative outcomes among men were reported by Tiggemann and Kuring (2004). In sum, the Surveillance subscale has been used reliably in samples of men, but further refinement of this assessment tool to capture men's particular experiences of habitual body monitoring and self-surveillance seems warranted.

Evidence has accumulated for the Surveillance subscale as a useful and valid measure of self-surveillance in a variety of samples: American women (preadolescent and adolescent: Lindberg et al., 2006; college-aged: Tylka & Hill, 2004; middle-aged: McKinley, 2006), Australian women (adolescent: Slater & Tiggemann, 2002; college-aged: Tiggemann & Kuring, 2004; middle-aged and older: Tiggemann & Lynch, 2001), British women (college-aged: Calogero, 2009), Swiss adolescent girls (Knauss, Paxton, & Alsaker, 2008), Nepali mothers and daughters (Crawford et al., 2009), heterosexual and lesbian women (Kozee & Tylka, 2006), women of color (Breitkopf, Littleton, & Berenson, 2007), pregnant women (Johnston-Robledo & Fred, 2008), menopausal women (McKinley & Lyon, 2008), deaf women (Moradi & Rottenstein, 2007), low-income women (Breitkopf et al., 2007), aerobic instructors and aerobic participants (Prichard & Tiggemann, 2005), former ballet dancers (Tiggemann & Slater, 2001), exotic dancers (Downs et al., 2006), sorority group members (Basow et al., 2007), and heterosexual and gay men (Martins et al., 2007; McKinley, 1998; Tiggemann & Kuring 2004). Although this coverage of studies is not exhaustive, it does provide an overview of the range of samples in which self-surveillance has been measured and discussed.

An additional consideration on the construct of self-surveillance is warranted. Scholars have also referred to the self-surveillance construct as *body surveillance* in the literature, and thus readers may see either of these labels used to describe this dimension of the OBCS. Indeed, even journal editors and reviewers appear to have different preferences for the label of this construct and scale. This tendency to use different labels for the same construct and measurement tool is potentially confusing and counterproductive, so it is important to review the original literature here in an attempt to clarify the issue. McKinley and Hyde (1996) described self-surveillance as one of the key components of women's objectified body consciousness. Drawing from the work of Bartky (1990), Spitzack (1990), and others, they labeled this dimension *self-surveillance* to capture the self-policing and vigilant self-monitoring that is engaged in response to social cues and social constructions that communicate to women that their bodies are being watched and evaluated. In their original article, McKinley and Hyde referred to self-surveillance as the phenomenon under investigation, and they use the label *Surveillance Scale* (or subscale) when referring to the items constituting this dimension. These authors have occasionally referred to body surveillance as another way of describing this particular view of the body, but the predominant terms used have been self-surveillance and Surveillance subscale. Individual researchers have referred to this construct with one of these three labels, and sometimes the same researcher has used different labels for the same construct in independent studies—the author of this chapter included.

Although the use of different labels for the same construct does not undermine the findings, it does interfere with interpretation by scholars unfamiliar with the area, and it suggests that scholars have a less precise understanding of the construct. Consistent terminology seems imperative to provide a more stringent analysis and interpretation of both the construct and the findings. Scholars of objectification are encouraged to come to some agreement on the labels for these constructs. One recommendation to take forward in future work is to refer to the actual construct as *self-surveillance* and the scale as the *Surveillance subscale*, consistent with the labels presented in McKinley and Hyde's (1996) original framework and the language commonly called upon by scholars of objectification to describe the self-policing practice that stems from adopting an external perspective on the self (Bartky, 1990; Berger, 1972; de Beauvoir, 1952; Spitzack, 1990).

The Body Shame subscale of the OBCS has become a standard measure of body shame as a key consequence of self-objectification and self-surveillance. In a single study of women's objectification, it is quite common to see the scores on the Surveillance subscale set to predict the scores on the Body Shame subscale. As mentioned earlier, the Control Beliefs subscale has not been positioned as centrally in the study of self-objectification and is not always reliable; therefore, it has not been used as consistently in studies of self-objectification.

EXPERIMENTAL INDUCTIONS OF SELF-OBJECTIFICATION

Objectification theory proposes that women not only develop a chronic tendency to view themselves through the lens of an observer but also encounter instances of sexual objectification to different degrees on a daily basis in their immediate social environments. Situations that would be defined as sexual objectification include gazing or leering at women's bodies, sexual comments about women's bodies, whistling or honking the car horn at women, being photographed with a cell phone, exposure to sexualized media imagery or pornography, sexual harassment, sexual violence, and rape. Situational experiences of sexual objectification call immediate attention to women's bodies, placing women's own bodies on display and producing a *state* of self-objectification.

Whereas trait self-objectification (as measured by the SOQ) refers to a chronic tendency to view one's own body through an objectified lens across situations, state self-objectification refers to a temporary condition in which individuals are viewing themselves as objects in response to environmental cues (Fredrickson & Roberts, 1997). Researchers have risen to the challenge of creating experimental inductions (or manipulations) of some of these situations in the laboratory to conduct controlled investigations of the immediate and long-term effects of state self-objectification.

To induce a state of self-objectification, researchers have typically created situations in which women are exposed to imagined or actual sexual objectification, after or during which they complete a battery of measures of relevant psychological constructs. To confirm that a state of self-objectification has been induced, researchers commonly administer the Twenty Statements Test (Fredrickson et al., 1998), which asks women to make up to 20 different statements about themselves and their identity that complete the sentence "I am _____." Responses to these statements are coded by independent judges into different categories to determine the percentage of appearance-based attributes indicated relative to attributes unrelated to appearance. The categories typically used to code these statements include (a) body size and shape, (b) other physical appearance, (c) physical competence, (d) traits or abilities, (e) states or emotions, or (f) uncodable. If respondents are in a state of self-objectification, then they should provide more appearance-based responses relative to other responses, compared with respondents in control conditions (in which state self-objectification was not induced). A proper debriefing to assess the respondents' knowledge and experience during the study is also important.

Two other methods for assessing whether respondents are in a state of self-objectification come from research that has adapted the SOQ or Surveillance subscale to assess bodily experience in the moment. The instructions for the SOQ have been modified such that respondents are instructed to rank order the 10 body attributes according to how important each attribute is to their own physical self-concept "right now" (Calogero & Jost, 2010). Items from the Surveillance subscale have been modified to assess momentary states of self-surveillance, such as "Right now I am thinking about how I look" (Breines, Crocker, & Garcia, 2008). Satisfactory reliability estimates have been provided for both modified scales. Thus, state versions of the SOQ or Surveillance subscale may provide alternative options to researchers for confirming an experimental induction of state self-objectification or simply for measuring state self-objectification in nonexperimental settings. In the following sections, several common methods for inducing state self-objectification for research purposes are reviewed.

The Swimsuit–Sweater Paradigm

A commonly used experimental induction of state self-objectification is to have women try on a bathing suit in front of a full-length mirror in a dressing room. Compared with women who try on a sweater in the same setting, the women who try on a bathing suit in front of a mirror report significantly more state self-objectification. In turn, this state of self-objectification has been causally linked to more negative body image, more disordered eating, prolonged body focus, and diminished cognitive performance. These associations have been demonstrated among White college women (Fredrickson et al., 1998; Gapinski, Brownell, & LaFrance, 2003; Quinn, Kallen, & Cathey, 2006; Quinn, Kallen, Twenge, & Fredrickson, 2006) as well as African American, Hispanic, and Asian American college women (Hebl, King, & Lin, 2004), and even among men when wearing Speedos (Hebl et al., 2004). Thus, this induction of a state of self-objectification has been shown to be highly potent in getting women to view themselves more from an external observational standpoint compared with conditions in which self-objectification is not activated.

Exposure to Objectified Media Images

Another common induction of state self-objectification was created based on the proposition in objectification theory that exposure to sexualized depictions of women in the media causes women to self-objectify. In these studies, women are exposed to images of models that vary in size or posture or type of clothing, and then they complete measures of self-objectification, body image, and/or other psychological outcomes. Not surprisingly, in most cases, these studies demonstrate that exposure to these ultra-thin, sexualized images of *other* women's bodies increases women's negative perceptions of their *own* bodies. For example, Harper and Tiggemann (2008) found that exposure to advertisements featuring a thin-idealized woman produced higher levels of state self-objectification (as measured by the Twenty Statements Test), weight-related appearance anxiety, negative mood, and body dissatisfaction in Australian college women compared with advertisements that did not feature these thin-idealized images of women. Thus, in support of objectification theory, exposure to sexualized media depictions of women induced a state of self-objectification and produced a variety of negative outcomes.

Mere Exposure Situations

Self-objectification has also been induced in more subtle and unobtrusive ways. One less obtrusive method is based on the idea that not only the objectifying media images but also the objectifying words presented by the media may cause women to self-objectify. Indeed, reading contemporary women's magazines for appearance and beauty advice has been related to more self-objectification (Kim & Ward, 2004; Morry & Staska, 2001). Roberts and Gettman (2004) controlled women's exposure to objectifying words by modifying the robust Scrambled Sentence Test to covertly present body-objectifying or non-body-objectifying words to women. In this common priming procedure, a set of five scrambled words is presented with one target word embedded among those five words. Respondents are instructed to form a grammatically correct sentence using four of the five words given. A series of these sentences is provided for any particular set of target words, thereby repeatedly exposing respondents to a target word each time they attempt to create a sentence. The target words are preselected to represent and cognitively activate a particular psychological construct. However, respondents are unaware that they are being exposed to specific types of words during this task.

Using this methodology to induce self-objectification, Roberts and Gettman (2004) exposed respondents in the body objectifying condition to words such as *posing, sexiness, weight, slender,* and *thinness.* Respondents in the non-body-objectifying condition were exposed to words such as *playing, fitness, health, stamina,* and *coordinated.* In addition, a neutral condition was included to establish baseline levels of self-objectification, which exposed respondents to words such as *here, tasty, together, fine,* and *music.* In each condition, women were exposed to the target words in 15 of the 25 sentences. Roberts and Gettman found that exposure to the body-objectifying words activated state self-objectification, which, in turn, was associated with more appearance-related thoughts and negative outcomes, compared with exposure to the non-body-objectifying words. These findings suggest that merely exposing women to text-based stimuli that emphasizes appearance and body size (e.g., magazine covers, billboards) induces a state of self-objectification that produces a variety of negative outcomes.

Another subtle induction of self-objectification was created based on the proposition in objectification theory that women internalize the male gaze in particular. That is, it is the anticipation of being viewed as sexual objects by men that leads women to adopt an objectified view of their own bodies insofar as they must monitor and measure their appearance prior to such evaluations. Calogero (2004) experimentally investigated women's anticipation of the male gaze by creating a situation in which women were led to believe that they would be interacting with an unknown person for a few minutes. Some women were led to believe that they would be interacting with a man, whereas some women were led to believe that they would be interacting with a woman. In addition, women in a neutral condition did not receive any information about a potential interaction. In this study, when women anticipated an interaction with a male stranger, they reported more body shame and social physique anxiety compared with women who anticipated interacting with a female stranger. Thus, in support of objectification theory, merely anticipating the male gaze was sufficient to induce a state of self-objectification, producing many of the expected negative outcomes.

According to objectification theory, women experience multiple unstructured physical and social contexts on a daily basis, which comprise subtle features that have the potential to trigger or diminish self-objectification (Fredrickson & Roberts, 1997). To test this more general assumption, Tiggemann and Boundy (2008) investigated whether incidental exposure to a number of features that women readily encounter in their physical and social environments triggers self-objectification and the associated negative outcomes. These researchers experimentally altered the physical context of the laboratory setting so that women completed questionnaires in a room that either included objectifying features (e.g., mirrors, scales, and fashion magazine covers) or no objectifying features. Some of the women also received an appearance compliment, another common element of women's social environments, to determine the impact of positive attention to appearance on self-objectification. Results demonstrated that a single mere exposure to these common objectifying cues (which did not explicitly direct women to think about their appearance) triggered state self-objectification, although this was found only among women high in trait self-objectification. In addition, all of the women reported more positive mood after receiving an appearance compliment, but women high in trait self-objectification who were complimented also reported higher body shame compared with the other women. Thus, this study not only supports objectification theory but also improves the external validity of this theoretical framework for explaining women's self-objectification.

RECENT ADVANCES

There have been several advances in the assessment of self-objectification and theoretically related phenomena over the past decade. In particular, the measurement of (a) experiences of sexual objectification and (b) self-objectification among adolescent girls has been especially important for testing objectification theory and extending its application to other age groups. Several of the most promising advances are reviewed in this section.

Experiences of Sexual Objectification

Objectification theory takes as its starting point that women are chronically sexually objectified in Westernized societies, and few empirical investigations have tested the link between experiences of sexual objectification and self-objectification or its proposed consequences. Research that has investigated these links has demonstrated that interpersonal encounters of sexual objectification (e.g., sexualized gazing, sexual commentary, sexual harassment) predict higher levels of self-objectification and self-surveillance (Hill & Fischer, 2008; Kozee & Tylka, 2006; Kozee, Tylka, Augustus-Horvath, & Denchik, 2007; Moradi, Dirks, & Matteson, 2005). Two recent scale developments are reviewed next that may further help to close this gap in self-objectification research.

The Interpersonal Sexual Objectification Scale (ISOS; Kozee et al., 2007) is a 15-item measure with a 5-point response format (ranging from 1 = *never* to 5 = *almost always*) that assesses the frequency of sexually objectifying events encountered within the respondents' recent history (i.e., in the past year). The ISOS contains two dimensions: (a) Body Evaluation (example item: "How often have you been whistled at while walking down the street?") and (b) Unwanted Explicit Sexual Advances (example item: "How often has someone made a degrading sexual gesture towards you?"). Kozee et al. (2007) demonstrated excellent psychometric properties for the ISOS across a series of construct validation studies with predominantly White college-age women. Both the ISOS total score and the subscale scores have good internal consistency and test–retest reliability over a 3-week period. In addition, the ISOS was related to measures of sexist degradation and unfair sexist events (within relationships, schools, and work) as well as to self-objectification and body shame, and the ISOS was unrelated to socially desirable responding. It is important to note also that the ISOS accounted for unique variance in self-surveillance and internalization of the thin ideal, even when other measures of sexual objectification were included in the model.

There are other validated measures of the experience of sexist events in the literature, for example, the Schedule of Sexist Events (Klonoff & Landrine, 1995) and the sexual objectification subscale of the Daily Sexist Events Scale (Swim, Cohen, & Hyers, 1998). However, an advantage of the ISOS is that it allows women to report encounters of interpersonal sexual objectification without having to label them as instances of sexual objectification. Thus, as the ISOS undergoes further validation with more diverse samples of women, this scale would seem particularly well suited to the study of the objectification processes proposed by objectification theory.

Another scale developed to measure recent and lifetime experiences of sexual objectification is the Cultural Sexual Objectification Scale (CSOS; Hill & Fischer, 2008). The CSOS is a three-dimensional measure that presents 40 short scenarios to be rated on the basis of a 6-point response format (ranging from 1 = *never* to 6 = *almost all the time*), with a few items using a 3-point response format (ranging from 1= *never* to 3 = *more than once*). The three dimensions are (a) Ubiquitous Sexualized Gaze/Harassment (example item: "How many times has a man made sexual comments about your body?"), (b) Sexual Assault by Men (example item: "How many times have you had sexual intercourse when you didn't want to because a man threatened or used physical force?"), and (c) Sexual Harassment/Assault by Women (example item: "How many times has a woman made crude sexual remarks about your body?").

Although there is obvious conceptual (and in some cases actual) overlap between items on the ISOS and the CSOS, the CSOS does offer some unique advantages for testing sexually diverse samples of women. In particular, Hill and Fischer (2008) compared the responses of heterosexual and lesbian women on the CSOS and demonstrated that the two groups of women did not differ in their experiences of being gazed at or harassed or being sexually assaulted by men; however, lesbian women reported significantly more experiences of being sexually harassed or assaulted by women than heterosexual women. Thus, because the CSOS includes items that assess sexually objectifying events perpetrated by other women, it is possible to examine a more comprehensive picture of women's experiences of sexual objectification.

Self-Objectification in Daily Life

Another recent advancement in the assessment of objectification is the application of experience sampling methodology to measure daily experiences of self-objectification. Breines et al. (2008) measured experiences of self-objectification in the daily lives of American college-age women over a 2-week period to determine what happens to women when they self-objectify. Women reported on their level of state self-objectification and various aspects of their well-being three to four times a day while they were engaged in particular activities using a handheld computer programmed with the Experience-Sampling Program (see Breines et al., 2008). By encouraging the women to complete the questionnaires in a variety of contexts throughout the day, this methodology allowed for the assessment of self-objectification when women were actually engaged in a variety of activities that may be objectifying to them to varying degrees (referred to as event-contingent sampling), such as studying, socializing, exercising, eating, or working. A particular strength of the experience-sampling methodology is that it allows for within-person comparisons over time, which means that other individual difference variables (e.g., neuroticism, social anxiety) can be ruled out as alternative explanations for women's responses throughout the day.

Breines et al. (2008) demonstrated that daily experiences of self-objectification across a variety of contexts negatively affect women's well-being as indicated by their diminished feelings of vitality, flow, and positive affect. However, this study also found that a particular subgroup of women seemed to benefit from self-objectifying: Women with high self-esteem and who based their self-worth to a large degree on their appearance reported greater well-being when they self-objectify compared with other women, in part because they feel less unattractive (i.e., ugly) when they self-objectify. The use of experience-sampling methodology to assess both the short-term and long-term effects of living in sexually objectifying social environments has great potential to advance the field of objectification research.

Self-Objectification in Adolescent Girls

To understand the developmental trajectory of self-objectification and how an external perspective on the body is eventually internalized, measurement tools to assess constructs relevant to self-objectification in younger age groups are sorely needed. One of the few adolescent measures of self-objectification is the eight-item Objectified Relationship With Body (ORB) subscale of the Adolescent Femininity Ideology Scale (AFIS; Tolman, Impett, Tracy, & Michael, 2006; Tolman & Porche, 2000). Sample items include "I think that a girl has to be thin to feel beautiful" and "I often wish my body were different," which are rated using a 6-point response format (ranging from 1 = *strongly disagree* to 6 = *strongly agree*). Studies using this AFIS subscale have demonstrated strong evidence for the link between young girls' objectified body–self relations and mental health. For example, Tolman et al. (2006) found that higher ORB scores predicted much lower self-esteem and higher depressed mood among early adolescent girls. Thus, in addition to the OBC-Youth Scale described earlier (Lindberg et al., 2006), the ORB subscale of the AFIS offers another option for self-objectification research with adolescents.

Social Objectification

Objectification has also been studied as a response to social power over others, whereby perceivers approach social targets as objects, a means to an end, to attain goals, and to reap personal benefits. Findings from six studies demonstrated that feeling powerful (e.g., having the capacity to influence others, control of resources, ability to reward/punish) led respondents to appraise and approach social targets on the basis of their usefulness and instrumentality to them, regardless of their other valuable attributes and qualities, referred to as *social objectification* (Gruenfeld, Inesi, Magee, & Galinsky, 2008). To assess social objectification of a target, Gruenfeld et al. (2008) developed the Objectification Scale, a 10-item scale with a 7-point response format (ranging from 1 = *disagree strongly* to 7 = *agree strongly*), with items such as "I think more about what this person can do for me than what I can do for him/her." The broader focus on instrumentality with the Objectification Scale extends the study of objectification to other social domains beyond the sexual arena, which is timely and imperative (for a discussion of racial objectification, see Moradi & Subich, 2003).

In some instances, Gruenfeld et al. (2008) found that social objectification of targets produced positive effects for those targets when the needs of the perceiver matched the skills and goals of the target. That is, some targets were evaluated and rewarded on the basis of their actual skills and competency instead of other attributes (e.g., age, gender, race) when those particular skills were instrumental to the perceiver's goals. On the basis of these findings, it was suggested that reports on the negative consequences of self-objectification may be overstated, apparently because in some cases being instrumental benefits everyone. These conclusions create a slippery slope. Because self-objectification was not actually measured in these studies, it seems too early and too far of a leap to conclude that self-objectification may not be so negative. Moreover, that an imbalance of power is necessary for objectification to occur is well known (Foucault, 1979), and these empirical findings underscore this idea. Whether or not the person becomes complicit in the objectification because of the anticipated social rewards or potential upward mobility does not undo the objectification of the person. Reducing a person to the status of "mere instrument" in the service of a more powerful person positions her in a vulnerable and subjugated role. Indeed, the fact that men perceive women's bodies as instrumental to their needs—and it is these very bodily attributes that some women have come to value highly in themselves and that will bring them particular social rewards—is a clear instance when the matching of goals between the more socially powerful (men) and the less socially powerful (women) would not reduce the psychic costs associated with self-objectifying, or effectively alter the target's upward mobility and social status (Bartky, 1990; Fredrickson & Roberts, 1997). Future research on objectifying behavior across broader social domains should continue to measure the effects of this behavior on the social targets as well as refine the assessment of the objectifying behavior itself.

Self-Objectification and Social Self-Consciousness

There is some conceptual overlap between measures of public self-awareness and self-objectification, and this is borne out in some of the empirical studies that have measured these constructs together. For example, McKinley and Hyde (1996) demonstrated moderate to high correlations between self-surveillance and public self-consciousness ($r = .73$) and between self-surveillance and public body consciousness ($r = .46$). More recent research showed correlations among self-surveillance, public self-consciousness, and public body consciousness ranging between .47 and .69 (Calogero & Watson, 2009). However, Calogero and Watson (2009) also found low to moderate correlations between self-objectification (as measured by the SOQ) and public self-consciousness ($r = .34$), public body consciousness ($r = .28$), and self-surveillance ($r = .37$). Thus, self-objectification, and to a lesser extent self-surveillance, are distinct from other types of public self-awareness. More research is needed to clarify these conceptual and operational issues.

A final scale warrants consideration here. The Appearance Orientation subscale of the Multidimensional Body–Self Relations Questionnaire (Brown, Cash, & Mikulka, 1990) has been used as a measure of self-objectification. Davis, Dionne, and Shuster (2001) stated that this scale is similar to the SOQ in that it reflects concern about appearance without an evaluative component. Although there is some conceptual overlap, an inspection of the items of the Appearance Orientation subscale suggests that this scale might be closely linked to the Surveillance subscale but not the SOQ. The Appearance Orientation subscale includes items related to appearance improvement and does not require respondents to prioritize appearance relative to competence. Thus, the value assigned to appearance may be differentially represented on the basis of whether the Appearance Orientation subscale or the SOQ is used. In sum, as highlighted throughout this chapter, judicious scale selection and cautious interpretation are recommended within this research area.

CONCLUSION

Scholars of objectification are encouraged to consider more consistent and systematic use of labels for the constructs of self-objectification and self-surveillance. In addition, researchers are encouraged to use the SOQ and the Surveillance subscale judiciously in the measurement of an objectified body–self relationship as these scales may not represent interchangeable constructs. When administration of only one of the two measures is possible or appropriate, it is necessary to carefully consider the specific phenomenon under investigation in order to select the most appropriate tool. When selecting a measure, one should always give careful consideration to the psychometric qualities of the instrument and the validation sample for the specific scale. More broadly, although current measurement tools have helped to illuminate the experience and consequences of self-objectification, revisiting and refining the conceptualization and operationalization of self-objectification is imperative for advancing research in this area (see Chapter 10, this volume). Most of the research on objectification theory has been with young, middle-class, White, heterosexual, able-bodied, college women from Australia and North America. Further research is needed to validate measures of self-objectification in more diverse samples, especially cross-cultural, clinical, and minority populations for whom appearance concerns and body focus may be highly salient but phenomenologically different. Indeed, further refinement of the assessment tools would widen and improve understanding of the psychology of objectification.

REFERENCES

Aubrey, J. S. (2006). Exposure to sexually objectifying media and body self-perceptions among college women: An examination of the selective exposure hypothesis and the role of moderating variables. *Sex Roles, 55,* 159–172. doi:10.1007/s11199-006-9070-7

Bartky, S. (1990). *Femininity and domination.* New York, NY: Routledge.

Basow, S. A., Foran, K. A., & Bookwala, J. (2007). Body objectification, social pressure, and disordered eating behavior in college women: The role of sorority membership. *Psychology of Women Quarterly, 31,* 394–400. doi:10.1111/j.1471-6402.2007.00388.x

Berger, J. (1972). *Ways of seeing.* London, England: Penguin.

Breines, J. G., Crocker, J., & Garcia, J. A. (2008). Self-objectification and well-being in women's daily lives. *Personality and Social Psychology Bulletin, 34,* 583–598. doi:10.1177/0146167207313727

Breitkopf, C. R., Littleton, H., & Berenson, A. (2007). Body image: A study in a tri-ethnic sample of low income women. *Sex Roles, 56,* 373–380. doi:10.1007/s11199-006-9177-x

Brown, T. A., Cash, T. F., & Mikulka, P. J. (1990). Attitudinal body image assessment: Factor analysis of the Body–Self Relations Questionnaire. *Journal of Personality Assessment, 55,* 135–144. doi:10.1207/s15327752jpa5501&2_13

Buchanan, T. S., Fischer, A. R., Tokar, D. M., & Yoder, J. D. (2008). Testing a culture-specific extension of objectification theory regarding African American women's body image. *Counseling Psychologist, 36,* 697–718. doi:10.1177/0011000008316322

Cafri, G., Thompson, J. K., & Jacobsen, P. B. (2006). Appearance reasons for tanning mediate the relationship between media influence and UV exposure and sun protection. *Archives of Dermatology, 142,* 1067–1069. doi:10.1001/archderm.142.8.1067

Cafri, G., Thompson, J. K., Roehrig, M., van den Berg, P., Jacobsen, P. B., & Stark, S. (2006). An investigation of appearance motives for tanning: The development and evaluation of the Physical Appearance Reasons for Tanning Scale (PARTS) and its relation to sunbathing and indoor tanning intentions. *Body Image, 3,* 199–209. doi:10.1016/j.bodyim.2006.05.002

Calogero, R. M. (2004). A test of objectification theory: Effect of the male gaze on appearance concerns in college women. *Psychology of Women Quarterly, 28,* 16–21. doi:10.1111/j.1471-6402.2004.00118.x

Calogero, R. M. (2009). Objectification processes and disordered eating in British women and men. *Journal of Health Psychology, 14*, 394–402. doi:10.1177/1359105309102192

Calogero, R. M., Davis, W. N., & Thompson, J. K. (2005). The role of self-objectification in the experience of women with eating disorders. *Sex Roles, 52*, 43–50. doi:10.1007/s11199-005-1192-9

Calogero, R. M., Herbozo, S., & Thompson, J. K. (2009). Complementary weightism: The potential costs of appearance-related commentary for women's self-objectification. *Psychology of Women Quarterly, 33*, 120–132. doi:10.1111/j.1471-6402.2008.01479.x

Calogero, R. M., & Jost, J. T. (2010). *Exposure to sexist ideology, self-objectification, and the protective function of the need to avoid closure.* Manuscript submitted for publication.

Calogero, R. M., & Watson, N. (2009). Self-discrepancy and chronic social self-consciousness: Unique and interactive effects of gender and real-ought discrepancy. *Personality and Individual Differences, 46*, 642–647. doi:10.1016/j.paid.2009.01.008

Crawford, M., Lee, I.-C., Portnoy, G., Gurung, A., Khatti, D., Jha, P., & Regmi, A. C. (2009). Objectified body consciousness in a developing country: A comparison of mothers and daughters in the US and Nepal. *Sex Roles, 60*, 174–185. doi:10.1007/s11199-008-9521-4

Daubenmier, J. J. (2005). The relationship of yoga, body awareness, and body responsiveness to self-objectification and disordered eating. *Psychology of Women Quarterly, 29*, 207–219. doi:10.1111/j.1471-6402.2005.00183.x

Davis, C., Dionne, M., & Shuster, B. (2001). Physical and personality correlates of appearance orientation. *Personality and Individual Differences, 30*, 21–30. doi:10.1016/S0191-8869(00)00006-4

de Beauvoir, S. (1952). *The second sex* (H. M. Parshley, Trans.). New York, NY: Vintage Books.

Downs, D. M., James, S., & Cowan, G. (2006). Body objectification, self-esteem, and relationship satisfaction: A comparison of exotic dancers. *Sex Roles, 54*, 745–752. doi:10.1007/s11199-006-9042-y

Fairchild, K., & Rudman, L. A. (2008). Everyday stranger harassment and women's objectification. *Social Justice Research, 21*, 338–357. doi:10.1007/s11211-008-0073-0

Foucault, M. (1979). *Discipline and punish: The birth of a prison.* New York, NY: Vintage Books.

Fredrickson, B. L., & Roberts, T. A. (1997). Objectification theory: Toward understanding women's lived experience and mental health risks. *Psychology of Women Quarterly, 21*, 173–206. doi:10.1111/j.1471-6402.1997.tb00108.x

Fredrickson, B. L., Roberts, T. A., Noll, S. M., Quinn, D. M., & Twenge, J. M. (1998). That swimsuit becomes you: Sex differences in self-objectification, restrained eating, and math performance. *Journal of Personality and Social Psychology, 75*, 269–284. doi:10.1037/0022-3514.75.1.269

Gapinski, K. D., Brownell, K. D., & LaFrance, M. (2003). Body objectification and "fat talk": Effects on emotion, motivation, and cognitive performance. *Sex Roles, 48*, 377–388. doi:10.1023/A:1023516209973

Grabe, S., Hyde, J. S., & Lindberg, S. M. (2007). Body objectification and depression in adolescents: The role of gender, shame, and rumination. *Psychology of Women Quarterly, 31*, 164–175. doi:10.1111/j.1471-6402.2007.00350.x

Grippo, K. P., & Hill, M. S. (2008). Self-objectification, habitual body monitoring, and body dissatisfaction in older European American women: Exploring age and feminism as moderators. *Body Image, 5*, 173–182. doi:10.1016/j.bodyim.2007.11.003

Gruenfeld, D. H., Inesi, M. E., Magee, J. C., & Galinsky, A. D. (2008). Power and the objectification of social targets. *Journal of Personality and Social Psychology, 95*, 111–127. doi:10.1037/0022-3514.95.1.111

Hallsworth, L., Wade, T., & Tiggemann, M. (2005). Individual differences in male body-image: An examination of self-objectification in recreational body builders. *British Journal of Health Psychology, 10*, 453–465. doi:10.1348/135910705X26966

Harper, B., & Tiggemann, M. (2008). The effect of thin ideal media images on women's self-objectification, mood, and body image. *Sex Roles, 58*, 649–657. doi:10.1007/s11199-007-9379-x

Harrison, K., & Fredrickson, B. L. (2003). Women's sport media, self-objectification, and mental health in Black and White adolescent females. *Journal of Communication, 53*, 216–232. doi:10.1111/j.1460-2466.2003.tb02587.x

Hebl, M. R., King, E. B., & Lin, J. (2004). The swimsuit becomes us all: Ethnicity, gender, and vulnerability to self-objectification. *Personality and Social Psychology Bulletin, 30*, 1322–1331. doi:10.1177/0146167204264052

Hill, M. S., & Fischer, A. R. (2008). Examining objectification theory: Lesbian and heterosexual women's experiences with sexual and self-objectification. *Counseling Psychologist, 36*, 745–776. doi:10.1177/0011000007301669

Jackson, K. M., & Aiken, L. S. (2000). A psychosocial model of sun protection and sunbathing in young women: The impact of health beliefs, attitudes, norms, and self-efficacy for sun protection. *Health Psychology, 19*, 469–478.

John, D. H., & Ebbeck, V. (2008). Gender-differentiated associations among objectified body consciousness, self-conceptions and physical activity. *Sex Roles, 59*, 623–632. doi:10.1007/s11199-008-9473-8

Johnston-Robledo, I., & Fred, V. (2008). Self-objectification and lower income pregnant women's breastfeeding attitudes. *Journal of Applied Social Psychology, 38*, 1–21.

Kim, J. L., & Ward, L. M. (2004). Pleasure reading: Associations between young women's sexual attitudes and their reading of contemporary women's magazines. *Psychology of Women Quarterly, 28*, 48–58.

Klonoff, E. A., & Landrine, H. (1995). The Schedule of Sexist Events: A measure of lifetime and recent sexist discrimination in women's lives. *Psychology of Women Quarterly, 19,* 439–472. doi:10.1111/j.1471-6402.1995.tb00086.x

Knauss, C., Paxton, S. J., & Alsaker, F. D. (2008). Body dissatisfaction in adolescent boys and girls: Objectified body consciousness, internalization of the media body ideal and perceived pressure from media. *Sex Roles, 59,* 633–643. doi:10.1007/s11199-008-9474-7

Kozee, H. B., & Tylka, T. L. (2006). A test of objectification theory with lesbian women. *Psychology of Women Quarterly, 30,* 348–357. doi:10.1111/j.1471-6402.2006.00310.x

Kozee, H. B., Tylka, T. L., Augustus-Horvath, C. L., & Denchik, A. (2007). Development and psychometric evaluation of the interpersonal sexual objectification scale. *Psychology of Women Quarterly, 31,* 176–189. doi:10.1111/j.1471-6402.2007.00351.x

Lindberg, S. M., Hyde, J. S., & McKinley, N. M. (2006). A measure of objectified body consciousness for preadolescent and adolescent youth. *Psychology of Women Quarterly, 30,* 65–76. doi:10.1111/j.1471-6402.2006.00263.x

Martins, Y., Tiggemann, M., & Kirkbride, A. (2007). Those Speedos become them: The role of self-objectification in gay and heterosexual men's body image. *Personality and Social Psychology Bulletin, 33,* 634–647. doi:10.1177/0146167206297403

McKinley, N. M. (1998). Gender differences in undergraduates' body esteem: The mediating effect of objectified body consciousness and actual/ideal weight discrepancy. *Sex Roles, 39,* 113–123. doi:10.1023/A:1018834001203

McKinley, N. M. (2006). The developmental and cultural contexts of objectified body consciousness: A longitudinal analysis of two cohorts of women. *Developmental Psychology, 42,* 679–687.

McKinley, N. M., & Hyde, J. S. (1996). The Objectified Body Consciousness Scale: Development and validation. *Psychology of Women Quarterly, 20,* 181–215. doi:10.1111/j.1471-6402.1996.tb00467.x

McKinley, N. M., & Lyon, L. A. (2008). Menopausal attitudes, objectified body consciousness, aging anxiety, and body esteem: European American women's body experiences in midlife. *Body Image, 5,* 375–380.

Mitchell, K. S., & Mazzeo, S. E. (2009). Evaluation of a structural model of objectification theory and eating disorder symptomatology among European American and African American undergraduate women. *Psychology of Women Quarterly, 33,* 384–395. doi:10.1111/j.1471-6402.2009.01516.x

Moradi, B., Dirks, D., & Matteson, A. (2005). Roles of sexual objectification experiences and internalization of standards of beauty in eating disorder symptomatology: A test and extension of objectification theory. *Journal of Counseling Psychology, 52,* 420–428. doi:10.1037/0022-0167.52.3.420

Moradi, B., & Huang, Y.-P. (2008). Objectification theory and psychology of women: A decade of advances and future directions. *Psychology of Women Quarterly, 32,* 377–398. doi:10.1111/j.1471-6402.2008.00452.x

Moradi, B., & Rottenstein, A. (2007). Objectification theory and deaf cultural identity attitudes: Roles in deaf women's eating disorder symptomatology. *Journal of Counseling Psychology, 54,* 178–188. doi:10.1037/0022-0167.54.2.178

Moradi, B., & Subich, L. M. (2003). A concomitant examination of the relations of perceived racist and sexist events to psychological distress for African American women. *Counseling Psychologist, 31,* 451–469. doi:10.1177/0011000003031004007

Morry, M. M., & Staska, S. L. (2001). Magazine exposure: Internalization, self-objectification, eating attitudes, and body satisfaction in male and female university students. *Canadian Journal of Behavioural Science, 33,* 269–279. doi:10.1037/h0087148

Muehlenkamp, J. J., & Saris-Baglama, R. N. (2002). Self-objectification and its psychological outcomes for college women. *Psychology of Women Quarterly, 26,* 371–379.

Noll, S. M. (1996). *The relationship between sexual objectification and disordered eating: Correlational and experimental tests of body shame as a mediator.* Unpublished doctoral dissertation, Duke University, NC.

Noll, S. M., & Fredrickson, B. L. (1998). A mediational model linking self-objectification, body shame, and disordered eating. *Psychology of Women Quarterly, 22,* 623–636. doi:10.1111/j.1471-6402.1998.tb00181.x

Piran, N., & Cormier, H. C. (2005). The social construction of women and disordered eating patterns. *Journal of Counseling Psychology, 52,* 549–558. doi:10.1037/0022-0167.52.4.549

Pope, H. G., Gruber, A. J., Mangweth, B., Bureau, B., deCol, C., Jouvent, R., & Hudson, J. I. (2000). Body image perception among men in three countries. *American Journal of Psychiatry, 157,* 1297–1301. doi:10.1176/appi.ajp.157.8.1297

Prichard, I., & Tiggemann, M. (2005). Objectification in fitness centers: Self-objectification, body dissatisfaction, and disordered eating in aerobic instructors and aerobic participants. *Sex Roles, 53,* 19–28. doi:10.1007/s11199-005-4270-0

Quinn, D. M., Kallen, R. W., & Cathey, C. (2006). Body on my mind: The lingering effect of state self-objectification. *Sex Roles, 55,* 869–874. doi:10.1007/s11199-006-9140-x

Quinn, D. M., Kallen, R. W., Twenge, J. M., & Fredrickson, B. L. (2006). The disruptive effect of self-objectification on performance. *Psychology of Women Quarterly, 30,* 59–64. doi:10.1111/j.1471-6402.2006.00262.x

Roberts, T., & Gettman, J. Y. (2004). Mere exposure: Gender differences in the negative effects of priming a state of self-objectification. *Sex Roles, 51,* 17–27. doi:10.1023/B:SERS.0000032306.20462.22

Siever, M. D. (1994). Sexual orientation and gender as factors in socioculturally acquired vulnerability to body dissatisfaction and eating disorders. *Journal of Consulting and Clinical Psychology, 62,* 252–260. doi:10.1037/0022-006X.62.2.252

Sinclair, S. L., & Myers, J. E. (2004). The relationship between objectified body consciousness and wellness in a group of college women. *Journal of College Counseling, 7,* 159–161.

Slater, A., & Tiggemann, M. (2002). A test of objectification theory in adolescent girls. *Sex Roles, 46,* 343–349. doi:10.1023/A:1020232714705

Spitzack, C. (1990). *Confessing excess: Women and the politics of body reduction.* Albany, NY: State University of New York Press.

Steer, A., & Tiggemann, M. (2008). The role of self-objectification in women's sexual functioning. *Journal of Social and Clinical Psychology, 27,* 205–225. doi:10.1521/jscp.2008.27.3.205

Strelan, P., & Hargreaves, D. (2005). Women who objectify other women: The vicious circle of objectification? *Sex Roles, 52,* 707–712. doi:10.1007/s11199-005-3737-3

Swim, J. K., Cohen, L. L., & Hyers, L. L. (1998). Experiencing everyday prejudice and discrimination. In J. K. Swim & C. Stangor (Eds.), *Prejudice: The target's perspective* (pp. 37–60). San Diego, CA: Academic Press.

Thompson, J. K., & Cafri, G. (2007). *The muscular ideal: Psychological, social, and medical perspectives.* Washington, DC: American Psychological Association. doi:10.1037/11581-000

Tiggemann, M., & Boundy, M. (2008). Effect of environment and appearance compliment on college women's self-objectification, mood, body shame, and cognitive performance. *Psychology of Women Quarterly, 32,* 399–405. doi:10.1111/j.1471-6402.2008.00453.x

Tiggemann, M., & Kuring, J. K. (2004). The role of body objectification in disordered eating and depressed mood. *British Journal of Clinical Psychology, 43,* 299–311. doi:10.1348/0144665031752925

Tiggemann, M., & Lynch, J. E. (2001). Body image across the life span in adult women: The role of self-objectification. *Developmental Psychology, 37,* 243–253. doi:10.1037/0012-1649.37.2.243

Tiggemann, M., & Slater, A. (2001). A test of objectification theory in former dancers and non-dancers. *Psychology of Women Quarterly, 25,* 57–64. doi:10.1111/1471-6402.00007

Tolman, D. L., Impett, E. A., Tracy, A. J., & Michael, A. (2006). Looking good, sounding good: Femininity ideology and adolescent girls' mental health. *Psychology of Women Quarterly, 30,* 85–95. doi:10.1111/j.1471-6402.2006.00265.x

Tolman, D. L., & Porche, M. V. (2000). The Adolescent Femininity Ideology Scale: Development and validation of a new measure for girls. *Psychology of Women Quarterly, 24,* 365–376. doi:10.1111/j.1471-6402.2000.tb00219.x

Tylka, T. L., & Hill, M. S. (2004). Objectification theory as it relates to disordered eating among college women. *Sex Roles, 51,* 719–730. doi:10.1007/s11199-004-0721-2

II

SEXUAL AND SELF-OBJECTIFICATION

3

THE SEXUALIZATION OF GIRLS AND WOMEN AS A PRIMARY ANTECEDENT OF SELF-OBJECTIFICATION

LINDA SMOLAK AND SARAH K. MURNEN

By definition, the sexualization and objectification of girls and women in patriarchal societies, including the United States, are related. *Objectification* is typically defined as a culture's tendency to treat women's bodies as objects rather than as active, autonomous entities (e.g., Fredrickson & Roberts, 1997; McKinley & Hyde, 1996). Objectification can take a variety of forms. For example, women's bodies might be viewed as vessels for reproduction, as in Margaret Atwood's (1986) novel *The Handmaid's Tale*. However, in the 21st century, the most common form of objectification is *sexual objectification*—that is, women's bodies are treated as objects for the sexual pleasure of men. Insomuch as a culture endorses sexual objectification, societal messages will pressure women to engage in practices that increase their heterosexual appeal, despite the potential risks associated with a sexualized appearance.

Sexual objectification, or *sexualization*, is an antecedent to self-objectification, which leads to self-surveillance and body shame (see Fredrickson & Roberts, 1997; McKinley & Hyde, 1996). Within the framework of objectification theory, this means that sexualization needs to be a common and pervasive phenomenon. In fact, sexualization needs to be frequent and widespread enough to approximate a social norm. Sexualization facilitates women's development of the belief that a sexy appearance is important not

53

only to appeal to men but also to be successful in all areas of life. This belief is key to internalizing the sexual gaze, that is, self-objectification. As a pervasive influence, sexualization exists in multiple forms and is directed at many girls and women from a variety of sources. Sexualization makes it clear to girls and women that being a sex object is a primary role. Furthermore, sexualization teaches women that attracting a man, which requires sex appeal, will ensure financial stability and personal safety. In other words, sexualization teaches girls and women that there are rewards for being sexy. Furthermore, there are punishments, or at least fewer opportunities, for not following the sexy norms.

The overarching goal of this chapter is to describe sexualization, focusing on U.S. culture. More specifically, we begin by describing how sexualization meets the criteria for a social norm. Next we describe specific forms of sexualization at various points in the life span. We adopt a developmental perspective to emphasize two points. First, as social norm theory and objectification theory indicate, sexualization of girls begins early, is frequent, and has multiple sources. Second, sexualization leading to self-objectification may be part of gender role development. Then, we describe the rewards/benefits and punishments/costs associated with sexualization norms. This leads to a discussion of why women might view sexiness as a source of power and might, therefore, actively participate in their own sexualization. We conclude by identifying several key research questions.

SEXUALIZATION AS A SOCIAL NORM

The meaning and basis of sexualization can be conceptualized in a variety of ways. In this chapter, the focus is on the sexualization of women as a social norm. This implies that both men and women have come to expect and accept that women will be treated as and behave like sexual objects for the pleasure of men.

Defining Sexualization

Sexualization is the culturally sanctioned appropriation of another person's sexuality. The American Psychological Association's (APA's) Task Force on the Sexualization of Girls (2007, p. 2) suggested that there are four components of sexualization: (a) sexual appeal is the sole determinant of a person's value; (b) sexual appeal is wholly based on physical attractiveness, which is narrowly defined; (c) someone is sexually objectified (objectification); or (d) sexuality is forced on a person. The final criterion is particularly applicable to children and adolescents.

Sexualization is distinct from healthy sexuality. Healthy sexuality involves mutual responsibility, respect, control, and pleasure within the context of an intimate relationship (APA, 2007). There is no mutuality in sexualization. One person is "using" the other for his or her own gratification without regard for the other's needs, interests, or desires. Healthy sexuality is life enhancing. It involves the ability to actively choose sexual activities and partners that provide pleasure without fear or shame (O'Sullivan, McCrudden, & Tolman, 2006). Sexualization is disempowering, limiting and constraining women's sexual options and defining what constitutes pleasure for women instead of facilitating women's own choices and preferences.

Social Norms and Sexualization

Evidence indicates that the sexualization of girls and women in American culture is a social norm. *Social norms* are perceived guidelines for behavior that are defined within social interactions and acquired through socialization processes. Typically, these norms are based on one's observation and evaluation of a peer group as to what constitutes "typical" behavior within the group. The existence of social norms implies that (a) there are expectations that represent misperceptions or misinformation about the frequency or meaning of specific behaviors, (b) one form of this misinformation and misperception consists of beliefs that the behaviors are more common than they actually are, and (c) these expectations influence one's own behavior (Berkowitz, 2003). Without intervention, beliefs in these social norms can result in unquestioning acceptance of the status quo as well as potentially dangerous behavior (e.g., engaging in unprotected sex, smoking cigarettes).

The sexualization of girls and women is a ubiquitous phenomenon, occurring in clothing, appearance-enhancing products and procedures, media, and messages from peers and parents (Levin & Kilbourne, 2008). Feminist theorists (e.g., Lorber, 2010; Sheffield, 2007) argue that sexualization is directed primarily at girls and women in patriarchal societies. It supports and helps perpetuate the status quo and gender stratification, and it supports the economy through the sale of clothing, makeup, hair products, diet and body-shaping products, and even plastic surgery (Levin & Kilbourne, 2008). Furthermore, by limiting women's options and keeping them dependent on men, sexualization maintains women's subordinate societal position. Because of its function in maintaining social roles, sexualization has come to be viewed as normal and even natural. For example, evolutionary psychologists argue that sexual attractiveness is supportive of procreation and therefore reflects natural selection (Buss et al., 1990; Singh, 1993). That is, sexualization is seen as a natural process that serves reproductive fitness. Within evolutionary theory, reproductive roles lead women to want men to provide protection for them and their offspring. This will cause women to sexualize themselves (i.e., self-objectify) to attract powerful men. Sexier women are also viewed as normative because they can supposedly make men want to potentially relinquish their "natural" promiscuity and invest their resources in an individual woman and her children. Some evolutionary theorists even argue that there is a female body shape, marked by an "hourglass" figure, that is inherently attractive to men and should, therefore, naturally be sought by women (Singh, 1993). Thus, this theory normalizes sexualization and self-objectification while supporting status quo gender roles.

Others argue that commercial culture promotes the importance of women's sexiness. Women are taught to be sexy, but not necessarily sexual, a position that is not completely consistent with the idea of a natural sexiness and sexuality. There has been a recent emphasis on the extreme sexualization of women in the United States, a process Paul (2005) referred to as "pornification." Among the many ways that pornography has become more widely accepted in society is the appearance of beauty practices in popular culture that used to be portrayed only in pornography, such as wearing thong underwear and stiletto heels (Jeffreys, 2005; Paul, 2005). Women are being encouraged to accept a masculinized view of sex that legitimizes their role as sex objects (Paul, 2005). Paul wrote,

> "Today, the pornography industry has convinced women that wearing a thong is a form of emancipation, learning to pole dance means embracing your sexuality, and taking your boyfriend for a lap dance is what every sexy and supportive girlfriend should do" (p. 110).

Levy (2005) wrote about some girls' and women's acceptance of "raunch culture" as evident in their participation in such cultural events as *Girls Gone Wild* videos. Yet, if girls and women have to choose between being asexual, as schools encourage in abstinence-only education, or being an object of male sexual fantasy, as commercial culture promotes, the role of sex object might be the more interesting choice. While commercial culture has encouraged this sexy image as a form of power, it is questionable whether this image truly is empowering (Gill, 2008; Paul, 2005). Popular images of the sexy women rarely convey the potential degradation and violence that can be part of women's sexual experience in a male-dominated society (Gill, 2008).

Sexualization of girls and women shows variability across cultures and time. Such variability, particularly across brief periods of time or across cultures, is also inconsistent with the argument that sexualization is a natural phenomenon. For example, Reichert and Carpenter (2004) found that the sexualization of women in advertisements increased significantly between 1983 and 2003. There are numerous cultures in which women are subject to punishment if they appear publicly in revealing clothing. This suggests that the sexualization of girls and women may be more of a cultural than biological phenomenon and that a culture may develop norms concerning sexiness and appearance.

Sexualization makes women vulnerable, physically and psychologically. It is difficult to demonstrate physical competence, such as lifting, bending, or running, dressed in stiletto heels and a tight-fitting skirt. Engaging in the "beauty practices" necessary for meeting standards created by sexualization (which itself can be dangerous) means women's energy is diverted from other (perhaps more empowering) activities. And, as radical feminists have noted, sexy clothing, appearance, and behavior in women can be used to excuse sexual violence by men (Lorber, 2010). Women who are sexually objectified in our culture are seen, and treated, as if they are lower status, which further limits their opportunities (Hesse-Biber, Leavy, Quinn, & Zoino, 2006; Smolak & Murnen, 2007). As is often the case with social norms, then, the perception that sexualization is empowering is a false one. Feminist theorists view sexualization as a form of oppression of women (Brownmiller, 1975; Calogero, Boroughs, & Thompson, 2007; Jeffreys, 2005). It functions to keep women in a subordinate position in society, a position that defines women's success in terms of their appeal to men. At a cultural level, sexualization has costs to women and benefits to men. As part of social norms, the sexualization of girls and women helps to maintain current societal power relationships.

Yet, women also frequently view sexuality as a source of power. Third-wave feminists believe that any choice made by women is positive (Lorber, 2010). This includes adopting a "sexy girl" or "girlie girl" appearance. Unlike radical feminists, third-wave feminists do not view such roles as inherently problematic. Indeed, they argue that even pornography, stripping, and pole dancing do not reflect sexualization and can be empowering (e.g., McGhan, 2007; Pollet & Hurwitz, 2007). Girls and women who are judged as more attractive do indeed experience greater social success. And attractive, though not necessarily overtly sexy, women are more likely to be hired and paid more for jobs (Cawley, 2004; Engemann & Owyang, 2005). Thus, there are clear societal rewards for women who participate in their own sexualization and thereby support the continuation of the cultural sexualization of women.

How Is Sexualization Conveyed?

Given the role of media in conveying sexualization, theories that offer explanations of media influence, particularly on the development of social norms, are relevant. Cultivation theorists argue that television can provide people with the norms for behaviors, ranging from what levels and types of violence are common to what is the normative treatment of women in heterosexual relationships (Gerbner, Gross, Morgan, & Signorelli, 1994). The more one is exposed to sexualizing and objectifying media images of women, the more likely one is to internalize these images and use them to guide one's own self-related attitudes and behaviors. It is evident that television and magazines are awash in such images (e.g., Harrison & Hefner, 2008; Ward, 2003). It is not surprising, then, that television viewing has been related to attitudes about thinness, breast size, and breast augmentation surgery (Harrison & Hefner, 2008).

In addition to establishing norms and expectations, media may also provide models for comparison purposes. In social comparison theory, people's drive to self-evaluate leads them to compare themselves with other people (Festinger, 1954). People are particularly inclined to compare themselves with those whom they perceive to be similar or to embody some ideal. This might explain the impact of peers on attitudes about sexuality and appearance (Carlson Jones, 2004; Lefkowitz & Gillen, 2006) as well as some media influences (Harrison & Hefner, 2008). It is noteworthy that cognitive developmental theories of gender role development emphasize that young girls actively seek female role models to evaluate and shape their own behavior (e.g., Kohlberg, 1966). In other words, in trying to determine what it means to be a "girl" or a "woman," young girls will look for information from the older girls and women (who are similar to the younger girl because they are female) who may be modeling sexualized dress, appearance, and behavior. But media are not the sole source of sexualization messages. Sexualization also includes the personal, direct experiences that women have with sexual objectification in the form of men staring at them (e.g., ogling, leering), men commenting on their bodies in an evaluative way (e.g., catcalls), men touching them, and men raping them. This continuum of sexual violence is rooted in the cultural interest in keeping women in a subordinate position. Ironically, it also leads women to depend on men for protection (Sheffield, 2007).

Sexualization may also be more subtle. Social role theorists (e.g., Eagly, Wood, & Johannesen-Schmidt, 2004) argue that gender roles and gendered behaviors are intended to support cultural values and roles. The feminine role may have been rooted in reproductive roles related to pregnancy and child care, but it has evolved to meet contemporary societal needs. For example, the workplace in the United States is still generally designed to work best for people who either have no children or have grown children. If the family has young children, it is often easiest and most cost-effective if someone stays home with the children. Because women still typically make less money than men do (Bureau of Labor Statistics, 2009), it is often the woman who stays home in a heterosexual couple. Such women are financially dependent on men and therefore have to be appealing to them. In this way, socially defined roles require that women be sexy and attractive to men. As with all social roles, this one needs to be learned, and so sexualization needs to appear during childhood. Thus, sexualization is part of the role that young girls acquire, arguably part of gender role development per se. Indeed, recent conceptualization of the feminine gender role includes attractiveness (and particularly thinness) as a dimension (Mahalik et al., 2005). Thus, theories of gender role development (e.g, Bigler & Liben, 2007; Bussey & Bandura, 2004; Leaper & Friedman, 2007; C. L. Martin & Ruble, 2004) are applicable as etiological models of self-sexualization.

SEXUALIZATION ACROSS THE LIFE SPAN

There is much evidence that U.S. culture does endorse the sexual objectification of women. It is also evident that sexually objectifying messages and pressures are also aimed at adolescent girls. Yet, it is clearly the case that in most cultures, including that of the United States, children are not appropriate targets of adult male sexuality. The United States, for example, has a myriad of laws against using young girls in pornography or engaging in sexual relations with them, even if they "consent." It would be difficult to argue that American culture widely sanctions treating girls as true sex *objects*. It would be equally difficult to argue, however, that young girls are not sexualized. There are bikini bathing suits for even preschool girls, makeup kits for preschool and elementary school age girls, high heels for infant girls, and T-shirts that say things like "Future Hottie" or "Future Trophy Wife" or "Porn Star." Young girls, then, are in training to be sexual objects. They are acquiring a gender role that includes monitoring attractiveness (Mahalik et al., 2005). Their bodies are already "projects" (Brumberg, 1997), as they try to emulate the concerns of adult women. They worry about fat (Holub, 2008). They may wear adultlike underwear, including training bras (in sizes that will routinely fit first graders). Thus, developmentally, objectification may be less directly sexualized than it is in adulthood. The girls are being treated like bodies and body parts. They are taught to be sexy not in order to be sexual but in preparation to serve the sexualized gaze and desires of men when they are older and so that they will think of sexualization as "normal." Young girls may be experiencing the imposition of inappropriate sexuality rather than being treated as sex objects per se (APA, 2007).

It remains unclear how self-objectification develops, particularly prior to adolescence. One possibility is that sexualization of girls, including an emphasis on attractiveness that is evident even to preschoolers, is a precursor to self-objectification. Sexualization continues, and perhaps intensifies, beyond adolescence. This may contribute to the intensification and maintenance of self-objectification. Thus, it is important to identify sources of sexualization across the life span as a first step in generating research that will be crucial in tracing the development of self-objectification. Similarly, the argument that sexualization constitutes a social norm requires that we establish how common, pervasive, and continuous it is. The purpose of this section is to describe sexualization from childhood through adulthood.

A word about media: Media is not the sole source of sexualization messages, but it may be the single greatest source. Portrayals of sex, and the social scripts that surround it, are common on television. For example, Kunkel, Eyal, Finnerty, Biely, and Donnerstein (2005) reported that 87% of comedy series, 87% of drama series, 92% of movies, and 67% of talk shows had at least one scene with sexual content during a typical week. These researchers found that the portrayal of sexual content almost doubled from 1998 to 2005. Much of this content sexualizes women. With an emphasis on "spontaneous, glamorous, unmarried, nonrelational sex" (Ward, 2003, p. 355), along with the sexual objectification and degradation of women, prime-time television portrays the sexualization of women as normative.

Although much of this programming is intended for adults, it is obvious that children and adolescents often see it. Children may absorb more sophisticated messages from such shows than parents routinely believe they do. For example, in a study of children ages 2 to 6 role playing adults, Dalton et al. (2005) reported that children who watched PG-13 or R movies were more likely to purchase alcohol for adult dolls who were having friends over for the evening. Furthermore, it has long been true that some sexual content is aimed at teens, as exemplified by shows ranging from *Beverly Hills 90210* to *Gossip Girl*.

Magazine messages and photographs can be even more explicitly sexually objectifying. For example, "lad magazines" are aimed at men. They do not routinely include nudity but still contain pictures of and articles about attractive celebrity women as well as "guy" articles about sexual encounters, partying, and related topics. Lad magazines have emerged as a medium that is more mainstream than pornography but still conveys many of the same messages about the sexual objectification of women. An analysis of *Maxim* and *Stuff*, two lad magazines, found that most of the women pictured were shown as mere sex objects, posed in alluring and provocative positions with no purpose except to appeal to men (Krassas, Blauwkamp, & Wesselink, 2003). *Maxim* is an enormously popular magazine, and many relatively famous actresses (e.g., Melissa Joan Hart, Friedda Pinto, Jaime Pressley) have been portrayed on its covers (Paul, 2005). Magazines aimed at girls and women can also be sexually objectifying. Krassas, Blauwkamp, and Wesselink (2001) analyzed pictures in *Cosmopolitan* versus *Playboy* and found that the images in both magazines emphasized the "male gaze," reinforcing the idea that women should be concerned with being sexually attractive to men.

In magazines aimed at adolescent girls, the dominant themes are that it is important for women to attract men, that women rather than men maintain romantic relationships, and that sexual activity is more acceptable for men than women (the sexual double standard; Ward, 2003). Magazines teach girls that being sexually attractive to men should be of supreme importance. Furthermore, magazines specify how girls can be sexy, including attaining a narrowly defined body ideal that features thin hips and waist with large breasts (Levine & Murnen, 2009). This unrealistic body type is often the focus of body shame that results from self-objectification.

Sexualization at Different Stages of Development

Sexualization of girls and women is evident at virtually all stages of the life span. The specific goals and manifestation of sexualization may vary somewhat at different stages of development. For example, very young girls are being trained to be sexual objects, whereas young adult women actually function as sexual objects.

Preschool

Even preschool children have learned that body fat is undesirable, especially for girls and women. Furthermore, there are some preschool girls who express weight concerns and who try to engage in dietary restraint to control weight; often these girls have mothers who are concerned about their own and their daughters' weights and so model dietary restraint and try to control their daughters' food intake (Fisher, Sinton, & Birch, 2009). Although girls this age may not be aware of the sexualization basis of such maternal behavior, they are learning that it is important to look good. This message is paired with the availability of "sexy" clothes for infants and preschoolers, including stiletto heels (e.g., Heelarious.com) and bikinis as well as makeup kits and play vanity tables. Indeed, some celebrities' preschool age daughters routinely wear high-heel shoes, a selection of which can easily be found online (e.g., in shopping websites such as Zappos.com), along with designer clothing and accessories. There are even beauty pageants in which preschoolers can be judged on their attractiveness while posing and posturing for an audience (e.g., the Cinderella Scholarship Pageant; http://cinderellapageant.com/index.html). Hence, at this stage of development, the messages linking sexualization and attractiveness may be separate, yet they are both present and will soon be integrated, perhaps in the form of Barbie.

Childhood

Young children play with toys, and Barbie continues to be the toy of choice for girls. According to Mattel, Inc. (http://www.mattel.com), only about 10% of 3- to 10-year-old American girls do not own a Barbie, whereas the average 3- to 6-year-old American girl owns 12 Barbies. Barbie is a global presence, with annual retail sales of about $3 billion. Barbie has been criticized because her physical proportions are unrealistic, with an extraordinarily large bust relative to a tiny waist (Dittmar, Halliwell, & Ive, 2006). Current Barbie dolls include a sexualized "Dallas Cowboys Cheerleaders" version as well as a line of "Fashionista" dolls with names like "Sassy," "Wild," and "Glam." The online advertisements for the Barbie Fashionista dolls (e.g., Amazon.com, n.d.) encourage daughters (ages 3 and up) to "strike a pose." Mattel's "So In Style" line of dolls are not only sexy, with styleable hair, but also have little sisters who can look up to them and try to imitate them. Mattel refers to Barbie as a "fashion icon" who has had an estimated 1 billion fashions produced for her and her friends. Indeed, the main intended activity for girls playing with Barbie is dressing Barbie and changing her clothes, emphasizing the importance of the right clothes (Wolf, 1991). Thus, Barbie's image is a sexualized, appearance-oriented one. Other dolls, such as Bratz, may be even more sexualized, but few products are more common or have the longevity of Barbie. Furthermore, there are additional products that encourage girls to learn sexualizing beauty routines, such as Barbie heads that allow the girls to style hair and apply makeup.

Dittmar et al. (2006) showed 5- and 8-year-old girls images of Barbie dolls, Emme dolls, or no dolls. Compared with Barbie dolls, Emme dolls have more realistic body proportions, those of a size 16 adult woman. The 5-year-olds who were exposed to Barbie reported lower body esteem as well as a greater desire to be thin than did the girls in the other conditions. This immediate negative effect was not evident among the 8-year-old girls, but the reaction of the younger girls suggests that a foundation for body dissatisfaction may have already been laid by exposure to Barbie dolls (Dittmar et al., 2006). This effect of a short-term exposure is likely intensified by the consistent, continuous play with Barbie that most American girls experience over the course of several years. Indeed, this early exposure to Barbie may be one lived experience that contributes to girls thinking that striving for an unattainable body shape is normal and natural.

Barbie's message is reinforced by websites (Levin & Kilbourne, 2008). For example, Mattel maintains a website called My Scene (http://myscene. everythinggirl.com/home.aspx), which features animated teen girls dressed in clingy clothes, heavily styled hair, and makeup who discuss their fashion style, flirtation techniques, and shopping preferences. "Makeover" websites (e.g., the Young Woman makeover game) also show girls how they can look "better" and more similar to the dolls they play with. There are also clothing stores (e.g., ShopJustice.com) that cater to elementary school girls, selling clothes and accessories that enable them to dress like older adolescents or young adults. The clothing includes bandeau and tube tops for first graders as well as accessories such as body glitter.

The media are a source of information about sexualization for children. Murnen, Smolak, Mills, and Good (2003) reported that first- through fifth-grade girls were aware of sexualized images of female celebrities. Girls who were more aware of the images were more likely to want to look like the thin, sexy celebrities and have poorer body esteem. They were also more likely to think that it was important to look that way, evidencing the "training" effect of this early exposure. The girls' comments (e.g., "My dad thinks Shania is hot" in response to a photo of Shania Twain) indicated that they were aware of the appeal of the celebrities' looks to men.

Adolescent girls retrospectively report that they were first sexually harassed in elementary school (Bryant, 1993). In a study using cross-gender sexual harassment vignettes, Murnen and Smolak (2000) found that girls who reported higher frequency of sexual harassment also demonstrated lower global self-esteem and weight-shape self-esteem. These associations were not evident among the boys. These girls have already apparently learned that their value (as reflected in self-esteem) is linked to their ability to conform to boys' sexualized expectations.

Early Adolescence

Media exposure is also an important source of sexualization in early adolescence. Research suggests that 60% of middle school girls read "teen" magazines at least two to five times per month (Field et al., 1999). The majority of print advertisements in these magazines portray women as sexual objects (Stankiewicz & Rosselli, 2008). Levin and Kilbourne (2008) described a variety of these ads, including one for Converse "Chuck Taylor" sneakers portraying a young couple hugging with the boy grabbing the girls' buttocks. Indeed, only men's magazines are more likely to sexually objectify women in advertisements (Stankiewicz & Rosselli, 2008), a phenomenon that might affect boys' ideas about how girls ought to behave, look, and be treated. Adolescent boys believe that thinness influences a girl's attractiveness, a preference that reflects media images of women (Paxton, Norris, Wertheim, Durkin, & Anderson, 2005). That such ads are successful in convincing girls that they need to be beautiful is evident in the over $8 billion they spend annually on beauty products (Levin & Kilbourne, 2008).

There is also evidence that gender intensification occurs during early adolescence as sexual maturation leads to the increased expectation that girls will behave like women and boys will behave like men (Galambos, Almeida, & Petersen, 1990). Both adults and peers will increase pressure on girls to engage in appropriate girl activities (e.g., shaving legs, wearing makeup, dressing in ways that are attractive and in vogue). Given that being thin and sexy is part of femininity (Mahalik et al., 2005), girls may perceive themselves as needing to be "sexier" simply because they are approaching adulthood and look more like adult women. Visible pubertal development such as breast development is correlated with higher levels of peer sexual harassment, which is further positively correlated with self-surveillance (Lindberg, Grabe, &

Hyde, 2007). Thus, having an adult woman's body seems to be a signal to boys that they can increase their overt sexualization of peer girls. Although many girls and women often act as if sexualization is normative and acceptable (e.g., by not reporting incidents of sexual harassment), it is evident that experiences of sexualization are threatening and distressing events.

Adolescence

Sexual harassment is even more common in high school than in middle school (American Association of University Women [AAUW], 2001). Up to 90% of high school girls (and boys) report sexual harassment experiences (AAUW, 2001; Leaper & Brown, 2008). The most frequent forms of sexual harassment during high school, reported by 50% to 67% of the girls as occurring at least once, included unwanted romantic attention, demeaning comments about gender, teasing about appearance, and unwanted physical contact (Leaper & Brown, 2008). Such experiences do affect girls' behaviors and attitudes. Compared with boys, girls reported feeling more self-conscious and less confident following sexual harassment (AAUW, 2001). Furthermore, girls who perceive themselves as less typically feminine and less content with the feminine gender role are more likely to perceive themselves as victims of sexism, primarily from male peers (Leaper & Brown, 2008). One possibility is that male peers who notice the girls who stray from the culturally defined path attempt to bring them back in line via sexual harassment and sexist comments about academics and sports. This underscores the links among the sexualization of girls in the form of sexual harassment, sexist experiences, and enforcement of socially stratified gender roles.

Emerging Adulthood (17 to 25 Years)

As women move out of high school and into either college or the workplace, they are preparing for (or even engaging in) two potentially conflicting roles: romantic relationships and career initiation. First, this has long been seen as the period when one focuses on forming committed intimate relationships (Erikson, 1950). Relationships become more nuanced and complex as well as more sexual (Collins & van Dulmen, 2006; Lefkowitz & Gillen, 2006). Such relationships may benefit from traditional feminine gender role behaviors that are often conceptualized as supporting an investment in romantic relationships (Mahalik et al., 2005). Women are likely to view attractiveness as important for attracting a man and for maintaining a successful heterosexual relationship (e.g., McKinley, 1999).

Thus, the interest in romantic relationships may intensify the receptivity to and acceptance of sexualization. Women are exposed to media models of romantic relationships (Ward, 2003). If women are frequent viewers of sexually oriented shows, such as soap operas or music videos, they are not only more likely to engage in sexual behavior but also more likely to tolerate problematic behaviors such as sexual harassment (Ward, 2003).

The second role that receives attention during emerging adulthood is career development. Women who are thinner and more attractive are routinely more successful in their careers in terms of job title and salary (McKinley, 1999; Smolak & Murnen, 2004). Yet, looking sexy appears to be a double-edged sword for women, at least in the workplace. A substantial minority of women report experiencing sexual harassment at work (Gruber, 1990), and perhaps 17% have quit their jobs because of sexual harassment (Gutek & Nakamura, 1983). Some women, such as those working in temporary clerical positions, may find it difficult to a leave a job even when they are distressed by harassment (Rogers & Henson, 2007) and may be forced to tolerate the sexualization. The focus on appearance as a path to career success may actually contribute to at least the justification of sexual harassment, demonstrating how culturally endorsed sexualization can cost women no matter what choice they make.

Sexist events, including sexualizing comments and behaviors by men, are also fairly common experiences for college-age women (Landry & Mercurio, 2009). Indeed, college women experience more sexism and sexist events than college men do (Swim, Hyers, Cohen, & Ferguson, 2001). Higher perceived levels of sexist events are related to general psychological distress (Landry & Mercurio, 2009; Szymanski, Gupta, Carr, & Stewart, 2009).

Adulthood

Adult women clearly face sexual objectification as well as other forms of sexualization. Women have to contend with everyday instances of sexual objectification that threaten their psychological health. Using the Schedule of Sexist Events, Klonoff and Landrine (1995) found that some of the most common sexist events experienced by women involved being exposed to sexually degrading jokes (reported by 94%), being sexually harassed (reported by 82%), being called sexual names (reported by 82%), and being the victim of unwanted sexual advances (reported by 67%). The experience of sexist events measured by the Schedule of Sexist Events was found to be more highly related to the frequency of psychiatric and physical symptoms than the experience of stressors that were not gender related (Landrine, Klonoff, Gibbs, Manning, & Lund, 1995).

Glick, Larsen, Johnson, and Branstiter (2005) proposed that there are three categories of female stereotypes in North America: the traditional woman who is a nurturant caretaker, the nontraditional woman who is an assertive career woman, and the sexy woman. The nontraditional career woman (who is agentic and instrumental, like men) is a more recent development in stereotypes for women and is associated with the increased number of women in paid employment (Diekman & Eagly, 2000). All three stereotyped groups can be the targets of sexism. There are negative attributes associated with both the traditional and nontraditional stereotype. For example, "nice" traditional women are generally liked but are not viewed as competent (Diekman & Eagly, 2000). Women need agentic traits to be viewed as competent (Rudman, 1998). Yet, agentic women may be seen as less well suited than agentic men for feminine managerial jobs because they are not nice enough (Rudman & Glick, 2001). Thus, women are also punished for failing to follow the rules of sexual and self-objectification. Given these negative associations with the traditional and agentic roles, it might make sense for women to explore adherence to the sexy woman stereotype.

After all, sexuality is potentially a source of power for women. Some young feminists argue that female sexuality is an important source of women's empowerment that should be celebrated (Lorber, 2010; McGhan, 2007). An example of this is the very popular television show *Sex and the City*, which aired from 1998 to 2004 and celebrated female sexual agency and pleasure. The show centered on four women friends who were very outspoken about their sexual encounters. However, the show can be criticized from a feminist perspective in that "for a show about women it displays a singular obsession about men" (Wignall, 2000, p. 18). The characters on the show could be described as shallow and self-absorbed. In addition, at the conclusion of the show all four of the women were paired with men. Thus, what appeared to be sexual control and choice was firmly rooted in the broader sexualized social script. Nevertheless, the enormous popularity and longevity of the show (it aired for six seasons, is still in syndication, and has spawned two feature films) means that many women have been exposed to the sexualized ideals and roles portrayed on the show.

Although the sexy woman role might be promoted as a source of power on prime-time television, it is not associated with characteristics related to competence. Glick et al. (2005) found that women portrayed as sexy were not seen as competent for a high-status managerial job compared with women portrayed in more businesslike clothing. Olympic athletes shown in sexualized clothing versus athletic clothing were seen as less intelligent, less capable, and less strong (Gurung & Chrouser, 2007). Thus, one "value" of sexualization in the patriarchal American culture is that it contributes to the image of women as incompetent in realms other than sexual attractiveness to men, thereby protecting men's status.

IS SELF-OBJECTIFICATION MISGUIDED?

Women are socialized to accept the less invasive forms of sexualization as normal, and perhaps even desirable, indicators that they are fulfilling expected role norms. Current feminine gender role norms for women, including investment in appearance, pursuit of thinness, valuing romantic relationships, and being "nice in relationships" (Mahalik et al., 2005), might reflect sexualization. In complement, men are encouraged by norms of adopting a "playboy" mentality, exhibiting power over women, endorsing dominance and violence, and pursuing status (Mahalik et al., 2003) to treat women as objects for their sexual pleasure, underscoring their role in the sexualization of women.

The feminine and masculine gender role norms complement one another when it comes to defining gendered societal expectations for sexual behavior. Kim et al. (2007) defined the "heterosexual script" to include a set of interlocking expectations for the sexual behavior of women and men that maintain a sexist and heterosexist society. For example, men are stereotyped as the initiators of sexual activity who have uncontrollable sex drives, whereas women are the "good girl" gatekeepers of male desire. Masculine courtship strategies encourage men to display wealth and power to attract women who are sexual objects valued for their attractiveness, whereas feminine strategies call women either to use passive and indirect methods or to exploit their own bodies to attract men. Women are expected to desire a committed relationship, whereas men want sex without commitment. As shown in previous sections, the role expectations for women are very complicated, potentially unsatisfying, and potentially threatening to women's health and empowerment. Orenstein (2001) described this time of uncertain roles as one of flux. Under these conditions, a focus on one's own sexual attractiveness might give women a sense of personal control. Furthermore, attractiveness is associated with positive attributes. In a meta-analysis of the existing research, Eagly Ashmore, Makhijani, and Longo (1991) found that attractive women and men were assumed to be more popular and sociable. Young women who were asked to imagine their lives if they embodied the societal ideal for attractiveness thought their lives would be better in multiple ways. For example, more than half of the women associated the ideal with positive social attention and with achieving romantic and employment success (Engeln-Maddox, 2006).

As Dellinger and Williams (1997) concluded, women are not "cultural dopes." Women often understand the contradictions associated with various sexual objectification practices. The women in Dellinger and Williams's study made conscious decisions about whether to wear makeup to work. C. E. Martin (2007) described the process of "double consciousness" as being "an insightful, self-aware feminist on the one hand and a guilty, obsessive sheep on the other" (p. 223). Women with the ability to be critically conscious of the culture should be able to withstand some societal pressure. However, it is not realistic to expect complete resistance because the rewards for compliance are substantial and salient.

Rubin, Nemeroff, and Russo (2004) found some support for this idea in a qualitative study of self-proclaimed feminists. These researchers held focus groups with 25 feminist and/or womanist North American college women who agreed that feminists were more likely to celebrate bodily diversity among women and that a feminist perspective should lead to a conscious awareness of cultural messages as well as the development of strategies to resist these cultural pressures. They believed that feminism promoted ways to reclaim the body from the objectifying gaze through "emancipatory resistance," which might occur through athletics, dance, "taking up space," "moving with confidence," and redefining beauty. Despite an awareness of what a feminist perspective could offer women to help protect against the development of body image dissatisfaction in a sexually objectifying culture, the women felt that they were still susceptible to cultural messages about thinness. Some of the women discussed the split between their rational knowledge that beauty practices could be oppressive and their feelings of negativity about their bodies. One woman said,

> Before . . . when I wasn't a feminist, I bought it. I bought into the whole you should eat this, you should work out, look beautiful all the time. And now I realize what, that's it's just a bunch of bull, you know. I realized that, but I'm still buying into it, and I feel bad about buying into it. (Rubin et al., 2004, p. 33)

Rubin et al. (2004) described rejecting beauty ideals as a "radical act" (p. 28) due to the enormous pressure on young women from appearance norms. In a meta-analytic review of the research linking feminist identity and body-related thoughts, Murnen and Smolak (2009) found that across 26 studies, possessing feminist attitudes was associated with greater body satisfaction and less internalization of the media ideal. Some women do develop a critical consciousness through feminism or other means that allows them to resist or reinterpret sexist experiences. In addition, feminism can encourage people to join together in collective action to expose and eradicate forces that threaten to disrupt women's connection to their bodies.

CONCLUSION

Sexualization of women, and even girls, for the pleasure of men is a ubiquitous phenomenon. It is evident in all forms of media—from magazines to video games—as well as in normative, daily personal interactions. Even infants and preschoolers are "in training" to become sex objects. It is clear that by elementary school, girls not only are aware of this role but also understand some components of sexualization. Sexualization increases and becomes more blatant during adolescence and young adulthood. American culture's equation of youth with sexiness and attractiveness may lead to a decrease in sexualization as women enter middle age.

There are data linking sexualization with self-objectification in adulthood and even a bit of data concerning adolescents. The data are, however, overwhelmingly cross-sectional. This means one can only hypothesize how early and pervasive sexualization might lead to self-objectification and its concomitant psychological disturbances (e.g., depression, anxiety, eating disorders). There is also no information currently available on how sexualization might interact with other variables, such as tendencies for social comparison or self-silencing, to produce, intensify, or maintain self-objectification. Indeed, there are many more questions than answers. It is imperative that researchers gather prospective data, preferably beginning in childhood, to begin to answer these questions.

In addition, most of the available data rely on White, middle-class samples. If researchers wish to decompose cultural messages about sexualization and the impact of these messages, cross-cultural data as well as data from U.S. ethnic and socioeconomic groups may prove invaluable. Examinations of sexualization messages, which may be more or less pervasive than in European American or middle-class culture, and their relationship to self-objectification in other groups are needed. Such research may help to identify the specific components of sexualization that are crucial for the development of self-sexualization (e.g., media vs. peer messages). It may also reveal the mechanisms through which the relationship between sexualization and self-objectification develops.

Finally, we argue that it is not premature to begin to work to counteract the pervasive sexualization of girls and women, both in terms of the messages per se and girls' understanding of those messages (see Chapter 9, this volume). Successful prevention programs can actually contribute to knowledge of the link between sexualization and self-objectification because they use experimental designs to evaluate the effectiveness of altering risk and protective factors in reducing sexualization messages and their internalization. Thus, prevention programs can serve the dual purposes of reducing sexualization and self-objectification while contributing to the empirical literature describing and explaining the link.

REFERENCES

Amazon. (n.d.). *Fashionista Barbie*. Retrieved from http://www.amazon.com/s/ref=nb_sb_noss?url=node%3D166118011&field-keywords=fashionista+barbie

American Association of University Women. (2001). *Hostile hallways: Bullying, teasing, and sexual harassment in schools*. Washington, DC: AAUW Educational Foundation.

American Psychological Association. (2007). *Report of the APA Task Force on the Sexualization of Girls*. Washington, DC: Author. Retrieved from http://www.apa.org/pi/wpo/sexualization_report_summary.pdf

Atwood, M. (1986). *The handmaid's tale*. New York, NY: Random House.

Berkowitz, A. (2003). Applications of social norms theory to other health and social justice issues. In H. W. Perkins (Ed.), *The social norms approach to preventing school and college age substance abuse* (pp. 259–279). San Francisco, CA: Jossey-Bass.

Bigler, R. S., & Liben, L. S. (2007). Developmental intergroup theory: Explaining and reducing children's social stereotyping and prejudice. *Current Directions in Psychological Science, 16*, 162–166. doi:10.1111/j.1467-8721.2007.00496.x

Brownmiller, S. (1975). *Against our will: Men, women, and rape*. New York, NY: Fawcett Books.

Brumberg, J. J. (1997). *The body project: An intimate history of American girls*. New York, NY: Random House.

Bryant, A. (1993). Hostile hallways: The AAUW survey on sexual harassment in America's schools. *Journal of School Health, 63*, 355–357. doi:10.1111/j.1746-1561.1993.tb07153.x

Bureau of Labor Statistics. (2009). *Median weekly earnings of full-time wage and salary workers by detailed occupation and sex*. Retrieved from http://www.bls.gov/cps/cpsaat39.pdf

Buss, D. M., Abbott, M., Angleitner, A., Asherian, A., Biaggio, A., Blanco-Villasenor, A., . . . Yang, K. (1990). International preferences in selecting mates: A study of 37 cultures. *Journal of Cross-Cultural Psychology, 21*, 5–47. doi:10.1177/0022022190211001

Bussey, K., & Bandura, A. (2004). Social cognitive theory of gender development and functioning. In A. H. Eagly, A. Beall, & R. Sternberg (Eds.), *The psychology of gender* (2nd ed., pp. 92–119). New York, NY: Guilford Press.

Calogero, R., Boroughs, M., & Thompson, J. K. (2007). The impact of Western beauty ideals on the lives of women and men: A sociocultural perspective. In V. Swami & A. Furnham (Eds.), *The body beautiful: Evolutionary and sociocultural perspectives* (pp. 259–298). New York, NY: Palgrave Macmillan.

Carlson Jones, D. C. (2004). Body image among adolescent girls and boys: A longitudinal study. *Developmental Psychology, 40*, 823–835. doi:10.1037/0012-1649.40.5.823

Cawley, J. (2004). The impact of obesity on wages. *Journal of Human Resources, 39*, 451–474. doi:10.2307/3559022

Collins, W. A., & van Dulmen, M. (2006). Friendships and romance in emerging adulthood: Assessing distinctiveness in close relationships. In J. J. Arnett & J. J. Tannner (Eds.), *Emerging adults in America: Coming of age in the 21st century* (pp. 219–234). Washington, DC: American Psychological Association. doi:10.1037/11381-009

Dalton, M., Bernhardt, A., Gibson, J., Sargent, J., Beach, M., Adachi-Medjia, A., & Heatherton, T. (2005). Use of cigarettes and alcohol by preschoolers while role-playing adults. *Archives of Pediatrics & Adolescent Medicine, 159,* 854–859. doi:10.1001/archpedi.159.9.854

Dellinger, K., & Williams, C. L. (1997). Makeup at work: Negotiating appearance rules in the workplace. *Gender & Society, 11,* 151–177. doi:10.1177/089124397011002002

Diekman, A. B., & Eagly, A. H. (2000). Stereotypes as dynamic constructs: Women and men of the past, present, and future. *Personality and Social Psychology Bulletin, 26,* 1171–1188. doi:10.1177/0146167200262001

Dittmar, H., Halliwell, E., & Ive, S. (2006). Does Barbie make girls want to be thin? The effect of experimental exposure to images of dolls on the body image of 5- to 8-year old girls. *Developmental Psychology, 42,* 283–292. doi:10.1037/0012-1649.42.2.283

Eagly, A. H., Ashmore, R. D., Makhijani, M. G., & Longo, L. C. (1991). What is beautiful is good, but . . . : A meta-analytic review of research on the physical attractiveness stereotype. *Psychological Bulletin, 110,* 109–128. doi:10.1037/0033-2909.110.1.109

Eagly, A. H., Wood, W., & Johannesen-Schmidt, M. C. (2004). Social role theory of sex differences and similarities: Implications for the partner preferences of women and men. In A. H. Eagly, A. E. Beall, & R. J. Sternberg (Eds.), *The psychology of gender* (2nd ed., pp. 269–295). New York, NY: Guilford Press.

Engeln-Maddox, R. (2006). Buying a beauty standard or dreaming of a new life? Expectations associated with media ideals. *Psychology of Women Quarterly, 30,* 258–266. doi:10.1111/j.1471-6402.2006.00294.x

Engemann, K., & Owyang, M. (2005, April). So much for that merit raise: The link between wages and appearance. *The Regional Economist.* St. Louis, MO: Federal Reserve Bank of St. Louis. Retrieved from Research.stlouisfed.org/publications/regional/05/04/appearance.pdf

Erikson, E. H. (1950). *Childhood and society.* New York, NY: Norton.

Field, A., Camargo, C., Taylor, C., Berkey, C., Frazier, L., Gillman, M., & Colditz, G. (1999). Overweight, weight concerns, and bulimic behaviors among girls and boys. *Journal of the American Academy of Child and Adolescent Psychiatry, 38,* 754–760. doi:10.1097/00004583-199906000-00024

Festinger, L. (1954). A theory of social comparison processes. *Human Relations, 7,* 117–140. doi:10.1177/001872675400700202

Fisher, J. O., Sinton, M., & Birch, L. L. (2009). Early experience with food and eating: Influencing risk for the development of disordered eating and problems of energy balance. In L. Smolak & J. K. Thompson (Eds.), *Body image, eating disorders, and obesity in youth: Assessment, treatment, and prevention* (2nd ed., pp. 17–34). Washington, DC: American Psychological Association. doi:10.1037/11860-001

Fredrickson, B. L., & Roberts, T. A. (1997). Objectification theory: Toward understanding women's lived experiences and mental health risks. *Psychology of Women Quarterly, 21*, 173–206. doi:10.1111/j.1471-6402.1997.tb00108.x

Galambos, N., Almeida, D., & Petersen, A. (1990). Masculinity, femininity, and sex role attitudes in early adolescence: Exploring gender intensification. *Child Development, 61*, 1905–1914. doi:10.2307/1130846

Gerbner, G., Gross, L., Morgan, M., & Signorelli, N. (1994). Growing up with television: The cultivation perspective. In J. Bryant & D. Zillmann (Eds.), *Media effects: Advances in theory and research* (pp. 17–41). Hillsdale, NJ: Erlbaum.

Gill, R. (2008). Empowerment/sexism: Figuring female sexual agency in contemporary advertising. *Feminism and Psychology, 18*, 35–60. doi:10.1177/0959353507084950

Glick, P., Larsen, S., Johnson, C., & Branstiter, H. (2005). Evaluations of sexy women in low-and high-status jobs. *Psychology of Women Quarterly, 29*, 389–395. doi:10.1111/j.1471-6402.2005.00238.x

Gruber, J. (1990). Methodological problems and policy implications in sexual harassment research. *Population Research and Policy Review, 9*, 235–254. doi:10.1007/BF00162837

Gurung, R. A. R., & Chrouser, C. J. (2007). Predicting objectification: Do provocative clothing and observer characteristics matter? *Sex Roles, 57*, 91–99. doi:10.1007/s11199-007-9219-z

Gutek, B., & Nakamura, C. (1983). Gender roles and sexuality in the world of work. In E. Allgeier & N. McCormick (Eds.), *Changing boundaries: Gender roles and sexual behavior* (pp. 182–201). Mountain View, CA: Mayfield.

Harrison, K., & Hefner, V. (2008). Media, body image and eating disorders. In S. L. Calvert & B. J. Wilson (Eds.), *Handbook of children, media, and development* (pp. 381–406). Malden, MA: Blackwell-Wiley. doi:10.1002/9781444302752.ch17

Hesse-Biber, S., Leavy, P., Quinn, C. E., & Zoino, J. (2006). The mass marketing of disordered eating and eating disorders: The social psychology of women, thinness, and culture. *Women's Studies International Forum, 29*, 208–224. doi:10.1016/j.wsif.2006.03.007

Holub, S. C. (2008). Individual differences in the anti-fat attitudes of preschoolchildren: The importance of perceived body size. *Body Image, 5*, 317–321. doi:10.1016/j.bodyim.2008.03.003

Jeffreys, S. (2005). *Beauty and misogyny: Harmful cultural practices in the West.* New York, NY: Routledge.

Kim, J. L., Sorsoli, C. L., Collins, K., Zylbergold, B. A., Schooler, D., & Tolman, D. (2007). From sex to sexuality: Exposing the heterosexual script on primetime network television. *Journal of Sex Research, 44*, 145–157.

Klonoff, E. A., & Landrine, H. (1995). The Schedule of Sexist Events: A measure of lifetime and recent sexist discrimination in women's lives. *Psychology of Women Quarterly, 19*, 439–472.

Kohlberg, L. (1966). A cognitive-developmental analysis of children's sex-role concepts and attitudes. In E. E. Maccoby (Ed.), *The development of sex differences* (pp. 82–173). Stanford, CA: Stanford University Press.

Krassas, N. R., Blauwkamp, J. M., & Wesselink, P. (2001). Boxing Helena and corseting Eunice: Sexual rhetoric in *Cosmopolitan* and *Playboy* magazines. *Sex Roles, 44,* 751–771. doi:10.1023/A:1012254515434

Krassas, N. R., Blauwkamp, J. M., & Wesselink, P. (2003). "Master your Johnson:" Sexual rhetoric in *Maxim* and *Stuff* magazines. *Sexuality & Culture, 7,* 98–119. doi:10.1007/s12119-003-1005-7

Kunkel, D., Eyal, K., Finnerty, K., Biely, E., & Donnerstein, E. (2005). *Sex on TV 5: A biennial report to the Kaiser Family Foundation.* Menlo Park, CA: Kaiser Family Foundation.

Landrine, H., Klonoff, E. A., Gibbs, J., Manning, V., & Lund, M. (1995). Physical and psychiatric correlates of gender discrimination: An application of the Schedule of Sexist Events. *Psychology of Women Quarterly, 19,* 473–492. doi:10.1111/j.1471-6402.1995.tb00087.x

Landry, L., & Mercurio, A. (2009). Discrimination and women's mental health: The mediating role of control. *Sex Roles, 61,* 192–203. doi:10.1007/s11199-009-9624-6

Leaper, C., & Brown, C. (2008). Perceived experiences with sexism among adolescent girls. *Child Development, 79,* 685–704. doi:10.1111/j.1467-8624.2008.01151.x

Leaper, C., & Friedman, C. K. (2007). The socialization of gender. In J. Grusec & P. Hastings (Eds.), *Handbook of socialization theory and research* (pp. 561–587). New York, NY: Guilford Press.

Lefkowitz, E. S., & Gillen, M. M. (2006). "Sex is just a normal part of life": Sexuality in emerging adulthood. In J. J. Arnett & J. L. Tanner (Eds.), *Emerging adults in American: Coming of age in the 21st century* (pp. 235–256). Washington, DC: American Psychological Association. doi:10.1037/11381-010

Levin, D., & Kilbourne, J. (2008). *So sexy, so soon: The new sexualized childhood and what parents can do to protect their kids.* New York, NY: Ballantine.

Levine, M. P., & Murnen, S. K. (2009). "Everybody knows that mass media are/are not (pick one) a cause of eating disorders": A critical review of evidence for a causal link between media, negative body image, and disordered eating in females. *Journal of Social and Clinical Psychology, 28,* 9–42. doi:10.1521/jscp.2009.28.1.9

Levy, A. (2005). *Female chauvinist pigs: Women and the rise of raunch culture.* New York, NY: Free Press.

Lindberg, S. M., Grabe, S., & Hyde, J. S. (2007). Gender, pubertal development, and peer sexual harassment predict objectified body consciousness in early adolescence. *Journal of Research on Adolescence, 17,* 723–742.

Lorber, J. (2010). *Gender inequality: Feminist theory and politics* (4th ed.). New York, NY: Oxford University Press.

Mahalik, J., R., Locke, B. D., Ludlow, L. H., Diemer, M. A., Scott, R. P. J., Gottfried, M., & Freitas, G. (2003). Development of the Conformity to Masculine Norms Inventory. *Psychology of Men & Masculinity, 4*, 3–25. doi:10.1037/1524-9220.4.1.3

Mahalik, J. R., Mooray, E. B., Coonerty-Femiano, A., Ludlow, L. H., Slattery, S. M., & Smiler, A. (2005). Development of the Conformity to Feminine Norms Inventory. *Sex Roles, 52*, 417–435. doi:10.1007/s11199-005-3709-7

Martin, C. E. (2007). *Perfect girls, starving daughters: The frightening new normalcy of hating your body*. New York, NY: Free Press.

Martin, C. L., & Ruble, D. (2004). Children's search for gender cures: Cognitive perspective on gender development. *Current Directions in Psychological Science, 13*, 67–70. doi:10.1111/j.0963-7214.2004.00276.x

McGhan, M. (2007). Dancing toward redemption. In S. Shaw & J. Lee (Eds.), *Women's voices, feminist visions: Classic and contemporary readings* (pp. 284–288). Boston, MA: McGraw-Hill.

McKinley, N. M. (1999). Women and objectified body consciousness: Mothers' and daughters' body experience in cultural, developmental, and familial contexts. *Developmental Psychology, 35*, 760–769. doi:10.1037/0012-1649.35.3.760

McKinley, N. M., & Hyde, J. S. (1996). The Objectified Body Consciousness Scale: Self-objectification, body shame, and disordered eating. *Psychology of Women Quarterly, 22*, 623–636.

Murnen, S. K., & Smolak, L. (2000). The experience of sexual harassment among grade-school students: Early socialization of female subordination? *Sex Roles, 43*, 1–17. doi:10.1023/A:1007007727370

Murnen, S. K., & Smolak, L. (2009). Are feminist women protected from body image problems? A meta-analytic review of relevant research. *Sex Roles, 60*, 186–197. doi:10.1007/s11199-008-9523-2

Murnen, S. K., Smolak, L., Mills, J. A., & Good, L. (2003). Thin, sexy women and strong, muscular men: Grade-school children's responses to objectified images of women and men. *Sex Roles, 49*, 427–437. doi:10.1023/A:1025868320206

Orenstein, P. (2001). *Flux: Women on sex, work, love, kids, and life in a half-changed world*. New York, NY: Anchor.

O'Sullivan, L., McCrudden, M., & Tolman, D. (2006). To your sexual health! Incorporating sexuality into the health perspective. In J. Worell & C. D. Goodheart (Eds.), *Handbook of girls' and women's psychological health* (pp. 192–199). New York, NY: Oxford University Press.

Paul, P. (2005). *Pornified: How pornography is transforming our lives, our relationships, and our families*. New York, NY: Times Books.

Paxton, S. J., Norris, M., Wertheim, E. H., Durkin, S. J., & Anderson, J. (2005). Body dissatisfaction, dating and importance of thinness to attractiveness in adolescent girls. *Sex Roles, 53*, 663–675. doi:10.1007/s11199-005-7732-5

Pollet, A., & Hurwitz, P. (2007). Strip till you drop. In S. Shaw & J. Lee (Eds.), *Women's voices, feminist visions: Classic and contemporary readings* (pp. 548–551). Boston, MA: McGraw-Hill.

Reichert, T., & Carpenter, C. (2004). An update on sex in magazine advertising: 1983 to 2003. *Journalism & Mass Communication Quarterly, 81*, 823–837.

Rogers, J. K., & Henson, K. (2007). "Hey, why don't you wear a shorter skirt": Structural vulnerability and the organization of sexual harassment in temporary clerical employment. In S. Shaw & J. Lee (Eds.), *Women's voices, feminist visions: Classic and contemporary readings* (pp. 486–497). Boston, MA: McGraw-Hill.

Rubin, L. R., Nemeroff, C. J., & Russo, N. F. (2004). Exploring feminist women's body consciousness. *Psychology of Women Quarterly, 28*, 27–37. doi:10.1111/j.1471-6402.2004.00120.x

Rudman, L. A. (1998). Self-promotion as a risk factor for women: The costs and benefits of counter-stereotypical impression management. *Journal of Personality and Social Psychology, 74*, 629–645. doi:10.1037/0022-3514.74.3.629

Rudman, L. A., & Glick, P. (2001). Prescriptive gender stereotypes and backlash toward agentic women. *Journal of Social Issues, 57*, 743–762. doi:10.1111/0022-4537.00239

Sheffield, C. J. (2007). Sexual terrorism. In L. L. O'Toole, J. R. Shiffman, & M. L. K. Edwards (Eds.), *Gender violence: Interdisciplinary perspectives* (2nd ed., pp. 111–130). New York, NY: New York University Press.

Singh, D. (1993). Adaptive significance of female physical attractiveness: Role of waist-to-hip ratio. *Journal of Personality and Social Psychology, 65*, 293–307. doi:10.1037/0022-3514.65.2.293

Smolak, L., & Murnen, S. K. (2004). A feminist approach to eating disorders. In J. K. Thompson (Ed.), *Handbook of eating disorders and obesity* (pp. 590–605). Hoboken, NJ: Wiley.

Smolak, L., & Murnen, S. K. (2007). Feminism and body image. In V. Swami & A. Furnham (Eds.), *The body beautiful* (pp. 236–258). London, England: Palgrave Macmillan.

Stankiewicz, J. M., & Rosselli, F. (2008). Women as sex objects and victims in print advertisements. *Sex Roles, 58*, 579–589. doi:10.1007/s11199-007-9359-1

Swim, J. K., Hyers, L. L., Cohen, L. L., & Ferguson, M. J. (2001). Everyday sexism: Evidence for its incidence, nature, and psychological impact from three daily diary studies. *Journal of Social Issues, 57*, 31–53. doi:10.1111/0022-4537.00200

Szymanski, D., Gupta, A., Carr, E., & Stewart, D. (2009). Internalized misogyny as a moderator of the link between sexist events and women's psychological distress. *Sex Roles, 61*, 101–109. doi:10.1007/s11199-009-9611-y

Ward, L. M. (2003). Understanding the role of entertainment media in the sexual socialization of American youth: A review of empirical research. *Developmental Review, 23*, 347–388. doi:10.1016/S0273-2297(03)00013-3

Wignall, A. (2000, April 16). *Can a feminist really love* Sex and the City? Retrieved March 9, 2009, from http://www.guardian.co.uk/ lifeandstyles/2008/apr/16/women.film

Wolf, N. (1991). *The beauty myth*. New York, NY: Morrow.

4

THE BIRTHMARK: AN EXISTENTIAL ACCOUNT OF THE OBJECTIFICATION OF WOMEN

JAMIE L. GOLDENBERG AND TOMI-ANN ROBERTS

In the short story *The Birthmark* (1843/1946), Nathaniel Hawthorne's character Georgiana has a crimson birthmark on her left cheek that resembles a "bloody hand." This one "visible mark of earthly imperfection" provides the impetus for anxiety that haunts Georgiana's husband and Georgiana herself. Indeed, it ultimately drives him, encouraged by Georgiana, to surgically remove the offensive mark, leaving Georgiana dead. This story, written in another time, depicts the unrealistic expectations for flawless beauty in women that are still, and perhaps even more, pervasive today. Moreover, accompanying such expectations, the characters in the story experience marked psychological distress in response to a perfectly natural "imperfection" on a woman's body.

In this chapter, we argue that the curiously dual reactions to women's bodies—threat toward their natural functions yet also idealized evaluations of their physical appearance—are flip sides of the same existential coin. Our perspective emphasizes existential threats associated with women's "imperfect"

The authors wish to thank Shona Tritt for drawing the connection between an existential account of the objectification of women and Nathaniel Hawthorne's short story *The Birthmark*.

(menstruating, childbearing, and lactating) bodies and with men's sexual attraction to them. We suggest that the sexual and self-objectification of women's bodies serves an existential function: It strips women of their more natural and potentially threatening qualities and emphasizes a safer, idealized attractiveness. However, in doing so, such defensive treatment demeans women by treating them as objects. Moreover, the objectification of women promotes a number of perceptions and self-perceptions that, like the removal of Georgiana's birthmark, result in devastating consequences for women.

In this chapter, we also take a step back and ask a question that has not yet been addressed in empirical psychology: Why are women so often objectified, but men rarely so? In disciplines outside of psychology, explanations for the objectification of women center on inequities in power between men and women worldwide. For example, Dworkin (1987) argued that women are socialized into heterosexual womanhood, which is the same as being socialized into subordination. For Dworkin, heterosexuality is organized around male dominance, which is heterosexual maleness, and female subordination, which is heterosexual femaleness. Women are socialized to be heterosexual females, and hence sexualized to the liking of heterosexual men, which is to be subordinate, which is to be unable to meaningfully consent to what is actually their own subordination. To the extent that women are complicit in this arrangement, it is because they have formed a kind of slave mentality or because they want to escape punishment or curry favor.

Such explanations, while offering important insights, fail in two ways that are important to psychology. First, they do not provide an understanding of the psychic function of objectification. And second, they do not adequately explain why many women themselves willingly participate in the self-objectification of their own bodies. In contrast, our existential framework borrows theoretically from more psychoanalytic-oriented feminist thinkers, such as Dorothy Dinnerstein (1976), who argued that men have subordinated women across culture and time because women, in giving life, also give death. The threat men feel toward women's life-and-death-giving "powers" is the impetus behind their efforts to control women. For if men can control women's bodies, they are also in effect controlling nature and mortality itself. Dinnerstein's view offers an existential beginning, and we believe our theory helps complete a functional understanding of this phenomenon, providing new insights into the question of why women are objectified and why they objectify themselves.

To begin, we discuss terror management theory, the social psychological theory on which we base our existential answer to the question, Why are women so often objectified, but men rarely so? In particular, we discuss recent extensions of terror management theory to explain ambivalence toward the physical body. We then use terror management theory to explain reactions to women's bodies in particular, both the threat posed by the physicality of women's bodies and objectification as a response to this threat. Although we take a functional approach to objectification, we by no means discount consequences of it. Thus, we discuss consequences of sexual and self-objectification. We conclude with a consideration of alternative means of coping with the existential threat associated with women's bodies.

THE PARADOX OF THE PHYSICAL BODY: EXISTENTIAL THREAT AND SOLUTION

Terror management theory (e.g., Greenberg, Pyszczynski, & Solomon, 1986; Solomon, Greenberg, & Pyszczynski, 2004), which is based on the theoretical insights of Ernest Becker (1973), starts with the basic premise that awareness of mortality causes unbearable anxiety in human beings. For a species biologically programmed for survival, the intelligence to understand and foresee the inevitability of its own death poses the potential for paralyzing terror. Rather than experience the anxiety that the awareness of mortality could engender, human beings have used these same cognitive capabilities that render them aware of mortality (i.e., symbolic thought) to develop a symbolic solution to mortality. That is, they manage their terror. Specifically, terror management theory suggests that it is through the creation of and participation in a meaningful cultural reality that individuals raise themselves to a higher level of existence. Individuals obtain psychological protection from the problem of death to the extent that they believe they are living up to meaningful cultural standards and values. To date, over 300 experiments conducted in more than a dozen countries provide support for this position. For example, reminders of mortality cause individuals to like others less who criticize their cultural beliefs (e.g., Greenberg et al., 1990), to express more discomfort when they themselves transgress cultural norms (Greenberg, Simon, Porteus, Pyszczynski, & Solomon, 1995), and to behave in ways that are perceived as culturally valued (Ben-Ari, Florian, & Mikulincer, 1999).

Goldenberg, Pyszczynski, Greenberg, and Solomon (2000; see also Goldenberg, 2005) extended this basic position of terror management theory by suggesting that any reminders that humans are biological animals and thus vulnerable, as all biological organisms are, to death and decay undermine the management of terror and thus pose a psychological problem. This conclusion resonates with other psychological research, such as Freud's theory of personality rooted in the problem of the id and contemporary empirical psychology on the emotion of disgust (e.g., Haidt, Rozin, McCauley, & Imada, 1997; Rozin, Haidt, & McCauley, 1993). Both types of research suggest that humans are fundamentally troubled by the recognition of the animal within.

Empirical research has supported Goldenberg and colleagues' position that the awareness of mortality underlies negative reactions to human physicality. For example, Goldenberg et al. (2001, Study 1) showed that when people are reminded of their mortality (mortality salience), they respond with greater disgust to body products and animals. Further, Goldenberg et al. (2001, Study 2) found that death reminders cause people to like an essay that argues that humans are distinct from animals by emphasizing human culture to a greater extent than a control condition (i.e., people not reminded of death beforehand), and also to like it substantially more than an essay that discusses the biological similarities between humans and animals. More recently, Cox, Goldenberg, Pyszczynski, and Weise (2007) found that the accessibility of death-related thoughts increases when people are reminded of their animal nature and then asked to answer questions about bodily products and functions. In addition, a handful of experiments have shown that priming mortality salience even leads to the avoidance of physical sensation and bodily movements under certain conditions (Goldenberg, Hart, et al., 2006; Goldenberg, Heflick, & Cooper, 2008). Taken together, these findings provide empirical support for the proposition that people are threatened by their physical nature and that existential concerns underlie these threats.

However, it is also clear that we do not always respond to our physical selves with outright animosity; rather, very often reactions to our bodies are marked with a great deal of ambivalence (see Goldenberg, Kosloff, & Greenberg, 2006). The physicality of human existence can offer either a reminder of death or an affirmation of life. Thus, on one hand, we can distance from, deny, and devalue the aspects of humanity that are perceived as most "creaturely," or animal-like, and hence vulnerable. On the other hand, given that humans also must live in, and are indeed drawn to, the world of the physical, people can ameliorate these threatening connotations by imbuing the threatening aspects of nature with symbolic meaning and value, so that these threatening creaturely aspects can be embraced with minimal threat. Thus, whereas some aspects of our physicality are confined to private quarters, discussed only in euphemisms or as the brunt of jokes, other aspects are often viewed with more favorable reactions.

It becomes apparent that negative and positive reactions to the physicality of humans are tied to a common source (i.e., existential terror) when we consider how the same behavior can be viewed with negative or with favorable attitudes, as a function of existential factors. Several studies have illustrated such ambivalence in response to sex. For example, Goldenberg, Cox, Pyszczynski, Greenberg, and Solomon (2002) demonstrated that when people were situationally induced to associate the physical aspects of sex with an animal act, by reading the creaturely essay described previously in which people were reminded of their similarities to other animals, reminders of mortality decreased their reported appeal for the physical aspects of sex (Goldenberg et al., 2002, Study 2). However, after reading the essay that described people as distinct from other species, reminders of death had no significant effect on the appeal of the physical aspects of sex (and even showed a trend toward increased appeal in this condition). Further, after the creaturely essay prime, thinking about physical sex increased the accessibility of death-related thoughts for participants, whereas it did not subsequent to the essay describing humans as unique (Goldenberg et al., 2002, Study 1).

In this research, the more romantic aspects of sex were not distanced from at all, supporting the idea that symbolic meaning can ameliorate otherwise threatening aspects of humans' physical nature. This point was made more succinctly by Goldenberg, Pyszczynski, McCoy, Greenberg, and Solomon (1999, Study 3), who showed that while highly neurotic individuals showed heightened death-thought accessibility after contemplating the physical aspects of sex, when they were asked to think about love before thinking about physical sex, death was no longer highly accessible. Additional evidence that the physicality of sex is stripped of its threatening aspects when embedded in a symbolic context is illustrated by the finding that when people derive self-esteem from their physical body, then mortality reminders actually lead to greater interest in the physical aspects of sex (Goldenberg, McCoy, Pyszczynksi, Greenberg, & Solomon, 2000).

We therefore maintain that there are two ways to defend against the threatening aspects of human physicality. People can deny, conceal, and certainly devalue their more creaturely features, or they can depotentiate the threatening connotations of the physical body by imbuing those very aspects of nature with symbolic, cultural meaning and value. It is in these two strategies of defense that one can better understand the duality of cultural reactions toward women and their bodies, which range, for example, from confinement to menstrual huts to the idealization of the female nude in art. But why is it that women have been so disproportionately the target of both defenses—both condemned for their base animal nature and worshiped for their goddesslike purity and beauty? Like Dinnerstein (1976), we suggest that women's more obvious role in reproduction and their ability to inspire physical lust reactions in men provide at least a partial explanation for the content and intensity of reactions to women.

THE BIRTHMARK

Although women's and men's bodies are alike in many of the biological functions they perform, there is a repertoire of bodily activities that are solely the responsibility of women. Specifically, as evolutionary theorists have pointed out, women bear a great deal more of the burden associated with the reproduction of our species than do men (Trivers, 1972). Women menstruate, they carry the fetus in their own body for 9 months, they experience childbirth, and their body provides for the child with lactation. Although women's role as childbearer has been celebrated, it has also been used as a means to discriminate against them. Plato attributed weakness in women to a "wandering uterus" searching for a fetus, and the prevailing medical opinion of the 19th and early 20th centuries was that women were mercilessly affected by their reproductive hormones, thereby rendering them unfit for certain intellectual and educational opportunities (Cayleff, 1992; Fausto-Sterling, 1992). Our theoretical perspective suggests that women's association with reproduction is threatening because it makes salient human creatureliness.

Menstruation

Perhaps the most obvious example of such reactions to women are found in long-standing, far-reaching taboos associated with menstruation, ranging from physical isolation (e.g., menstrual huts) and restricted activities (e.g., no contact with hunting tools in tribal cultures, no swimming in more developed modern cultures) to hygiene rituals (e.g., mikvah baths), consumer products emphasizing cleanliness (e.g., powder-fresh "sanitary napkins"), euphemistic speech (e.g., "the rag," "Aunt Flo"), and secrecy (e.g., discrete small-sized tampons and "soundproof" maxi-pad wrappers).

Empirical evidence corroborates these cultural observations linking menstruation to disgust and contamination beliefs. For example, Rozin, Haidt, McCauley, Dunlop, and Ashmore (1999) found that male and female participants in their study responded with a disgust reaction to an unused tampon (that was unwrapped in front of them), refusing to touch it to their lips upon request. In a study designed to test more implicit reactions to menstruation, we (Roberts, Goldenberg, Power, & Pyszczynski, 2002) found that male and female participants exhibited negative reactions to a woman who inadvertently dropped a wrapped tampon out of her backpack. Not only was the woman viewed as less competent and less likable than when the same woman dropped a less "offensive" but equally feminine item—a hair barrette—from her bag, but the mere presence of the tampon also led participants to distance themselves physically from the woman by sitting farther away from her. Thus, clearly people have disgust-style negative responses to the perfectly healthy phenomenon of menstruation, but what about other aspects of women's reproductive responsibilities, such as pregnancy and lactation? And, importantly, do existential concerns play a role in such reactions?

Pregnancy

Pregnancy, on the surface, is something that most people would describe as a beautiful, happy occurrence. Nevertheless, as with menstruation, there are strong expectations for women to conceal their pregnant bodies. When pregnancy is not appropriately concealed, reactions are often negative. For example, in the early 1990s, actor Demi Moore's nude, pregnant, cover photograph on *Vanity Fair* inspired much controversy, but another nude, nonpregnant Demi Moore cover pose did not. More recently, the Federal Communications Commission received a series of "indecency" complaints about NBC's coverage of the 2004 Athens Summer Olympics, which depicted a woman with an enlarged, "pregnant" belly at the opening ceremonies (de Moraes, 2004), and Barbie's friend Midge (a pregnant and happily married Barbie doll) was pulled from Wal-Mart shelves across the country following complaints from customers (Associated Press, 2002).

Thus, while there is anecdotal evidence that people's attitudes toward pregnancy are not entirely positive, according to the present analysis, concerns about creatureliness underlie such negative reactions. Goldenberg, Cox, Arndt, and Goplen (2007) provided empirical evidence in two experiments. In the first, reactions to the two aforementioned *Vanity Fair* (1991, 1992) covers with Demi Moore posing pregnant or not were assessed as a function of the creatureliness essay manipulation. In line with our position, priming the similarities between humans and animals led to more negative reactions to the pregnant image but did not affect reactions to the image in which she was not pregnant. In a second experiment, participants evaluated actor Gwyneth Paltrow's talent, competence, and intelligence in response to viewing a photo of her fully clad, pregnant or not, again as a function of a creatureliness manipulation. This study showed that not only do concerns about creatureliness inspire stronger reactions to a provocative pregnant pose, but a woman's competence is devalued under such conditions.

Breasts

Breast-feeding, too, although medically advocated and considered the healthiest choice for both mothers and babies (Rubin et al., 1990; Walker, 1993), can inspire negative reactions in Western culture. In the United States, women who breast-feed their children in public are often frowned upon (e.g., Forbes, Adams-Curtis, Hamm, & White, 2003; Yalom, 1997) or explicitly asked to leave public establishments (e.g., coffee shops: Helderman, 2004; retail shops: Spencer, 2005; even obstetrician/gynecologists' offices: Whitely, 2001); and breast milk, like menstrual blood, is often perceived as dirty (Morse, 1989) or disgusting (Fallon & Rozin, 1983).

Cox, Goldenberg, Arndt, and Pyszczynski (2007) provided direct support for the proposition that breast-feeding serves as a reminder of the physical, animal nature of humanity and that this is threatening because it raises existential mortality concerns. In two studies, the salience of mortality enhanced negative reactions to breast-feeding. In the first, after being reminded of death, breast-feeding in public was rated as a more severe transgression; in the second study, mortality salience led participants to dislike a woman who breast-fed her baby in private and physically distance from her, compared with a woman who bottle-fed her baby. In addition, in the second study, participants were given the opportunity to set up chairs to engage in a "getting acquainted exercise" with the purported task partner. Participants reminded of their mortality showed more behavioral avoidance of the breast-feeding partner, opting to place their chairs farther apart.

Two more studies provided critical evidence that creaturely concerns are instrumental in such reactions. In particular, a third experiment demonstrated that priming breast-feeding in conjunction with mortality rendered thoughts associated with human creatureliness more accessible. A fourth study provided evidence for a causal role of creaturely concerns on breast-feeding reactions by showing that people expressed increased negativity toward a picture of a breast-feeding female (but not the same female not pictured breast-feeding) after reading an essay that primed human–animal similarities. This last study took advantage of two nearly identical magazine covers (with one showing actor Pierce Brosnan with his wife and child, and the other showing the same poses except that the wife is breast-feeding) to demonstrate the effect.

Our argument that women's bodies are more likely to provoke an existential threat is incomplete without consideration of one additional factor: Heterosexual men are sexually attracted to them. Thus, women's bodies are not only threatening on account of their reproductive aspects, but these same bodies, and some of the same body parts, pose the potential to inspire lust in men. Of course, women are attracted to men, too, but in contrast to women's attraction to men, men's attraction has been shown to emphasize physical features of arousal (i.e., an erect penis) more prominently (e.g., Buss, 1989; Buss & Schmitt, 1993; Clark & Hatfield, 1989), and thus is perhaps more likely to pose a threat in itself.

Indeed, the findings from a series of studies by Landau et al. (2006) demonstrated that mortality salience reduced men's, but not women's, attractiveness ratings of sexually alluring women and led men to downplay their sexual, but not friendly, intent toward a friendly, attractive woman. Another study provided support for the possibility that the threat of sexual attraction may be specific to men: In contrast to men, women did not respond to mortality salience with a decreased attraction to a sexually seductive male. Landau et al. also provided direct evidence that male lust plays a critical role in such reactions. After being asked to think about a time when male participants had experienced lust compared with excitement in response to a sporting event, mortality reminders led men to recommend more lenient penalties to a male who had aggressed against a woman but not to a male who had aggressed against another man. These somewhat chilling findings suggest that male lust indeed poses an existential threat, and that men's defenses in the face of this threat can include derogatory attitudes and even aggression toward women. In other words, it is at least in part because of intense desire, combined with distinctly human concerns about death, that men sometimes distance from their attraction to women and instead devalue them.

Thus, there is a growing body of evidence to support the claim that the reproductive aspects of women's bodies, as well as men's sexual attraction to them, can provoke a threat that is exacerbated by experimental primes highlighting the awareness of human mortality and/or creatureliness. It follows from the framework provided by terror management theory that a solution to this problem lies in humankind's capacity to imbue that which is threatening with symbolic value.

DISTANCING FROM WOMEN'S CREATURELY BODIES: OBJECTIFICATION AS A SOLUTION

Just as there is a long tradition of construing women as closer to nature, there are also ample cultural examples of women being elevated above nature, idealized, even worshipped as goddesses. So stereotypes about women are paradoxical, because they contain both negative and seemingly positive judgments. As Glick and Fiske (1996) have shown, women are simultaneously perceived as less competent and valuable than men, but women are also idealized in, for example, their roles as wives and mothers. On the one hand, as we have shown with respect to menstruation, pregnancy, and breast-feeding, women's reproductive and bodily functions are viewed with derision, but, on the other hand, other aspects of their bodies are revered as cultural symbols of beauty and male desire.

Our position is that objectification of women serves to strip women of their connection to nature. As we suggested at the outset, in addition to concealing and devaluing the more creaturely aspects of women's bodies, following from terror management theory, we suggest that the threat can also be diffused by symbolic drapery that transforms the threat. We would like to argue that the objectification of women is one such form of drapery that enables a transformation of natural, creaturely women into objects of beauty and desire.

As described earlier in this volume (see Chapter 1), objectification occurs when a woman's body, body parts, or sexual functions are separated from her person or regarded as if they are capable of representing her (Bartky, 1990). Of course, objectification occurs in obviously cruel and dehumanizing ways, for example, when women's bodies are targeted for violent pornographic treatment or used in the sex trade industry. But the sexual objectification of women's bodies also occurs in a more seemingly benign, and many would argue, even benevolent fashion and is so widespread as to be part of everyday life. As any quick glance at the many forms of media bombarding us daily would attest, women's bodies and body parts are used as decorative features, meant to draw our attention and get us to purchase products.

What we learn by scrutinizing these ubiquitous presentations of women is that women's bodies are acceptable and deemed beautiful only under certain conditions. For example, Wolf (1991) described how the images of the idealized female bodies to which people are exposed by the American media are invariably of youth, slimness, and Whiteness, and these images are increasingly broadcast worldwide. In other cultures, such as the Karen people of Upper Burma, the standard of feminine beauty involves an elongated neck with stacks of golden necklaces. Regardless of the particular features deemed essential by a culture for feminine beauty, we believe that it is specifically when the more creaturely features and functions of women's bodies are actually or symbolically removed from the presentation that the female body is publicly acceptable and attractive.

Iris Marion Young (1992) once wrote of women's breasts, "Cleavage is good; nipples are a no-no" (p. 220). Breasts are multidimensional. They are not only a source of food for offspring but also the objects of sexual desire. It is interesting that people do not seem capable of sustaining both of these orientations toward breasts at once. The maternal breast and the sexualized breast never speak to one another (e.g., one cannot purchase a nursing bra at Victoria's Secret). Attitudes toward women's breasts illustrate the second way we have argued that women's corporeal bodies can be managed—imbue them with symbolic meaning. Studies indeed show that the extent to which both men and women view breasts as objects to be enjoyed by men predicts negative attitudes toward breast-feeding. In one qualitative study, a mother negatively disposed toward breast-feeding her infant was quoted as saying, "Yuck, those are for your husband!" (Morse, 1989, p. 229). In a more recent quantitative investigation, Ward, Merriwether, and Caruthers (2006) found that the more men engaged with popular men's magazines, the more they construed women as sexual objects, and this attitude predicted more negative views toward breast-feeding and more concern that breast-feeding interferes with sexual relations.

In an experimental context we have provided evidence for a direct connection between the creaturely aspects of women's bodies, menstruation in this case, and the tendency to objectify women. In the tampon-drop experiment, Roberts et al. (2002) found that not only were negative reactions exhibited in response to the individual woman who dropped the tampon, but when the participants were asked to describe their expectations for women's bodies in general, those who had seen the tampon rather than the hair barrette were particularly likely to rate physical appearance as especially important relative to health and functioning. Thus, the reaction to the tampon in this study generalized beyond the woman who dropped it to women in general and took the form of viewing women in a more objectified light. That is, when reminded of women's more creaturely nature, both men and women endorsed a less natural, more appearance-oriented standard for women's bodies. In addition, other research has provided evidence for the role of mortality concerns in objectification of women's bodies. Grabe, Routledge, Cook, Anderson, and Arndt (2005) found that although men tended to objectify women at high levels in all conditions of their experiment, when concerns about mortality were primed, women objectified other women to the same extent as men did.

Construing women as objects also requires downplaying their explicit sexuality as well. Putting "beautiful" (good) women on an objectified pedestal may also serve the function of protecting men from the threat associated with their own animalistic urges toward them. Desiring a virginal, well-groomed, sanitized, deodorized, and goddesslike creature should not be so threatening. After all, there is no chance of contamination or pollution in interacting with such a creature. Another study by Landau et al. (2006) provided evidence consistent with this; in that study mortality salience led men to decrease their interest in a seductive woman, but this effect was eliminated when the woman appeared more wholesome.

This position fits with the findings of Glick and Fiske (2001), who observed that prejudice against women takes the form not only of overtly hostile sexism but also benevolent sexism: "characterizing women as pure creatures who ought to be protected, supported, and adored and whose love is necessary to make a man complete" (p. 109). The primary theoretical explanation for benevolent sexism is that it enables interaction between the sexes while simultaneously pacifying women. Although we agree that sexism involves dual reactions toward women, our work leads us to differ somewhat in explanation for these dual reactions. In addition to pacifying women, we expect that such attitudes also protect men. Men's physical, animal desires should be rendered less threatening if the target of these desires is construed as a pure and wholesome object of worship.

LIVING IN THE CREATURELY BODY:
SELF-OBJECTIFICATION AS A SOLUTION

On first thought, it may seem surprising that the women participants in the study by Roberts et al. (2002) responded to the tampon as did the men, by objectifying women, and that women in the study by Grabe et al. (2005) objectified other women as a function of mortality salience. However, according to the position that we have provided, objectification of women serves an important existential function: It strips them of their creaturely functions and thus provides psychic protection from the threat of death. Thus, women objectify other women (Strelan & Hargreaves, 2005); additionally, women also objectify their own bodies, or self-objectify (e.g., Fredrickson, Roberts, Noll, Quinn, & Twenge, 1998; Noll & Fredrickson, 1998). In other words, we suggest that women themselves participate willingly in the flight away from the existentially threatening, corporeal body.

Indeed, there is no shortage of evidence that women place more importance on appearance than men and that they engage in more efforts to attain standards for appropriate appearance (Dion, Dion & Keelan, 1990). Why do they do so? One answer is that there are tangible rewards offered to women who conform to cultural standards for appropriate and desirable women's bodies. It has long been established that women who are deemed attractive receive a host of positive interpersonal and even economic outcomes, compared with those considered more homely (e.g., Berscheid, Dion, Walster & Walster, 1971; Fiske, Bersoff, Borgida, Deaux, & Heilman, 1991). As Unger (1979) argued, physical beauty can function as a kind of currency for women.

However, our perspective suggests that by pursuing such standards for appearance, in addition to receiving extrinsic rewards, women are also afforded more psychic, existential protection. Indeed, a number of studies reveal that reminders of mortality promote appearance striving among women. For example, mortality salience has been found to lead women to restrict their consumption of high-fat (but nutritious) snack food (Goldenberg, Arndt, Hart, & Brown, 2005) and to increase their intentions to tan their skin (Routledge, Arndt, & Goldenberg, 2004). Further, in the context of tanning, primes that associate tanned skin with standards for attractiveness enhance this tendency (Cox et al., 2009; Routledge et al., 2004).

In a more recent series of studies, Goldenberg, Cooper, Heflick, Routledge, and Arndt (2009) provided support for the hypothesis that trait self-objectification, and not just behaviorally conforming to societal standards concerning appearance, serves an existential function. In the first study in this series, self-objectification was shown to predict the degree to which women reported liking an objectifying image (e.g., the *Sports Illustrated* swimsuit issue) when mortality was salient; higher self-objectification was associated with greater liking. In contrast, in response to an image portraying a competent, nonobjectified woman (*Sports Illustrated* with soccer player Mia Hamm on the cover), greater self-objectification was associated with decreased liking when mortality was salient. Thus, it appears that investment in self-objectification as a framework on women's physical selves is at least in part an effort to allay existential threats. Sexually objectifying images are the cultural icons in this project, likely serving as reinforcers for this psychic work.

A second study in this series expanded on the first by examining whether an objectifying image could facilitate a more receptive reaction to a health appeal for high self-objectifiers in the context of a mortality reminder (Goldenberg, Cooper, et al., 2009). This hypothesis was based on prior research demonstrating that self-affirmations can facilitate nondefensive receptivity to health recommendations (because health threats pose a threat to the self; e.g., Sherman, Nelson, & Steele, 2000). To the extent that reminders of mortality motivate women to clarify and affirm their important values and beliefs (e.g., Landau, Greenberg, Sullivan, Routledge, & Arndt, 2009), objectifying images should allow for such self-affirmations among high self-objectifiers when an awareness of mortality is primed. As hypothesized, and consistent with the first study, high self-objectifiers responded to a death-related health communication with increased intentions to engage in breast self-exams and greater receptivity to the health communication. Moreover, these effects occurred independent of level of body esteem, suggesting that it was not the positivity or negativity of women's feelings about their bodies that influenced these reactions but the degree that they valued appearance.

In a last study, Goldenberg, Cooper, et al. (2009) also examined how women respond not only to the objectifying images but also to an experience in which they themselves are objectified. Although receiving a compliment on one's appearance in the context of a competence-oriented domain would usually be considered inappropriate, even demeaning, Goldenberg, Cooper, et al. hypothesized that such a situation might actually boost the self-esteem of high-self objectifiers when thoughts of mortality have been activated. Indeed, high-objectifying women respond to a compliment about their outfit in the midst of a performance task with increased state self-esteem after a subliminal prime of mortality. The pattern was reversed in a no-feedback condition. These studies provide direct evidence that objectification provides existential protection, at least among women committed to self-objectification as a defense.

CONSEQUENCES OF OBJECTIFICATION
AND SELF-OBJECTIFICATION

Although we have argued that objectification serves a defensive function, there are clearly consequences for the individual who is objectified and who self-objectifies (see Chapters 1, 6, and 7, this volume). More generally, social psychologists have demonstrated that striving to meet external standards to be accepted is in itself undermining to a person's autonomy, good health, and well-being (Crocker & Wolfe, 2001; Deci & Ryan, 1995; Leary, Tchividjian, & Kraxberger, 1994; Schimel, Arndt, Pyszczynski, & Greenberg, 2001). From our perspective, the psychic effort to self-objectify creates an inherent problem with one's own natural, nonobjectified body. For example, Roberts (2004) and Roberts and Waters (2004) found that women who held a more self-objectified perspective on their own bodies also held more negative attitude toward menstruation, including disgust, contempt, embarrassment, and shame. Further studies have shown that women's self-objectification predicts a constellation of attitudes dubbed *reproductive shame*—more positive attitudes toward artificially suppressing menstruation and breast augmentation, and more negative attitudes toward breast-feeding, including beliefs that public breast-feeding is indecent, as well as concerns that breast-feeding negatively affects women's sexual attractiveness (Johnston-Robledo, Fricker, & Pasek, 2007; Johnston-Robledo, Sheffield, Voigt, & Wilcox-Constantine, 2007). In addition, Roberts and Gettman (2004) found that priming women with objectifying words (e.g., *weight, attractive, appearance*) as opposed to words associated with health and functioning (e.g., *fitness, stamina, vitality*) led them to experience more body shame and disgust, and to rate the physical aspects of sex as less appealing, whereas no differences were found for men.

In addition, as mentioned previously, research has demonstrated that priming existential concerns associated with mortality and human creatureliness leads women to avoid important health behaviors that involve their breasts in a context in which they are not objectified: breast self-exams and mammography. In these studies, priming creatureliness with an essay that describes the biological similarities between humans and animals in a context in which thoughts about death are activated on account of a salient health threat, women decrease breast self-exam intentions and behavior (Goldenberg, Arndt, Hart, & Routledge, 2008) and report greater discomfort when undergoing a mammogram (Goldenberg, Routledge, & Arndt, 2009). Moreover, these effects were independent of any concerns about cancer, and thus again suggest that women are willing to risk their health in the face of a need to avoid the creatureliness of the physical body.

In addition to the well-researched consequences of objectifying one's self, there are consequences for women in terms of how they are perceived by others. Our perspective suggests that favorable evaluations of women require that they conceal the natural aspects of the physical body, whereas men can belch, pass gas, even urinate in public, grow obese, or let hair grow on their bodies instead of their head, and expect far less ostracism and derision. Indeed, research has demonstrated that the same natural bodily functions are evaluated more negatively in women. In a study in which a male or female experimenter excused him- or herself to either use the restroom or get some paperwork, results showed that participants rated the female experimenter more negatively in the bathroom condition than the control group, but no differences were found for the male experimenter (Roberts & MacLane, 2002). Other studies have shown that body hair on women elicits greater disgust than on men, and its removal is considered obligatory for women but not for men (Tiggemann & Lewis, 2004).

Research indicates that in nearly all forms of media women are objectified more than men (e.g., van Zoonen, 1994; see Fredrickson & Roberts, 1997). The 2008 U.S. presidential race, in which women played a major role, was no exception. While there has been much research on perceptions of women as a function of attractiveness (with the general finding "what is beautiful is good," Jackson, Hunter, & Hodge, 1995; including in voting in [mock] presidential elections, Chiao, Bowman, & Gill, 2008; but see Heilman & Stopeck, 1985), the question of how focusing on a woman's appearance affects evaluations of her has for the most part escaped empirical scrutiny. However, Martha Nussbaum (1999) discussed the topic, and based on her treatise, Heflick and Goldenberg (2009) hypothesized that focusing on a woman's appearance will lead her to be perceived as less competent and, by virtue of becoming an object, less fully human. In light of the nation's obsession with vice presidential candidate Sarah Palin's appearance, Heflick and Goldenberg asked people to write about Sarah Palin or her physical appearance (about a month before the election), and then had people evaluate her on traits associated with competence and also traits associated with human nature (see Haslam, 2006). Both were decreased as a function of the appearance focus manipulation and also as a function of a continuous measure of the degree to which they wrote about her appearance. To examine the generalizability of the psychological process, the researchers also had people evaluate actor Angelina Jolie and found the same effects. The only differences among perceptions of the target women were, one, Palin was perceived as less competent than Jolie, and two, focusing on Palin's appearance reduced the likelihood that people intended to vote for the McCain–Palin ticket.

A MORE HUMAN AND HUMANE ALTERNATIVE?

In this chapter, we present the somewhat controversial position that objectification provides a psychic defense against an existential threat associated with women's bodies and their role in reproduction. Although we take a functional approach, we are by no means suggesting that this is a politically or culturally acceptable solution, and we do not believe that it is the only solution. We also do not discount the more decidedly feminist perspectives that emphasize power inequities between men and women; we merely suggest these explanations are incomplete without additional consideration of an existential account of the problem.

But is there a solution to the phenomena we describe? To the extent that the need to defend against the threat of one's mortality is at the crux of one's troubles with women's bodies, women's role in reproduction should provide not only a threat but also a resolution. These so-called creaturely aspects of women's bodies are all involved in the creation of life, and thus recognizing the life-creating potential in women's bodies offers a solution to the problem by confronting death with life—head on, rather than with denial. If we can encourage positive attitudes toward women's real, naked, menstruating, lactating bodies, we may not only undermine pressure to objectify them but also improve women's well-being and men's relationships with them (see Chapter 9, this volume).

Some tentative evidence exists to support this proposition. For example, Rempel and Baumgartner (2003) showed that women who expressed more comfortable and accepting attitudes toward menstruation were more likely to feel comfortable with their own sexuality. Furthermore, those women who reported engaging in sexual activity during menses were more interested in and aroused by both romantic and more unconventional sexual activities with their partners and were less sensitive to disgust. Another set of studies showed that the practice of yoga enhances women's *embodiment* (defined as attending to and responding to sensations from within the body), and this body responsiveness is, in turn, predictive of lower self-objectification, greater satisfaction with the body, and fewer disordered eating attitudes (Daubenmier, 2005; Impett & Daubenmier, 2006).

Men, too, can benefit from greater acceptance of women's corporeal bodies. Schooler and Ward (2006) showed that men who were more comfortable with women's "real bodies" (defined as endorsement of scale items assessing positive attitudes toward body functions, smells, and hair) reported greater sexual assertiveness and were more often involved in committed relationships. Furthermore, although men who were more accepting of women's real bodies reported no more oral sex or vaginal sex experience, they did report significantly more kissing and caressing experience. In other words, men who are more comfortable with women's actual creaturely bodies appear to enjoy a higher degree of intimacy with them.

As we have acknowledged, however, existential influences do not exist in a vacuum. Thus, while associating women's bodies with life also offers a solution to the existential threat, in light of the very real power inequities that exist between men and women, there are likely additional pressures to cope with the threat in a way that undermines women's significance rather than enhances it. But for now we remain optimistic that, at least in theory, there is an alternative solution to the objectification of women that also goes to the heart of the human existential predicament.

CODA

In closing, we suggest that women's bodies pose a potential threat because of their association with nature, and thus with the existential anxiety surrounding the human awareness of mortality. In *The Birthmark*, Hawthorne wrote, "The crimson hand expressed the ineludible gripe in which mortality clutches the highest and purest of earthly mould, degrading them into kindred with the lowest, and even with the very brutes, like whom their visible frames return to dust." It follows that objectification, in transforming the natural, flawed, biological body into a cultural symbol, can function as a defense against this threat. Unfortunately, though, to be an object is to be denied one's humanity—indeed, one's life. Thus, it is not surprising that in the end the successful removal of Georgiana's birthmark removed her very life.

REFERENCES

Associated Press. (2002, December 24). Pregnant doll pulled from Wal-Mart after customers complain. *USA Today*. Retrieved from http://www.usatoday.com/money/industries/retail/2002-12-24-pregnant-doll_x.htm

Bartky, S. L. (1990). *Femininity and domination: Studies in the phenomenology of oppression*. New York, NY: Routledge.

Becker, E. (1973). *The denial of death*. New York, NY: Free Press.

Ben-Ari, O. T., Florian, V., & Mikulincer, M. (1999). The impact of mortality salience on reckless driving: A test of terror management mechanisms. *Journal of Personality and Social Psychology, 76*, 35–45. doi:10.1037/0022-3514.76.1.35

Berscheid, E., Dion, K. L., Walster, E., & Walster, G. W. (1971). Physical attractiveness and dating choice: A test of the matching hypothesis. *Journal of Experimental Social Psychology, 7*, 173–189. doi:10.1016/0022-1031(71)90065-5

Buss, D. M. (1989). Sex differences in human mate preferences: Evolutionary hypotheses tested in 37 cultures. *Behavioral and Brain Sciences, 12*, 1–49. doi:10.1017/S0140525X00023992

Buss, D. M., & Schmitt, D. P. (1993). Sexual strategies theory: An evolutionary perspective on human mating. *Psychological Review, 100*, 204–232. doi:10.1037/0033-295X.100.2.204

Cayleff, S. E. (1992). She was rendered incapacitated by menstrual difficulties: Historical perspectives on perceived intellectual and physiological impairment among menstruating women. In A. J. Dan. & L. L. Lewis (Eds.), *Menstrual health in women's lives* (pp. 229–235). Chicago, IL: University of Illinois Press.

Chiao, J. Y., Bowman, N. E., & Gill, H. (2008). The political gender gap: Gender bias in facial inferences that predict voting behavior. *PLoS ONE, 3*(10), e3666. doi:10.1371/journal.pone.0003666.

Clark, R. D., & Hatfield, E. (1989). Gender differences in receptivity to sexual offers. *Journal of Psychology & Human Sexuality, 2*, 39–55. doi:10.1300/J056v02n01_04

Cox, C. R., Cooper, D. P., Vess, M., Arndt, J., Goldenberg, J. L., & Routledge, C. (2009). Bronze is beautiful but pale can be pretty: The effects of appearance standards and mortality salience on sun-tanning outcomes. *Health Psychology, 28*, 746–752.

Cox, C. R., Goldenberg, J. L., Arndt, J., & Pyszczynski, T. (2007). Mother's milk: An existential perspective on negative reactions to breastfeeding. *Personality and Social Psychology Bulletin, 33*, 110–122. doi:10.1177/0146167206294202

Cox, C. R., Goldenberg, J. L., Pyszczynski, T., & Weise, D. (2007). Disgust, creatureliness, and the accessibility of death related thoughts. *European Journal of Social Psychology, 37*, 494–507. doi:10.1002/ejsp.370

Crocker, J., & Wolfe, C. T. (2001). Contingencies of self-worth. *Psychological Review, 108*, 593–623. doi:10.1037/0033-295X.108.3.593

Daubenmier, J. J. (2005). The relationship of yoga, body awareness, and body responsiveness to self-objectification and disordered eating. *Psychology of Women Quarterly, 29*, 207–219. doi:10.1111/j.1471-6402.2005.00183.x

de Moraes, L. (2004, December, 16). A controversy of Olympic proportions? Well, not exactly. *The Washington Post*, p. C7.

Deci, E. L., & Ryan, R. M. (1995). Human autonomy: The basis for true self-esteem. In M. Kernis (Ed.), *Efficacy, agency, and self-esteem* (pp. 31–49). New York, NY: Plenum.

Dinnerstein, D. (1976). *The mermaid and the minotaur: Sexual arrangements and human malaise*. New York, NY: Harper Collins.

Dion, K. L., Dion, K. K., & Keelan, P. (1990). Appearance anxiety as a dimension of social-evaluative anxiety: Exploring the ugly duckling syndrome. *Contemporary Social Psychology, 14*, 220–224.

Dworkin, A. (1987). *Intercourse*. London, England: Arrow Books.

Fallon, A. E., & Rozin, P. (1983). The psychological bases of food rejection in humans. *Ecology of Food and Nutrition, 13,* 15–26.

Fausto-Sterling, A. (1992). *Myths of gender: Biological theories about women and men* (2nd ed.). New York, NY: Basic Books.

Fiske, S. T., Bersoff, D. N., Borgida, E., Deaux, K., & Heilman, M. E. (1991). Social science research on trial: Use of sex stereotyping research in Price Waterhouse v. Hopkins. *American Psychologist, 46,* 1049–1060. doi:10.1037/0003-066X.46.10.1049

Forbes, G. B., Adams-Curtis, L. E., Hamm, N. R., & White, K. B. (2003). Perceptions of the woman who breastfeeds: The role of erotophobia, sexism, and attitudinal variables. *Sex Roles, 49,* 379–388. doi:10.1023/A:1025116305434

Fredrickson, B. L., & Roberts, T. (1997). Objectification theory: Toward understanding women's lived experiences and mental health risks. *Psychology of Women Quarterly, 21,* 173–206. doi:10.1111/j.1471-6402.1997.tb00108.x

Fredrickson, B. L., Roberts, T., Noll, S. M., Quinn, D. M., & Twenge, J. M. (1998). That swimsuit becomes you: Sex differences in self-objectification, restrained eating and math performance. *Journal of Personality and Social Psychology, 75,* 269–284. doi:10.1037/0022-3514.75.1.269

Glick, P., & Fiske, S. T. (1996). The ambivalent sexism inventory: Differentiating hostile and benevolent sexism. *Journal of Personality and Social Psychology, 70,* 491–512. doi:10.1037/0022-3514.70.3.491

Glick, P., & Fiske, S. T. (2001). An ambivalent alliance: Hostile and benevolent sexism as complementary justifications for gender inequality. *American Psychologist, 56,* 109–118. doi:10.1037/0003-066X.56.2.109

Goldenberg, J. L. (2005). The body stripped down: An existential account of ambivalence toward the physical body. *Current Directions in Psychological Science, 14,* 224–228. doi:10.1111/j.0963-7214.2005.00369.x

Goldenberg, J. L., Arndt, J., Hart, J., & Brown, M. (2005). Dying to be thin: The effects of mortality salience and body-mass index on restricted eating among women. *Personality and Social Psychology Bulletin, 31,* 1400–1412. doi:10.1177/0146167205277207

Goldenberg, J. L., Arndt, J., Hart, J., & Routledge, C. (2008). Uncovering an existential barrier to breast self-exam behavior. *Journal of Experimental Social Psychology, 44,* 260–274. doi:10.1016/j.jesp.2007.05.002

Goldenberg, J. L., Cooper, D., Heflick, N. A., Routledge, C., & Arndt, J. (2009). *Is objectification always harmful? Reactions to objectifying images and feedback as a function of self-objectification and mortality salience.* Manuscript submitted for publication.

Goldenberg, J. L., Cox, C. R., Arndt, J., & Goplen, J. (2007). "Viewing" pregnancy as existential threat: The effects of creatureliness on reactions to media depictions of the pregnant body. *Media Psychology, 10,* 211–230.

Goldenberg, J. L., Cox, C., Pyszczynski, T., Greenberg, J., & Solomon, S. (2002). Understanding human ambivalence about sex: The effects of stripping sex of its meaning. *Journal of Sex Research, 39,* 310–320. doi:10.1080/00224490209552155

Goldenberg, J. L., Hart, J., Pyszczynski, T., Warnica, G. M., Landau, M. J., & Thomas, L. (2006). Terror of the body: Death, neuroticism, and the flight from physical sensation. *Personality and Social Psychology Bulletin, 32,* 1264–1277. doi:10.1177/0146167206289505

Goldenberg, J. L., Heflick, N. A., & Cooper, D. P. (2008). The thrust of the problem: Bodily inhibitions and guilt as a function of mortality salience and neuroticism. *Journal of Personality, 76,* 1055–1080. doi:10.1111/j.1467-6494.2008.00513.x

Goldenberg, J. L., Kosloff, S., & Greenberg, J. (2006). Existential underpinnings of approach and avoidance of the physical body. *Motivation and Emotion, 30,* 127–134. doi:10.1007/s11031-006-9023-z

Goldenberg, J. L., McCoy, S. K., Pyszczynksi, T., Greenberg, J., & Solomon, S. (2000). The body as a source of self-esteem: The effects of mortality salience on identification with one's body, interest in sex, and appearance monitoring. *Journal of Personality and Social Psychology, 79,* 118–130. doi:10.1037/0022-3514.79.1.118

Goldenberg, J. L., Pyszczynski, T., Greenberg, J., & Solomon, S. (2000). Fleeing the body: A terror management perspective on the problem of human corporeality. *Personality and Social Psychology Review, 4,* 200–218. doi:10.1207/S15327957PSPR0403_1

Goldenberg, J. L., Pyszczynski, T., Greenberg, J., Solomon, S., Kluck, B., & Cornwell, R. (2001). I am *not* an animal: Mortality salience, disgust, and the denial of human creatureliness. *Journal of Experimental Psychology: General, 130,* 427–435. doi:10.1037/0096-3445.130.3.427

Goldenberg, J. L., Pyszczynski, T., McCoy, S. K., Greenberg, J., & Solomon, S. (1999). Death, sex, love, and neuroticism: Why is sex such a problem? *Journal of Personality and Social Psychology, 77,* 1173–1187. doi:10.1037/0022-3514.77.6.1173

Goldenberg, J. L., Routledge, C., & Arndt, J. (2009). Mammograms and the management of existential discomfort: Threats associated with the physicality of the body and neuroticism. *Psychology & Health, 24,* 563–581. doi:10.1080/08870440701864546

Grabe, S., Routledge, C., Cook, A., Andersen, C., & Arndt, J. (2005). In defense of the body: The effect of mortality salience on female body objectification. *Psychology of Women Quarterly, 29,* 33–37. doi:10.1111/j.1471-6402.2005.00165.x

Greenberg, J., Pyszczynski, T., & Solomon, S. (1986). The causes and consequences of a need for self-esteem: A terror management theory. In R. F. Baumeister (Ed.), *Public and private self* (pp. 189–212). New York, NY: Springer-Verlag.

Greenberg, J., Pyszczynski, T., Solomon, S., Rosenblatt, A., Veeder, M., Kirkland, S., & Lyon, D. (1990). Evidence for terror management theory: II. The effects of mortality salience reactions to those who threaten or bolster the cultural worldview. *Journal of Personality and Social Psychology, 58,* 308–318. doi:10.1037/0022-3514.58.2.308

Greenberg, J., Simon, L., Porteus, J., Pyszczynski, T., & Solomon, S. (1995). Evidence of a terror management function of cultural icons: The effects of mortality salience on the inappropriate use of cherished cultural symbols. *Personality and Social Psychology Bulletin, 21*, 1221–1228. doi:10.1177/01461672952111010

Haidt, J., Rozin, P., McCauley, C. R., & Imada, S. (1997). Body, psyche and culture: The relationship between disgust and mortality. *Psychology and Developing Societies, 9*, 107–131. doi:10.1177/097133369700900105

Haslam, N. (2006). Dehumanization: An integrative review. *Personality and Social Psychology Review, 10*, 252–264. doi:10.1207/s15327957pspr1003_4

Hawthorne, N. (1946). The birthmark. In N. Arvin (Ed.), *Hawthorne's short stories* (pp. 147–164). New York, NY: Knopf. (Original work published 1843)

Heflick, N. A., & Goldenberg, J. L. (2009). Objectifying Sarah Palin: Evidence that objectification causes women to be perceived as less competent and less fully human. *Journal of Experimental Social Psychology, 45*, 598–601. doi:10.1016/j.jesp.2009.02.008

Heilman, M. E., & Stopeck, M. H. (1985). Being attractive, advantage or disadvantage? Performance-based evaluations and recommended personnel actions as a function of appearance, sex and job type. *Organizational Behavior and Human Decision Processes, 35*, 202–215. doi:10.1016/0749-5978(85)90035-4

Helderman, R. S. (2004, August 9). *Md. moms say no to coverup at Starbucks: Women push chain for policy allowing public breast-feeding in all U.S. stores.* Retrieved from http://www.washingtonpost.com/wp-dyn/articles/A50610-2004Aug8.html

Impett, E. A., & Daubenmier, J. J. (2006). Minding the body: Yoga, embodiment and well-being. *Sexuality Research and Social Policy, 3*, 39–48.

Jackson, L. A., Hunter, J. E., & Hodge, C. N. (1995). Physical attractiveness and intellectual competence: A meta-analytic review. *Social Psychology Quarterly, 58*, 108–122. doi:10.2307/2787149

Johnston-Robledo, I., Fricker, J., & Pasek, L. (2007). Indecent exposure: Self-objectification and young women's attitudes toward breastfeeding. *Sex Roles, 56*, 429–437. doi:10.1007/s11199-007-9194-4

Johnston-Robledo, I., Sheffield, K., Voigt, J., & Wilcox-Constantine, J. (2007). Reproductive shame: Self-objectification and young women's attitudes toward their reproductive functioning. *Women & Health, 46*, 25–39. doi:10.1300/J013 v46n01_03

Landau, M. J., Goldenberg, J. L., Greenberg, J., Gillath, O., Solomon, S., Cox, C., . . . Pyszczynski, T. (2006). The siren's call: Terror management and the threat of sexual attraction. *Journal of Personality and Social Psychology, 90*, 129–146. doi:10.1037/0022-3514.90.1.129

Landau, M. J., Greenberg, J., Sullivan, D., Routledge, C., & Arndt, J. (2009). The protective identity: Evidence that mortality salience heightens the clarity and coherence of the self-concept. *Journal of Experimental Social Psychology, 45*, 796–807. doi:10.1016/j.jesp.2009.05.013

Leary, M. R., Tchividjian, L. R., & Kraxberger, B. E. (1994). Self-presentation can be hazardous to your health: Impression management and health risk. *Health Psychology, 13*, 461–470. doi:10.1037/0278-6133.13.6.461

Morse, J. M. (1989). "Euch, those are for your husband!" Examination of cultural values and assumptions about breast feeding. *Health Care for Women International, 11*, 223–232. doi:10.1080/07399339009515890

Noll, S. M., & Fredrickson, B. L. (1998). A mediational model linking self-objectification, body shame, and disordered eating. *Psychology of Women Quarterly, 22*, 623–636. doi:10.1111/j.1471-6402.1998.tb00181.x

Nussbaum, M. C. (1999). *Sex and social justice.* New York, NY: Oxford University Press.

Rempel, J. K., & Baumgartner, B. (2003). The relationship between attitudes toward menstruation and sexual attitudes, desires, and behavior in women. *Archives of Sexual Behavior, 32*, 155–163. doi:10.1023/A:1022404609700

Roberts, T.-A. (2004). "Female trouble": The Menstrual Self-Evaluation Scale and women's self-objectification. *Psychology of Women Quarterly, 28*, 22–26. doi:10.1111/j.1471-6402.2004.00119.x

Roberts, T.-A., & Gettman, J. Y. (2004). Mere exposure: Gender differences in the negative effects of priming a state of self-objectification. *Sex Roles, 51*, 17–27. doi:10.1023/B:SERS.0000032306.20462.22

Roberts, T.-A., Goldenberg, J. L., Power, C., & Pyszczynski, T. (2002). "Feminine protection": The effects of menstruation on attitudes toward women. *Psychology of Women Quarterly, 26*, 131–139. doi:10.1111/1471-6402.00051

Roberts, T.-A., & MacLane, C. (2002, February). *The body disgusting: How knowledge of body functions affects attitudes toward women.* Paper presented at the Annual Society for Personality and Social Psychology Convention, Savannah, GA.

Roberts, T.-A., & Waters, P. L. (2004). Self-objectification and that "not so fresh feeling": Feminist therapeutic interventions for healthy female embodiment. *Women & Therapy, 27*, 5–21. doi:10.1300/J015v27n03_02

Routledge, C., Arndt, J., & Goldenberg, J. L. (2004). A time to tan: Proximal and distal effects of mortality salience on sun exposure intentions. *Personality and Social Psychology Bulletin, 30*, 1347–1358. doi:10.1177/0146167204264056

Rozin, P., Haidt, J., & McCauley, C. R. (1993). Disgust. In M. Lewis & J. Haviland (Eds.), *Handbook of emotions* (pp. 575–594). New York, NY: Guilford Press.

Rozin, P., Haidt, J., McCauley, C., Dunlop, L., & Ashmore, M. (1999). Individual differences in disgust sensitivity: Comparisons and evaluations of paper-and-pencil versus behavioral measures. *Journal of Research in Personality, 33*, 330–351. doi:10.1006/jrpe.1999.2251

Rubin, D. H., Leventhal, J. M., Krasilnikoff, P. A., Kuo, H. S., Jekel, J. F., Weile, B., . . . Berget, A. (1990). Relationship between infant feeding and infectious illness: A prospective study of infants during the first years of life. *Pediatrics, 85*, 464–471.

Schimel, J., Arndt, J., Pyszczynski, T., & Greenberg, J. (2001). Being accepted for who we are: Evidence that social validation of the intrinsic self reduces general defensiveness. *Journal of Personality and Social Psychology, 80*, 35–52. doi:10.1037/0022-3514.80.1.35

Schooler, D., & Ward, M. (2006). Average Joes: Men's relationships with media, real bodies and sexuality. *Psychology of Men & Masculinity, 7,* 27–41. doi:10.1037/1524-9220.7.1.27

Sherman, D. A. K., Nelson, L. D., & Steele, C. M. (2000). Do messages about health risks threaten the self? Increasing the acceptance of threatening health messages via self-affirmation. *Personality and Social Psychology Bulletin, 26,* 1046–1058. doi:10.1177/01461672002611003

Solomon, S., Greenberg, J., & Pyszczynski, T. (2004). The cultural animal: Twenty years of terror management theory and research. In J. Greenberg, S. L. Koole, & T. Pyszczynski (Eds.), *Handbook of experimental existential psychology* (pp. 13–34). New York, NY: Guilford Press.

Spencer, C. (2005, June 15). *Debate still rages on breast-feeding.* Retrieved from http://news.enquirer.com/apps/pbcs.dll/article?AID=/20050615/BIZ/506150316/1001

Strelan, P., & Hargreaves, D. (2005). Women who objectify other women: The vicious circle of objectification? *Sex Roles, 52,* 707–712. doi:10.1007/s11199-005-3737-3

Tiggemann, M., & Lewis, C. (2004). Attitudes toward women's body hair: Relationship with disgust sensitivity. *Psychology of Women Quarterly, 28,* 381–387. doi:10.1111/j.1471-6402.2004.00155.x

Trivers, R. L. (1972). Parental investment and sexual selection. In B. Campbell (Ed.), *Sexual selection and the descent of man* (pp. 136–179). Chicago, IL: Aldine.

Unger, R. K. (1979). Toward a redefinition of sex and gender. *American Psychologist, 34,* 1085–1094. doi:10.1037/0003-066X.34.11.1085

Vanity Fair. (1991, August). Cover titled "More Demi Moore."

Vanity Fair. (1992, August). Cover titled "Demi's Birthday Suit."

Van Zoonen, L. (1994). *Feminist media studies.* London, England: Sage.

Walker, M. (1993). A fresh look at the risk of artificial infant feeding. *Journal of Human Lactation, 9,* 97–107. doi:10.1177/089033449300900222

Ward, L. M., Merriwether, A., & Caruthers, A. (2006). Breasts are for men: Media use, masculinity ideology, and men's beliefs about women's bodies. *Sex Roles, 55,* 703–714.

Whitely, J. (2001, May 28). *Breast-feeding: Out in the open.* Retrieved from http://www.reviewjournal.com/lvrj_home/2001/May-28-Mon-2001/living/16082266.html

Wolf, N. (1991). *The beauty myth: How images of beauty are used against women.* New York, NY: Anchor Books.

Yalom, M. (1997). *A history of the breast.* New York, NY: Knopf.

Young, I. M. (1992). Breasted experience: The look and the feeling. In D. Leder (Ed.), *The body in medical thought and practice* (pp. 215–230). Boston, MA: Kluwer.

5

CONTINUITY AND CHANGE IN SELF-OBJECTIFICATION: TAKING A LIFE-SPAN APPROACH TO WOMEN'S EXPERIENCES OF OBJECTIFIED BODY CONSCIOUSNESS

NITA MARY McKINLEY

Scholars of objectification have acknowledged that the objectification of women's bodies is likely to vary across the life span. In this chapter, I take a life-span approach to examining both continuity and change in self-objectification across developmental age groups and as a function of the interactions among biology, psychology, and social contexts. In particular, drawing from my own scholarship on women's experiences of objectification, throughout this chapter I explore the development of an objectified body consciousness, which encompasses women's experiences of self-surveillance, body shame, and appearance control (McKinley, 1999; McKinley & Hyde, 1996). Thus, I primarily use the term *objectified body consciousness* to refer to women's objectified relationships with their bodies. When I use the term *self-objectification*, I refer to the construct as it was defined and measured by Noll and Fredrickson (1998; see Chapter 2, this volume). By studying objectified body consciousness across the life span, it is possible to consider the developmental processes and historical contexts that shape how girls and women come to view themselves as disembodied objects within a sexually objectifying cultural context, and how this develops into an objectified body consciousness that includes practices such as self-surveillance and outcomes such as body shame.

LIFE-SPAN DEVELOPMENTAL TASKS AND OBJECTIFIED BODY CONSCIOUSNESS

Life-span theories emphasize the importance of changing tasks and social roles at different developmental stages (e.g., Arnett, 2004; Erikson, 1959; Havighurst, 1953). These tasks and roles are likely to interact with the social context of objectification, and considering them can help one understand how objectified body consciousness may develop and shift across the life span.

Infants and Children

There is no theory on the connection between objectified body consciousness and the developmental tasks of infancy and early to middle childhood. Indeed, it remains unclear how such developmental tasks as learning to trust caregivers or developing a sense of autonomy and initiative (Erikson, 1959) would be related to developing an objectified view of one's body. However, some theories, such as that proposed by Havighurst (1953), suggest that children develop their sense of appropriate feminine and masculine roles in early childhood. Some researchers have suggested that concern with appearance may be a way to demonstrate femininity (Rodin, Silberstein, & Striegel-Moore, 1985), and this has been documented among samples of adults (e.g., Davis, Dionne, & Lazarus, 1996; Murnen & Smolak, 1997). Research on young girls, however, has not found such relationships. For example, Flannery-Schroeder and Chrisler (1996) found no associations between femininity and body esteem or eating-disordered symptoms in first, third, or fifth graders. These researchers noted problems with the measurement of feminine roles in young children, especially because of the confounding of presumed feminine traits with those traits typically associated with young children (e.g., dependence).

It may be that early connections between gender roles and body image are more subtle than might be documented by these survey studies or that the early gendering of bodies is simply invisible across a wide variety of social contexts. Considering the body as a critical site for gender construction, K. A. Martin (1998) observed five preschool classrooms and reported gender differences in the types of bodily controls exerted over girls' and boys' physicality in these social contexts. In particular, she documented five practices that seem to differentially shape girls' and boys' bodily behaviors: dressing up, permitted relaxed behaviors or requiring formal behaviors, controlling voices, verbal and physical instructions regarding children's bodies by teachers, and physical interactions among children. For example, Martin observed that teachers were more likely to give instructions to girls that directed them to change or alter a bodily behavior (e.g., sit here, be gentle, give it to me), whereas boys were given less directive and substantive instructions with regard to their bodily behavior (e.g., stop clapping, don't run, don't cry).

If one considers that objectified bodies are gendered bodies, the significance of these insights for the development of women's objectified body consciousness is fairly clear. These early experiences may "train" young girls to connect their bodily experience with discipline, direction, femininity, and external control, which may translate into an objectified sense of body consciousness later in life. According to K. A. Martin (1998), "gendering of the body in childhood is the foundation on which further gendering of the body occurs throughout the life course" (p. 495). Much more theory and data are needed to explore the precursors to and development of gendered and objectified views of the body among very young girls.

Adolescent Girls and Young Adult Women

The presumption of most theorists is that the period from adolescence through early adulthood is when girls and women fully manifest an objectified view of the self (e.g., Fredrickson & Roberts, 1997; Harter, 1999; McKinley & Hyde, 1996). Objectified body consciousness may be especially important during adolescence and young adulthood because of the developmental tasks and social roles specific to these life stages. In particular, adolescents and young adults focus on the tasks of developing an autonomous identity, feeling a sense of personal achievement, and fostering intimacy in close relationships (Arnett, 2004; Cross & Madson, 1997; Josselson, 1987; but see also Enns, 1991, for a critique of relationship models of women's identity).

Objectified body consciousness may be related to the developmental task of intimacy, or the establishment of (presumed heterosexual) romantic relationships. This task is emphasized as critical during young adulthood in life-span theories (Erikson, 1959; Havighurst, 1953). Critical to the present thesis is Feingold's (1990) finding that women's appearance is especially important to the establishment of heterosexual relationships, suggesting that taking an objectified view of the self may be more likely during periods of romantic relationship development. Research has supported this association. For example, undergraduate women whose self-worth was highly contingent on relationships reported significantly higher levels of body shame and self-surveillance (Sanchez & Kwang, 2007). In a separate study, undergraduate women who were supraliminally primed with words associated with romantic relationships (e.g., *romance, relationship, partner*) reported significantly higher levels of self-objectification than did women who were not primed (Sanchez & Broccoli, 2008). To further qualify and extend these associations, Smolak and Murnen (2008) demonstrated the highest levels of drive for thinness among undergraduate women who reported the greatest conformity to traditional romantic relationships norms and the highest self-surveillance. In sum, these studies support the idea that the developmental tasks of seeking and establishing intimate relationships may foster greater objectified body consciousness among young adult women.

Objectified body consciousness may be particularly strong in adolescence and young adulthood also because of the clash between the goals of attaining intimacy and striving for achievement and identity among women. Rodin et al. (1985) argued that intimacy and achievement are in conflict for women because women must be "feminine" (which patriarchal societies define as passive) to attract heterosexual partners, whereas achievement requires agency. However, the goals of intimacy and achievement may not be mutually exclusive for many women if the body becomes the site for achievement striving. Feminist theorists have argued that women's personal identity and sense of achievement are connected to the internalization of cultural beauty standards and working to achieve those standards. Appearance focus and body concerns are intricately tied to women's sense of achievement. For example, Bartky (1988) argued that through the social disciplining of the female body, women develop a sense of themselves as an individual not only by how they perceive they are viewed by others but also through the skills they learn in reproducing approved body standards. Engaging in self-surveillance and other appearance management practices (e.g., dieting, cosmetic surgery) in an attempt to meet feminine beauty ideals may be a way that women can work simultaneously on identity, achievement, and intimacy goals in a culturally acceptable way. In support of these views, both competitiveness (Striegel-Moore, Silberstein, Grunberg, & Rodin, 1990) and preference for nontraditional gender roles (Silverstein, Carpman, Perlick, & Purdue, 1990) have been associated with more eating disorder symptoms in undergraduate women.

In addition, feminist developmentalists have argued that adolescent girls are encouraged to facilitate and maintain important close relationships by "silencing the self," which serves to ignore individual needs (including bodily needs, personal achievement, and autonomy) in order to avoid interpersonal conflict (Brown & Gilligan, 1992; Jack & Dill, 1992). In a sample of late adolescent girls (ages 16 to 19), Impett, Schooler, and Tolman (2006) found a positive association between silencing the self (i.e., being inauthentic in relationships) and having an objectified relationship with one's body, which were conceptualized as two facets of conventional femininity ideology (see Chapter 2, this volume, for a description of the Adolescent Femininity Ideology Scale to measure self-objectification). Moreover, Tolman, Impett, Tracy, and Michael (2006) found that these two facets of femininity ideology explained more than half of the variance in early adolescent (ages 12 to 15) girls' self-esteem and half of the variance in depression. Most critical to the present thesis, the experience of an objectified relationship with one's body—or objectified body consciousness—was a significantly stronger predictor of these outcomes than being inauthentic in relationships, which further underscores the critical role of self–body relations in girls' adolescent development.

Longitudinal research that examines developmental changes in objectified body consciousness from preadolescence to adolescence to young adulthood is sorely needed. On the basis of cross-sectional research, it seems that late adolescence may be more worrisome with regard to self-objectification than early adolescence. In their cross-sectional study of ethnically diverse adolescent girls, Harrison and Fredrickson (2003) found that self-objectification was lower among 6th and 7th graders and higher among 8th to 12th graders; however, they found no developmental differences in body shame and no ethnic differences in these patterns of findings. In another cross-sectional study, Lindberg, Hyde, and McKinley (2006) found that 10- to 11-year-old girls had lower levels of self-surveillance than undergraduate women (ages 18 to 27 years). These developmental shifts are especially critical when one considers that young women will tend to surround themselves with like-minded women as they continue to develop their relationships and personal identity, which means highly self-objectified women may seek out other highly self-objectified women as their peer group, thereby perpetuating the experience of objectified body consciousness between and within women. For example, among a sample of undergraduate women at the same college, Basow, Foran, and Bookwala (2007) found that sorority women and women intending to rush for sorority reported significantly higher self-surveillance, body shame, and disordered eating compared with nonsorority women and women who did not intend to rush. In addition, sorority women and women who intended to rush reported more perceived social pressure to act and think like their friends than did nonsorority interested women. More research is needed, particularly longitudinal research, to clarify when the shifts and stabilization in objectified body consciousness occur in adolescence and early adulthood.

Middle-Aged Women

In middle age, fulfilling the task of generativity, or contributing to the next generation, is featured in most life-span theories (Erikson, 1959; Havighurst, 1953). Generative tasks can include actual parenting as well as acts of mentorship and contributing to society as a whole (Kotre, 1984). In contrast to previous developmental stages and tasks, fulfillment of generativity is not focused on how a person appears but rather on her contributions to society, and thus one might predict lower levels of objectified body consciousness among middle-aged women. Research has demonstrated some support for this prediction. In a cross-sectional study of adult women who ranged in age between 20 and 84 years old, Tiggemann and Lynch (2001) found that both self-objectification and self-surveillance decreased with age, whereas body shame did not. In contrast, Grippo and Hill (2008) did not find age to be related to self-objectification or self-surveillance in a sample of adult women ranging in age from 40 to 87 years. However, they did find that age moderated the relationship between self-surveillance and body satisfaction, such that there was a weaker relationship between these two variables for older women compared with middle-aged women. Thus, middle-aged women are still at risk of objectified body consciousness even when their primary developmental tasks are not so closely linked to appearance.

In my work comparing discrete samples of undergraduate women and their middle-aged mothers using both cross-sectional and longitudinal methods (McKinley, 1999, 2006), I examined changes in objectified body consciousness for two nonoverlapping cohorts: young adult women (mean age was 19 years at Time 1 and 29 years at Time 2) and middle-aged women (mean age was 47 years at Time 1 and 57 years at Time 2). At Time 1, the middle-aged women had lower levels of self-surveillance and body shame than the young women (McKinley, 1999). Although body shame was negatively related to body satisfaction in both age groups, self-surveillance was unrelated to body satisfaction among the middle-aged women. In a 10-year longitudinal follow-up of this cross-sectional work (Time 2; McKinley, 2006), there were no longer age differences in self-surveillance and body shame as both of these variables had decreased for the young women. However, self-surveillance continued to predict lower body esteem for the young women at Time 2, and the relationship between self-surveillance and body shame remained stronger among the young women compared with the middle-aged women. For the middle-aged cohort, there were no changes in self-surveillance or body shame from Time 1 to Time 2 and no changes in the relationships between these variables and body esteem. This lack of change could mean that developmental changes in objectified body consciousness occur in transitions as was found in the cross-sectional data (Tiggemann & Lynch, 2001) or that cohort effects are the more important influence for women in their 40s and 50s.

Older Women

In older age, the critical developmental tasks are focused on establishing ego integrity, which includes engaging in a life review and finding meaning for one's life (Erikson, 1959) as well as adapting to changing physical and social roles (Havighurst, 1953). Similar to the prediction for middle-aged women, one might expect that these developmental tasks would be protective against higher objectified body consciousness. In particular, this adjustment to the physical changes of old age may shift women's focus away from appearance concerns and more toward functionality and health (Tiggemann, 2004). Yet, this is not the full story. Clarke (2002) assessed perceptions of body weight in a sample of women ages 61 to 92 and found that weight and appearance are still central to women's identity and their perceived social value. The majority of women reported some degree of body dissatisfaction, a desire to lose weight for appearance reasons, and varied degrees of dieting behavior. Indeed, as women's natural bodies diverge more substantially from what they used to look like as well as from cultural appearance ideals, it is possible that women would experience greater objectified body consciousness (Chrisler & Ghiz, 1993; Dillaway, 2005).

There is very little research on the experience of objectified body consciousness among women in old age, and even when continuous age-range studies include women of this age group, they do not often examine them as a discrete entity. Tiggemann and Lynch's (2001) cross-sectional study mentioned earlier did examine roughly three age subgroups: 20 to 39 years, 40 to 69 years, and 70 to 85 years, with the oldest group having the lowest levels of self-objectification and self-surveillance and the youngest group having the highest levels, suggesting that objectified body consciousness becomes less important in old age. It is clear that more research is needed that examines the experience of objectified body consciousness among women in older age, especially as it may relate to their fulfillment (or lack thereof) of developmental tasks.

INTERACTION OF BIOLOGY AND CULTURE ON OBJECTIFIED BODY CONSCIOUSNESS

Different biological stages of a woman's life may create differential risk of higher objectified body consciousness. Both puberty and menopause are likely to be associated with changes in reproductive capacity and thus differences in sexual objectification (Fredrickson & Roberts, 1997). They are also both associated with a redistribution of body fat and weight gain, and are thus likely to be significant passages for women's body experience within a cultural context that values thinness (Tiggemann, 2004).

At puberty, girls add body fat, as well as secondary sexual characteristics associated with sexuality (Arnett, 2004). These changes are proposed to result in an intensification of the sexual objectification of girls' bodies, thereby increasing their objectified body consciousness (Fredrickson & Roberts, 1997; McKinley & Hyde, 1996). Lindberg et al. (2006) established that puberty was important in the experience of objectified body consciousness in that, among 10- to 11-year-old girls, more advanced pubertal status was associated with higher levels of self-surveillance and body shame. Lindberg, Grabe, and Hyde (2007) further demonstrated that among early adolescent girls, pubertal development predicted both increased peer sexual harassment and increased body mass index. In turn, peer sexual harassment predicted that higher self-surveillance and body mass index partially mediated the relationship between pubertal development and body shame. These findings suggest that both the increase in sexual objectification and the physiological changes associated with sexual maturity have important implications for the development of objectified body consciousness in girls.

Biological changes associated with menopause are likely to be associated with a shift in reproductive capacity, and thus a diminution of sexual objectification of older women (Fredrickson & Roberts, 1997), as well as a redistribution of fat (Tiggemann, 2004). As women age, they experience other physiological changes in skin and muscle tone that are socially constructed as degeneration (E. Martin, 1987). However, advertisers and experts exhort women to control their body size and the physiological changes that occur with aging (Chrisler & Ghiz, 1993; Spitzack, 1990). This may encourage more self-objectification and self-surveillance among some older women.

Thus, for middle-aged and older women, biology may interact in more complex ways with the cultural context that objectifies women's bodies and emphasizes youth and beauty but also emphasizes life tasks for this developmental period that are associated with generativity and ego integrity and are not appearance-laden. Yet, the desexualization of women in middle and old age at the cultural level, although decreasing opportunities to be sexually objectified, also renders older women's bodies largely invisible (Fredrickson & Roberts, 1997; McKinley, 1999). This might also negatively affect body esteem and contribute to an objectified relationship with the body. In addition, the physiological changes associated with aging are likely to call attention to women's bodies in negative ways because of the culture's emphasis on youth, which may increase objectified body consciousness. Older women can be considered attractive and thus suitable targets for objectification, but only to the extent that they do not look old (Chrisler & Ghiz, 1993; Spitzack, 1990).

No research has examined whether menopausal status is related to women's objectified body consciousness. However, I have shown in older women (ages ranging from 50 to 68 years), that more positive attitudes toward menopause were associated with lower levels of self-surveillance, whereas greater anxiety about age-related appearance changes was associated with higher levels of self-surveillance (McKinley & Lyon, 2008). More research is needed to examine whether women experience changes in objectified body consciousness as a function of menopause per se or as a function of the general aging process overall.

COHORT DIFFERENCES IN OBJECTIFIED BODY CONSCIOUSNESS

An important concept to life-span developmental research is that of cohort differences. *Cohort differences* refer to the unique historical experiences of a given age group. This is particularly important to consider when examining cross-sectional research because any age differences that may be found could represent either age-associated changes, such as differences in developmental tasks or biological differences, or differences based on the unique historical experiences of a given age group. Differing historical events, attitudes, and standards are likely to shape the specific body experiences of women of different cohorts, particularly those events experienced in young adulthood. For example, Duncan and Agronick (1995) studied multiple cohorts of women and found that events that occurred in their early adulthood were most salient compared with events occurring at other life stages.

Wolf (1991) argued that women's increasing participation in public life has led to a backlash in which greater emphasis has been placed on appearance and its association with achievement for women. Also, feminine beauty standards (e.g., ultra-thinness, large breasts) have become more extreme since 1959, making them more and more difficult to attain (Garner, Garfinkel, Schwartz, & Thompson, 1980; Wiseman, Gray, Mosimann, & Ahrens, 1992). Attaining these stringent body standards may require greater self-surveillance for the women of younger cohorts for whom these standards will be most relevant. More recent cohorts of adult women may place more importance on their appearance and thus objectify themselves more than women of earlier cohorts. Indeed, this possibility is consistent with evidence from cross-sectional research demonstrating lower levels of objectified body consciousness (McKinley, 1999; Tiggemann & Lynch, 2001) and differences in the strength of the relationships between objectified body consciousness and body satisfaction across different age groups (Grippo & Hill, 2008; McKinley, 1999).

LIMITATIONS AND FUTURE RESEARCH

This chapter demonstrates that we are in the early stages of applying a life-span approach to our understanding of the development of objectified body consciousness. Taking a life-span perspective provides a rich context for expanding knowledge of girls' and women's bodily experiences and the ways in which these experiences interact with the development of identity and self-concept within an objectifying culture. Research is needed to test more specifically some of the predictions of life-span theories, including how differences in life-span tasks and roles, differences in the interaction between biology and culture, and cohort differences magnify or diminish an objectified experience of body consciousness. Understanding how physiological changes associated with sexual maturity and aging may interact with sexual objectification, as well as with a cultural context that values thinness and a youthful appearance, underscores the complexity of women's experience of objectified body consciousness across the life span. A good example of this is Lindberg et al.'s (2006, 2007) studies that examine the relationship of pubertal status to objectified body consciousness. More research is needed to test the specific relationships between objectified body consciousness and gender role development in childhood, identity and intimacy development in adolescence and young adulthood, generativity in middle age, and adaptation to physical changes and shifting roles in old age. For example, researchers could examine the relationship between the adoption of gender roles and self-objectification, including the use of longitudinal data to examine the developmental sequence of learning/embodying these roles and the manifestation of objectified body consciousness. Longitudinal data could help determine whether self-objectification precedes or succeeds the development of an inauthentic self, thus further illuminating the role of objectified body consciousness in girls' and women's identity formation.

Further research is also needed to understand how the meeting and thwarting of achievement tasks (e.g., career success, job loss) and intimacy tasks (e.g., marriage, divorce) are related to the experience of objectified body consciousness. In addition, almost nothing is known about the relationship of menopause or other biological passages (e.g., pregnancy, childbirth, motherhood) with objectified body consciousness, or how these biological passages interact with developmental tasks and roles, which would be important to examine. For example, future investigations should examine whether young adult women who have become mothers experience their bodies differently from their peers who have not had children, and if so, why.

Research on the objectification of women, like many other areas of psychology, has focused largely on convenience samples of undergraduate students. Given that undergraduate women are presumed to be at a critical developmental stage when sexual objectification is likely to be especially salient, this is not surprising. Indeed, more developmental research would provide further evidence of some of the main tenets of objectification theory, such as the importance of the sexualization of women's bodies at different life stages (Fredrickson & Roberts, 1997). However, considering the life-span approach, more research with girls and women across the entire age spectrum is needed. Both cross-sectional and longitudinal studies are needed; however, particularly needed are longitudinal studies to demonstrate how women's and girls' bodily experiences change across the life span, and what differences might be accounted for by particular cohort effects. Longitudinal research can demonstrate how bodily experiences change over time, and therefore it provides the best type of data for testing hypotheses around developmental change. Longitudinal data would also help researchers predict prospectively the relationships among self-objectification, self-surveillance, body shame, body esteem, and other developmental outcomes. Because different cohorts may change differently over time, data collection from multiple overlapping cohorts (cross-sequential design) is preferred to capture more fully how women's objectified body consciousness changes over time.

It is also the case that almost all of the studies reviewed in this chapter have been conducted in the United States or Australia and have used participants who were primarily White, presumably middle-class, and presumably heterosexual. Thus, the findings summarized here reflect the objectified body consciousness of those girls and women almost exclusively. Some research has shown ethnic differences in objectified body consciousness (Breitkopf, Littleton, & Berenson, 2007), whereas other research has not (Harrison & Fredrickson, 2003; Hebl, King, & Lin, 2004). There is also some research on the experience of objectified body consciousness in lesbians (Haines et al., 2008; Kozee & Tylka, 2006), yet nothing with regard to the developmental trajectory of objectified body consciousness in lesbian girls and women. More research is needed to understand how more diverse samples of girls and women come to experience and embody sexual and self-objectification across the life span (McKinley, 2000).

CONCLUSION

The small body of research examining developmental differences and changes in objectified body consciousness highlights two key findings. First, objectified body consciousness is highest among girls and women in adolescence and young adulthood and lowest among older women. Second, the differences in self-surveillance and body shame between younger and older women suggest that the experience of an objectified relationship with the body may change for women over time. By considering the shifting developmental tasks and the unique historical events felt by particular cohorts, a life-span perspective on objectified body consciousness provides a more comprehensive framework for understanding the phenomenon. Indeed, learning how different life stages promote more or protect against self-objectification will help clarify the developmental pathways that increase girls' and women's risk of or resistance to developing objectified relationships with their bodies.

REFERENCES

Arnett, J. J. (2004). *Emerging adulthood: The winding road from the late teens through the twenties*. New York, NY: Oxford University Press.

Bartky, S. L. (1988). Foucault, femininity, and the modernization of patriarchal power. In I. Diamond & L. Quinby (Eds.), *Feminism and Foucault: Reflections on resistance* (pp. 61–86). Boston, MA: Northeastern University Press.

Basow, S. A., Foran, K. A., & Bookwala, J. (2007). Social contagion of eating disordered behavior in college women: The role of sorority living. *Psychology of Women Quarterly, 31*, 394–400.

Breitkopf, C. R., Littleton, H., & Berenson, A. (2007). Body image: A study in a tri-ethnic sample of low-income women. *Sex Roles, 56*, 373–380. doi:10.1007/s11199-006-9177-x

Brown, L. M., & Gilligan, C. (1992). *Meeting at the crossroads: Women's psychology and girls' development*. Cambridge, MA: Harvard University Press.

Chrisler, J. C., & Ghiz, L. (1993). Body image issues of older women. *Women & Therapy, 14*, 67–75. doi:10.1300/J015v14n01_07

Clarke, L. H. (2002). Older women's perceptions of ideal body weights: The tensions between health and appearance motivations for weight loss. *Ageing and Society, 22*, 751–773. doi:10.1017/S0144686X02008905

Cross, S. E., & Madson, L. (1997). Models of the self: Self-construals and gender. *Psychological Bulletin, 122*, 5–37. doi:10.1037/0033-2909.122.1.5

Davis, C., Dionne, M., & Lazarus, L. (1996). Gender-role orientation and body image in women and men: The moderating influence of neuroticism. *Sex Roles, 34*, 493–505. doi:10.1007/BF01545028

Dillaway, H. (2005). (Un)changing menopausal bodies: How women think and act in the face of a reproductive transition and gendered beauty ideals. *Sex Roles, 53*, 1–17. doi:10.1007/s11199-005-4269-6

Duncan, L. E., & Agronick, G. S. (1995). The intersection of life stage and social events: Personality and life outcomes. *Journal of Personality and Social Psychology, 69*, 558–568. doi:10.1037/0022-3514.69.3.558

Enns, C. Z. (1991). The "new" relationship models of women's identity: A review and critique for counselors. *Journal of Counseling and Development, 69*, 209–217.

Erikson, E. (1959). Growth and crises of the healthy personality. *Psychological Issues, 1* (Monograph 1), 50–100.

Feingold, A. (1990). Gender differences in effects of physical attractiveness on romantic attraction: A comparison across five research paradigms. *Journal of Personality and Social Psychology, 59*, 981–993. doi:10.1037/0022-3514.59.5.981

Flannery-Schroeder, E. C., & Chrisler, J. (1996). Body esteem, eating attitudes, and gender-role orientation in three age groups of children. *Current Psychology, 15*, 235–248. doi:10.1007/BF02686880

Fredrickson, B. L., & Roberts, T. (1997). Objectification theory: Toward understanding women's lived experiences and mental health risks. *Psychology of Women Quarterly, 21*, 173–206. doi:10.1111/j.1471-6402.1997.tb00108.x

Garner, D. M., Garfinkel, P. E., Schwartz, D., & Thompson, M. (1980). Cultural expectations of thinness in women. *Psychological Reports, 47*, 483–491.

Grippo, K. P., & Hill, M. S. (2008). Self-objectification, habitual body monitoring, and body dissatisfaction in older European American women: Exploring age and feminism as moderators. *Body Image, 5*, 173–182. doi:10.1016/j.bodyim.2007.11.003

Haines, M. E., Erchull, M. J., Liss, M., Turner, D. L., Nelson, J. A., Ramsey, L. R., & Hurt, M. M. (2008). Predictors and effects of self-objectification in lesbians. *Psychology of Women Quarterly, 32*, 181–187. doi:10.1111/j.1471-6402.2008.00422.x

Harrison, A., & Fredrickson, B. L. (2003). Women's sports media, self-objectification, and mental health in Black and White adolescents. *Journal of Communication, 53*, 216–232. doi:10.1111/j.1460-2466.2003.tb02587.x

Harter, S. (1999). *The construction of the self: A developmental perspective*. New York, NY: Guilford Press.

Havighurst, R. J. (1953). *Human development and education*. New York, NY: David McKay.

Hebl, M. R., King, E. B., & Lin, J. (2004). The swimsuit becomes us all: Ethnicity, gender, and vulnerability to self-objectification. *Personality and Social Psychology Bulletin, 30*, 1322–1331. doi:10.1177/0146167204264052

Impett, E. A., Schooler, D., & Tolman, D. L. (2006). To be seen and not heard: Femininity ideology and adolescent girls' sexual health. *Archives of Sexual Behavior, 35*, 129–142. doi:10.1007/s10508-005-9016-0

Jack, D. C., & Dill, D. (1992). The Silencing the Self Scale: Schemas of intimacy associated with depression in women. *Psychology of Women Quarterly, 16*, 97–106. doi:10.1111/j.1471-6402.1992.tb00242.x

Josselson, R. (1987). *Finding herself: Pathways to identity development in women*. San Francisco, CA: Jossey-Bass.

Kotre, J. (1984). *Outliving the self: Generativity and the interpretation of lives*. Baltimore, MD: Johns Hopkins University Press.

Kozee, H. B., & Tylka, T. L. (2006). A test of objectification theory with lesbian women. *Psychology of Women Quarterly, 30*, 348–357. doi:10.1111/j.1471-6402.2006.00310.x

Lindberg, S. M., Grabe, S., & Hyde, J. S. (2007). Gender, pubertal development, and peer sexual harassment predict objectified body consciousness in early adolescence. *Journal of Research on Adolescence, 17*, 723–742.

Lindberg, S. M., Hyde, J. S., & McKinley, N. M. (2006). A measure of objectified body consciousness for pre-adolescent and adolescent youth. *Psychology of Women Quarterly, 30*, 65–76. doi:10.1111/j.1471-6402.2006.00263.x

Martin, E. (1987). *The woman in the body: A cultural analysis of reproduction*. Boston, MA: Beacon Press.

Martin, K. A. (1998). Becoming a gendered body: Practices of preschools. *American Sociological Review, 63*, 494–511. doi:10.2307/2657264

McKinley, N. M. (1999). Women and objectified body consciousness: Mothers' and daughters' body experience in cultural, developmental, and familial context. *Developmental Psychology, 35*, 760–769. doi:10.1037/0012-1649.35.3.760

McKinley, N. M. (2000, August). Beauty, boon or beast? Dilemmas of lesbian body consciousness. In J. C. Cogan (Chair), *Disrupting the cultural narrative by daring to discuss lesbian beauty*. Symposium conducted at the annual meeting of the American Psychological Association, Washington, DC.

McKinley, N. M. (2006). The developmental and cultural contexts of objectified body consciousness: A longitudinal analysis of two cohorts of women. *Developmental Psychology, 54*, 159–173.

McKinley, N. M., & Hyde, J. S. (1996). The Objectified Body Consciousness Scale: Development and validation. *Psychology of Women Quarterly, 20*, 181–215. doi:10.1111/j.1471-6402.1996.tb00467.x

McKinley, N. M., & Lyon, L. A. (2008). Menopausal attitudes, objectified body consciousness, aging anxiety, and body esteem: European American women's body experiences in midlife. *Body Image: An International Journal of Research, 5*, 375–380.

Murnen, S. K., & Smolak, L. (1997). Femininity, masculinity, and disordered eating: A meta-analytic review. *International Journal of Eating Disorders, 22*, 231–242. doi:10.1002/(SICI)1098-108X(199711)22:3<231::AID-EAT2>3.0.CO;2-O

Noll, S. M., & Fredrickson, B. L. (1998). A mediational model linking self-objectification, body shame, and disordered eating. *Psychology of Women Quarterly, 22*, 623–636. doi:10.1111/j.1471-6402.1998.tb00181.x

Rodin, J., Silberstein, L., & Striegel-Moore, R. (1985). Women and weight: A normative discontent. In T. Sonderegger (Ed.), *Psychology and gender: Nebraska symposium on motivation* (pp. 265–306). Lincoln, NE: University of Nebraska Press.

Sanchez, D. T., & Broccoli, T. L. (2008). The romance of self-objectification: Does priming romantic relationships induce states of self-objectification among women? *Sex Roles, 59*, 545–554. doi:10.1007/s11199-008-9451-1

Sanchez, D. T., & Kwang, T. (2007). When the relationship becomes her: Revisiting women's body concerns from a relationship contingency perspective. *Psychology of Women Quarterly, 31*, 401–414. doi:10.1111/j.1471-6402.2007.00389.x

Silverstein, B., Carpman, S., Perlick, D., & Purdue, L. (1990). Nontraditional sex role aspirations, gender identity conflict, and disordered eating among college women. *Sex Roles, 23*, 687–695. doi:10.1007/BF00289256

Smolak, L., & Murnen, S. K. (2008). Drive for leanness: Assessment and relationship to gender, gender role and objectification. *Body Image, 5*, 251–260. doi:10.1016/j.bodyim.2008.03.004

Spitzack, C. (1990). *Confessing excess: Women and the politics of body reduction*. Albany, NY: State University of New York Press.

Striegel-Moore, R. H., Silberstein, L. R., Grunberg, N. E., & Rodin, J. (1990). Competing on all fronts: Achievement orientation and disordered eating. *Sex Roles, 23*, 697–702. doi:10.1007/BF00289257

Tiggemann, M. (2004). Body image across the adult life span: Stability and change. *Body Image: An International Journal of Research, 1*(1), 29–41. doi:10.1016/S1740-1445(03)00002-0

Tiggemann, M., & Lynch, J. E. (2001). Body image across the life span in adult women: The role of self-objectification. *Developmental Psychology, 37*, 243–253. doi:10.1037/0012-1649.37.2.243

Tolman, D. L., Impett, E. A., Tracy, A. J., & Michael, A. (2006). Looking good, sounding good: Femininity ideology and adolescent girls' mental health. *Psychology of Women Quarterly, 30*, 85–95. doi:10.1111/j.1471-6402.2006.00265.x

Wiseman, C. V., Gray, J. J., Mosimann, J. E., & Ahrens, A. H. (1992). Cultural expectations of thinness in women: An update. *International Journal of Eating Disorders, 11*, 85–89. doi:10.1002/1098-108X(199201)11:1<85::AID-EAT2260110112>3.0.CO;2-T

Wolf, N. (1991). *The beauty myth: How images of beauty are used against women.* New York, NY: Anchor Press.

III

CONSEQUENCES OF
SELF-OBJECTIFICATION

6

PERFORMANCE AND FLOW: A REVIEW AND INTEGRATION OF SELF-OBJECTIFICATION RESEARCH

DIANE M. QUINN, STEPHENIE R. CHAUDOIR,
AND RACHEL W. KALLEN

The young girl feels that her body is getting away from her, it is no longer the straightforward expression of her individuality; it becomes foreign to her; and at the same time she becomes for others a *thing:* on the street men follow her with their eyes and comment on her anatomy.
—Simone de Beauvoir (1952, p. 308, emphasis added)

We posit that in a culture that objectifies the female body, whatever girls and women do, the potential always exists for their thoughts and actions to be interrupted by images of how their bodies appear.
—Fredrickson and Roberts (1997, p. 180)

The quote from Fredrickson and Roberts (1997) directly captures how objectification by others and by the self interferes with performance. At its most basic, objectification is a disruption. Whatever task or thought in which a woman is engaged, objectification can disrupt and shift the woman's attention to her appearance. In this chapter, we first consider the implications of objectification theory for performance outcomes and review evidence supporting Fredrickson and Roberts's (1997) original claim that self-objectification usurps cognitive resources. We then discuss evidence to support three different reasons why self-objectification can be detrimental to performance. Finally, we draw on insights from the self-regulation literature (Carver & Scheier, 1998) to examine how these processes can be conceptualized within a single, parsimonious framework. We provide evidence from some of our most recent work to support this new framework and discuss how it can highlight useful new directions for future research.

SELF-OBJECTIFICATION AND PERFORMANCE

A number of studies have examined the ways that both trait and state self-objectification affect performance. In this section, we consider how self-objectification can interfere with at least three indices of performance: peak flow states, cognitive performance, and physical performance.

Flow States

Women who are high in trait self-objectification are chronically monitoring their appearance. Research has shown that high trait-level self-objectifiers spend a lot of time and emotional resources thinking about how they appear to others. Thus, theoretically, they may spend less time in states of intense focus in which they can "lose themselves" in intellectual, artistic, or physical endeavors. To explore this possibility, several studies have examined whether trait-level self-objectification is correlated with fewer experiences of flow states (i.e., states of intense concentration and focus). Different measures of flow states have been used, but they typically measure whether (or how frequently) people can devote their entire attention to a task, whether they often concentrate so intensely that they lose track of time, and whether they can act without thinking or self-consciousness.

In a study that surveyed college students, Tiggemann and Kuring (2004) found that trait self-objectification was related indirectly to self-reported flow states through self-surveillance. That is, self-objectification was related to greater levels of self-surveillance (i.e., frequently thinking about one's own appearance), which, in turn, was related to lower frequency of flow states. This was true for both male and female participants. Greenleaf (2005) found a correlation between self-surveillance and flow states for women ranging from 18 to 64 years old. In a more recent study of another large sample of women across the life span (18 to 65 years old), Szymanski and Henning (2007) found both a direct relationship between self-objectification and lower flow states and an indirect relationship through self-surveillance. Thus, the more time women spent thinking about their appearance and monitoring how they look to others, the less time they spent intensely focused on creative and physical tasks.

One study also examined the impact of state self-objectification on flow states. Using a daily diary approach, Breines, Crocker, and Garcia (2008) asked women to report on their state of self-objectification, their current feelings of positive affect, and their current feelings of flow (e.g., "I am so absorbed in what I am doing I have lost track of time") several times each day for 2 weeks. State self-objectification was measured as a function of current body monitoring (i.e., participants were asked the extent to which they were thinking about how they looked at the present moment). Thus, this study was able to track experiences of self-objectification in the lives of women as they were occurring. Results showed that increases in state self-objectification were related to decreases in flow experiences. Taken together with the above-mentioned research, there is converging evidence that self-objectification can lead to decreased flow experiences, states that are related to more positive achievement outcomes (e.g., Csikszentmihalyi & Csikszentmihalyi, 1988; Rathunde & Csikszentmihalyi, 1993). Much more work is needed, however, to examine the relationships among self-objectification, flow, and long-term achievement outcomes.

Cognitive Performance

Researchers have found that self-objectification can undermine cognitive performance (Fredrickson, Roberts, Noll, Quinn, & Twenge, 1998; Quinn, Kallen, Twenge, & Fredrickson, 2006). In the original manipulation of self-objectification, termed the *swimsuit–sweater paradigm*, participants were randomly assigned to try on and evaluate themselves while wearing either a one-piece swimsuit or a V-neck sweater, ostensibly as part of a consumer decision-making study. Although this manipulation requires all participants to focus on their body and appearance while wearing the garment, only the swimsuit condition elicits a state of self-objectification because it accentuates "their awareness of observers' perspectives on their bodies" (Fredrickson et al., 1998, p. 270). That is, only participants wearing the swimsuit should become intensely preoccupied with their body and appearance and consider how their bodies might appear from a third-person perspective.

Fredrickson et al. (1998) found that both male and female undergraduate participants in the swimsuit condition experienced a state of self-objectification. That is, for participants of both genders, the process of trying on and evaluating themselves in a mirror prompted them to feel as though they were defined by their body. However, only women's cognitive performance was affected by being in a state of self-objectification. Women in the swimsuit condition performed significantly worse on a math task than women in the sweater condition, whereas men's performance was not affected by condition (Fredrickson et al., 1998, Study 2).

Subsequent research has largely replicated this basic pattern of findings, suggesting that being in a state of self-objectification can have deleterious effects on cognitive performance. Because the study above used a math test as the performance measure, one important question was whether the performance effects were due to inducing self-objectification or, alternatively, due to inducing a state of "stereotype threat." A large body of research (for a review, see Quinn, Kallen, & Spencer, in press) has shown that when women take math tests, stereotypes about their inferior math skills are implicitly activated, and such stereotypes can suppress performance. To address this issue, Quinn, Kallen, Twenge, and Fredrickson (2006) ruled out stereotype threat as a plausible alternative explanation for the performance decrements demonstrated in a state of self-objectification. Using the swimsuit–sweater paradigm, these researchers demonstrated that undergraduate women in a state of self-objectification perform significantly worse on a cognitive task that has no gender stereotypes associated with it: the Stroop color-naming task. On the Stroop task, participants see different words flash up on a computer screen and their task is to simply name the color of the ink in which the words are printed. How quickly they can name the ink color is recorded. Because reading a word is done more quickly and automatically than naming the ink color, it is possible to get interference between the word content and ink color. For example, it takes a person longer to name the ink color when the word *red* is printed in blue ink than to name the color of the ink for the word *chair*. Use of the Stroop task in hundreds of psychological studies (for a review, see MacLeod, 1991) shows that decreases in attentional resources available for the task lead to slower overall responding (Engle, 2002; Kane & Engle, 2003). Thus, these findings suggest that the performance decrements demonstrated by Fredrickson et al. (1998) were not elicited solely because women were reminded about the negative stereotypes associated with their math ability but instead because they were not devoting their full attention to the task.

Whereas the seminal findings by Fredrickson et al. (1998) indicate that only women experience performance decrements due to self-objectification, work by Hebl, King, and Lin (2004) suggests that the deleterious consequences of self-objectification are not solely confined to women. Using an ethnically diverse sample of male and female undergraduate students, Hebl and colleagues demonstrated that being in a state of self-objectification can undermine cognitive performance for both men and women of Caucasian, African American, Hispanic, and Asian American ethnicities. They found that although men did better on a measure of math performance relative to women, both men and women in the swimsuit condition performed worse than their counterparts in the sweater condition. Further, these effects occurred across participants of all ethnicities. In summary, these findings suggest that no one is immune from experiencing detriments in cognitive performance due to self-objectification.

How do we reconcile these seemingly disparate findings obtained by Fredrickson et al. (1998) and Hebl et al. (2004)? Hebl et al. argued that the research by Fredrickson and colleagues used unbalanced manipulations of self-objectification for men and women. Whereas women wore a one-piece swimsuit that fit tightly to their bodies, men wore swim trunks that did not. To remedy this discrepancy, Hebl and colleagues asked their male participants to wear tight-fitting Speedo swimsuits while their female participants were asked to wear one-piece swimsuits, thereby equalizing the intensity of the objectifying situation. Thus, Hebl et al. argued that they found decrements in performance for both men and women because they subjected both genders to equally objectifying situations whereas Fredrickson et al. did not.

Because the data comparing the effects of self-objectification across both men and women are sparse, we cannot draw a firm conclusion about whether the harmful effects of self-objectification are confined solely to women or experienced by both genders. However, as Hebl et al. (2004) noted, even if these negative effects are "equal opportunity" outcomes, women are much more likely than men to experience states of self-objectification. Thus, although outcomes may be similar for both genders, women are more vulnerable to experiencing them on a frequent basis because of their disproportionately greater exposure to self-objectifying situations such as sexual harassment and catcalls (Kozee, Tylka, Augustus-Horvath, & Denchik, 2007; Swim, Hyers, Cohen, & Ferguson, 2001). It is therefore possible that many small instances of disrupted attention could compound to larger negative outcomes over time. Moreover, whereas wearing a Speedo swimsuit is a rare and novel situation for American men and represents the most extreme and revealing of garments, wearing a one-piece swimsuit is not only a normal occurrence for women but also the most conservative and body-covering option for American women's swimwear.

Other studies have used a variation of the swimsuit–sweater paradigm or an entirely new manipulation but have failed to demonstrate deleterious effects on cognitive performance. For example, Gapinski, Brownell, and LaFrance (2003) used the swimsuit–sweater paradigm; however, their manipulation also examined whether "fat talk"—body-disparaging comments that make body and appearance salient in a given situation—might exacerbate the negative effects of self-objectification. Specifically, in addition to trying on either a swimsuit or a sweater, undergraduate women were also exposed to a fat-talk manipulation in which a female confederate either defamed her own appearance (i.e., "I look totally fat in this! My stomach is sticking out") or made a similarly negative comment about her computer. Unlike prior research, results from this study failed to demonstrate an effect of the swimsuit–sweater manipulation on performance using measures of cognitive completion, logical reasoning, spatial orientation, and math ability. However, the results do indicate that women who are high in trait self-objectification and who heard fat-talk demonstrated worse cognitive functioning, whereas women who are low in trait self-objectification and who heard fat-talk demonstrated improved cognitive functioning compared with women in the control talk condition. Although this study does not replicate the findings of previous research, this study's deviation from the standard swimsuit–sweater paradigm prevents us from being able to draw direct comparisons across the study data. That is, the introduction of a conversation with a female confederate while trying on the garment may have significantly altered the experience of the participants, preventing them from being fully immersed in a potentially objectifying situation.

In considering the manipulations used to examine whether self-objectification usurps cognitive resources, the majority of studies have used the swimsuit–sweater paradigm. Although reliance on this paradigm allows for comparison of effects across studies, it does not allow researchers to understand whether these performance decrements might occur in less obtrusive situations. In response to this limitation, Tiggemann and Boundy (2008) examined whether altering subtle aspects of the physical and social environment could induce a state of self-objectification and yield cognitive deficits. In their study, undergraduate women were placed in either an objectifying environment filled with items designed to make their appearance salient—a bathroom scale, full-length mirrors, and fashion magazines—or a neutral lab environment. Further, participants either received an appearance-based compliment or received no compliment. Despite the fact that these subtle manipulations seemed to increase self-objectification, results indicate that neither of these study manipulations affected performance on logical reasoning or spatial orientation tasks. Thus, the extent to which self-objectification disrupts cognitive performance on a daily basis is still unclear.

Physical Performance

In addition to interfering with cognitive performance, some research suggests that self-objectification may also serve to hinder physical performance. Whereas several studies have examined the relationships between trait self-objectification and the frequency of participation in physical performance activities such as dancing (Tiggemann & Slater, 2001) and yoga (Daubenmier, 2005), only one study has examined women's proficiency in these activities. Fredrickson and Harrison (2005) examined the effect of self-objectification on physical performance in a throwing task. In this study, researchers examined adolescent girls' ability to throw a softball and found that girls who self-objectified to a greater degree also demonstrated lower throwing performance even after controlling for age and prior throwing experience. Because these researchers used a composite measure of self-objectification that assessed trait self-objectification, state self-objectification, and objectifying thoughts during the throwing task, we cannot disentangle the effect of these variables individually. However, results from this study provide preliminary evidence to suggest that the deleterious effects of self-objectification can have an impact on physical performance.

Summary

There is initial evidence for a relationship between trait self-objectification and the experience of less frequent flow states. In addition, state self-objectification is related to diminished cognitive performance, both on math tasks and on an attentional task (Stroop color naming). However, some experimental studies have failed to find an effect of state self-objectification on cognitive tasks or the effect only occurred when trait self-objectification was examined in combination with a state manipulation. Thus, although research on objectification has flourished in the past decade, there is still much more work to be done on examining when self-objectification interferes with performance outcomes.

HOW DOES SELF-OBJECTIFICATION INTERFERE WITH PERFORMANCE?

As reviewed here, there is evidence that self-objectification can interfere with various types of performance, leading women to achieve below their potential. However, it is not clear how self-objectification results in lowered performance outcomes. Objectification theory suggests three potential paths. First, self-objectification is theorized to result in a change in visual perspective. Specifically, a person objectifying the self takes a third-person perspective, viewing the self through the eyes of the other. We review the research evidence for perspective taking and whether it predicts worse performance. Second, when women self-objectify, they are thought to be actively monitoring their appearance and comparing their appearance with cultural standards of appearance. We review whether there is evidence of active appearance monitoring and then examine whether the monitoring itself is interfering with performance outcomes. Finally, self-objectification is theorized to lead to the experience of negative self-conscious emotions. Managing these emotions may be distracting and thus result in performance decrements. Once we have reviewed these possibilities, we present a framework to integrate what we know so far and to suggest directions for future work.

Taking a Third-Person Perspective on the Self

Although the change in perspective from the active first-person to the passive third-person perspective is a central part of objectification theory, surprisingly little research has directly examined this change in perspective; to date, only one published study has done so. Huebner and Fredrickson (1999) asked male and female college students to recall one of four different types of situations: studying alone, eating in a dining hall, giving a presentation, and being at a mixed-sex party. Once the event was recalled, participants were asked to rate the extent to which their memories were more observer oriented (as if seen by an observer or a "camera mounted somewhere on the wall") versus more field oriented (as seen "through your own eyes, from your own point of view"). Overall, women reported more observer, or third-person perspective, memories than men did. However, this gender difference was accounted for by memories of the mixed-sex party. In these public, unstructured situations, women had significantly more observer memories compared with men. In the other situations (studying alone, eating in the dining hall, and giving a class presentation), there were no gender differences. Thus, potentially objectifying situations do seem to prompt women to take an observer perspective on the self.

Although this study provides some preliminary evidence about the perspective-taking process purported to occur during self-objectification, we could find no research that manipulated or measured perspective taking in relation to performance or state self-objectification. In our own unpublished work, we have measured the extent of observer versus field memory in the same way as Huebner and Fredrickson (1999) after a swimsuit–sweater study but found no gender or condition differences (Quinn & Chaudoir, 2009). We have also asked participants to quickly draw the letter "E" on their foreheads while wearing the swimsuit. In previous work (e.g., Hass, 1984; Galinsky, Magee, Inesi, & Gruenfeld, 2006), changes in perspective taking have been shown by using this task. If a person is taking an observer perspective, they should draw the letter such that it would look correct to the observer ("E"). If a person is taking a first-person perspective, the E would look backward to an observer "Ǝ" but correct for the self. Again, using the swimsuit–sweater paradigm we did not find that women in the swimsuit condition were more likely to draw the E from an observer perspective. Indeed, we found just the opposite effect: Women in the self-objectification condition were the least likely to draw an observer E. Thus, women seem to be intensely self-focused during self-objectification.

In another series of studies in our lab, we directly manipulated perspective taking (Earnshaw, Quinn, & Kenny, 2009) to examine its effect on self-objectification processes. In these studies, we took pictures of female participants and then asked the participants to look at the picture and either imagine what a stranger would think about their appearance (third-person perspective on appearance) or imagine what they would do in the future (active first-person perspective). In line with objectification theory, taking a third-person perspective on appearance did lead to more thoughts of the self as a body and increased negative affect compared with taking an active first-person perspective on the self. However, in a follow-up task of person perception, it was not the case that participants in the third-person perspective condition were more likely to actually take others' perspectives into account when evaluating how others judged their appearance (i.e., metaperceptions of appearance). Indeed, although participants in the third-person perspective condition believed that others judged their appearance more negatively than those taking a first-person perspective, examination of the data showed that participants were relying on their own self-assessments rather than literally taking into account the judgments of outside observers. In a follow-up study, we compared participants on a manipulation of taking a third-person perspective on appearance versus taking a third-person perspective on the whole person. We found that participants taking a third-person perspective on their appearance—that is, self-objectification—were more self-focused in evaluating how others judged their appearance than those taking a third-person perspective on themselves as whole and complete persons. In short, we have some evidence that taking a third-person perspective on appearance leads women to think more about their own internalized appearance standards rather than specific others' standards.

In summary, there is currently no research that demonstrates that a change to the third-person visual perspective accounts for performance or attention shifts during state self-objectification. As discussed in more detail in the next section, thinking about how the self appears to others likely sets in motion a chain of cognitive and affective events that include both the activation and application of learned appearance standards to the self.

Appearance Monitoring

Another way in which self-objectification could interfere with performance and achievement is if women are focusing their attention on monitoring their appearance—thinking about how their body looks—rather than on a particular task or goal. Considerable evidence indicates that women who are high in trait self-objectification are also high in self-surveillance. Indeed, several studies use self-surveillance as *the* measure of self-objectification (see Chapter 2, this volume). However, there is very little research directly linking self-surveillance with decreased cognitive performance. As reviewed earlier, a few studies have shown a correlation between increased self-surveillance and decreased reports of flow experiences (e.g., Szymanski & Henning, 2007; Tiggemann & Kuring, 2004; Tiggemann & Slater, 2001). We could find no research that directly manipulates appearance monitoring and examines cognitive performance outcomes.

Negative Self-Conscious Emotions

A key feature of the model proposed by Fredrickson and Roberts (1997) entails the processes by which women may uniquely and disproportionately experience negative self-conscious emotions, such as shame, anxiety, and depression. As noted in Chapter 1 of this volume, there is ample evidence that self-objectification is related to negative self-conscious emotions, particularly shame. It should be noted that whereas the original theory of self-objectification discussed global feelings of shame (Fredrickson & Roberts, 1997), most of the follow-up work has specifically measured body shame. Is the experience of body shame and appearance anxiety interrupting women's concentration and resulting in overall decreased cognitive achievement and fewer experiences of flow? In the few studies that have examined the correlations between experiences of emotions and flow states, the data are a bit contradictory. Greenleaf and McGreer (2006) surveyed both sedentary and physically active women. For the sedentary women there was a strong negative correlation between appearance anxiety and flow states. Thus, the more appearance anxiety reported, the fewer flow states. For the physically active women, however, there was no significant correlation between appearance anxiety and flow states. Greenleaf (2005) did find a negative correlation between body shame and flow states for physically active women, but in this case the flow states were specifically related to flow in physical or sports activity and not to flow more generally. Finally, Szymanski and Henning (2007) found that both increased body shame and increased appearance anxiety are correlated with lower reported flow experiences. Thus, at the trait level, there is some evidence that negative self-conscious emotions are related to less reported flow states, but questions of how, when, and for whom negative emotions interfere with flow states remain.

Research using the swimsuit–sweater paradigm has shown that when wearing the swimsuit, women experience a state of self-objectification and this state leads to both increased body shame and decreased performance (Fredrickson et al., 1998; Quinn, Kallen, Twenge, & Fredrickson, 2006). However, these studies do not report any full correlation matrices, and there is no evidence that the experience of body shame or other self-conscious emotions mediates the effects on performance. Indeed, we specifically reanalyzed the data from Quinn, Kallen, Twenge, and Fredrickson (2006) and found that body shame was not correlated with performance on the Stroop task. Thus, negative self-conscious emotions and cognitive performance seem to be two important outcomes of state self-objectification, but they do not form a direct causal chain.

SELF-OBJECTIFICATION EFFECTS WITHIN A SELF-REGULATORY FRAMEWORK

Thus far, research has shown that a state of self-objectification can interfere with women's performance, and trait self-objectification is related to fewer flow experiences. Also, both state and trait self-objectification are related to more thoughts about the body and appearance and more negative self-conscious emotions about the body. However, there is little evidence to support the contention that taking a third-person perspective, engaging in appearance monitoring, and experiencing negative emotions act as direct mediators between self-objectification and performance outcomes. We suggest that objectification research could benefit by considering these findings within a conceptual framework that could integrate previous findings and elaborate on the potential mediating processes that might explain how self-objectification interferes with performance. We believe that using the control theory model of self-regulation (Carver & Scheier, 1981, 1998) provides one such framework.

Theoretically, self-objectification occurs when a person takes an observer's view of the self, thinking about how one's own body and appearance may be judged and evaluated by others. Taking such a third-person perspective of the self is not unusual: All people can and do think about the self as an object at various times. Duval and Wicklund (1972) argued that there are two basic states of awareness: objective self-awareness, in which a person's attention is focused on the self (e.g., attitudes, values, physiological sensations); and subjective self-awareness, in which the person's attention is focused on things external to the self (e.g., tasks, other people, scenery). Thus, self-objectification can be conceptualized as a special case of objective self-awareness, in which the focus of attention is the appearance of one's own body.

Focusing attention on the self is considered both a prerequisite to and a necessary ingredient of self-regulation (Baumeister, Heatherton, & Tice, 1994; Carver & Scheier, 1981). A shift in attention from the environment to the self is theorized to automatically initiate a self-regulatory feedback loop (Carver & Scheier, 1981), in which the current self is compared with salient standards. If the self is found to be discrepant from the standards, behavioral or environmental changes are instigated to bring it closer. Once changes are made, the self is compared with the standard again. If the standard has been met, the person disengages from the self-regulatory loop. If the standard has not been met, the loop continues. Continuing to focus on the self is crucial for successful self-regulation, but it comes at the cost of depleting cognitive resources (e.g., Muraven & Baumeister, 2000; Schmeichel, Vohs, & Baumeister, 2003).

If we consider self-objectification from a self-regulatory lens (see Figure 6.1), the following process may occur. First, when people experience self-objectification, they will temporarily take a third-person view of their body, focusing their attention on their body and appearance. Thus, they have entered a state of objective self-awareness, in which attention is focused on the self. According to objectification theory, this should be a more frequent experience for women than for men but does occur for both. For example, in several objectification studies in which self-objectification is manipulated by asking participants to wear swimsuits (versus sweater), both men and women

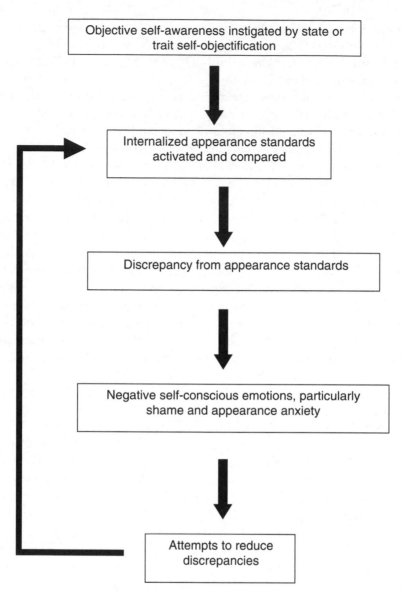

Figure 6.1. Self-objectification processes within a control theory self-regulatory framework.

in the swimsuits described themselves more in terms of their bodies than did men and women wearing sweaters (Fredrickson et al., 1998; Hebl et al., 2004). Moreover, there is quite a bit of research showing that high trait self-objectification is related to increased thoughts about appearance (Moradi & Huang, 2008).

Next, becoming objectively self-aware will automatically cue internalized appearance standards. Original work on objective self-awareness found that when people focus on the self, they automatically compare the self with the most salient self-relevant standard or goal (Scheier & Carver, 1983). Thus, for example, if one becomes self-aware while completing an intelligence test, one should automatically activate intelligence standards. In the case of self-objectification, appearance standards are the most self-relevant salient standards.

Once standards have been activated, people will compare themselves against their standards in search of any discrepancies. If no discrepancies arise, people will exit from the self-regulation loop. A large volume of research on body image (e.g., Cash & Pruzinsky, 2004) shows that women are held to much more stringent body and appearance standards than men. Thus, at this point in the self-objectification process, men who become objectively self-aware will be more likely to exit the self-regulatory loop than women because fewer men find major discrepancies between internalized standards of appearance and their own appearance (Hebl et al., 2004). Men, then, can go back to being primarily subjectively self-aware and focused on external tasks. In contrast, women, who are socialized to a practically impossible ideal image of beauty and thinness, will enter a self-regulatory loop.

However, once self-objectifying women compare the self with salient appearance standards, they are likely to experience a self-discrepancy (Breines et al., 2008). Indeed, Calogero and Watson (2009) showed that increased body monitoring is correlated with increased general self-discrepancies, especially the actual–ought self-discrepancy. In our own experimental work, we find that when a state of self-objectification is manipulated, women are not simply thinking more about their body but also thinking more *negative* thoughts about their bodies (Quinn & Chaudoir, 2009). Experiencing self-discrepancies of any kind is related to increased negative emotions (Higgins, 1987). Women experiencing self-objectification are likely to experience specific discrepancies from internalized appearance standards, which in turn should result in negative self-conscious emotions, such as shame and anxiety. As reviewed earlier, self-objectification is strongly related to experiences of body shame and appearance anxiety. Shame is thought to signify a loss of social status or social value with the person feeling inferior to others (e.g., Kemeny, Gruenewald, & Dickerson, 2004; Tangney, Miller, Flicker, & Barlow, 1996). When women feel discrepant from the very appearance standards that they have been socialized to believe are critically important to their evaluation by others, it is of no surprise that shame results.

Once a discrepancy has been noticed and negative self-conscious emotions have been experienced, the next stage in a self-regulatory feedback loop is an attempt to reduce the discrepancy to meet the salient standard (and, thereby, repair negative emotions). Although people can do little to immediately change the shape and size of their bodies, it is clear that attempts are made. For example, in the original swimsuit–sweater study, women in the swimsuit condition showed more restrained eating patterns during the study (Fredrickson et al., 1998). In our own recent work, we found that when women are wearing the swimsuit, they write about more intentions to diet and exercise than when they are wearing the sweater (Quinn & Chaudoir, 2009). Research on trait self-objectification has shown repeatedly that women chronically high in self-objectification also have elevated levels of eating disorder symptomatology. Thus, there is evidence that women are attempting to reduce the discrepancy from the standard by changing their bodies.

After an attempt at reducing the discrepancy has been made, the next step is to compare the self with the standard again. If the discrepancy has been reduced and the standard met, then a person will exit the feedback loop and return to subjective self-awareness, no longer focusing attention on the self. If the standard has not been met, the person will stay in the self-regulatory loop, continuing to attempt to reduce the discrepancy and meet the standard. Because a quick change in body is not possible (and, indeed, changing the body to meet the current female appearance standards is virtually impossible for most women), we speculate that women in a state of self-objectification remain stuck in the feedback loop, continuing to self-regulate. In terms of trait self-objectification, it may be that because the women themselves are chronically focusing on the self in relation to appearance standards, they are frequently reengaging themselves in this negative (and destructive) self-regulatory feedback loop. Being actively engaged in self-regulation, which explicitly focuses attention on the self, likely leads to the less frequent experiences of flow states. For state self-objectification, particularly when manipulated in a laboratory, there are very few ways to reduce the discrepancy, and thus women may stay in the self-regulatory loop for the duration of the experimental session. Indeed, we have shown that even at the end of a study, when women are no longer dressed in swimsuits, they are still thinking about their body and appearance (Quinn, Kallen, & Cathey, 2006). It is notable that the one published swimsuit–sweater study that did not find effects on performance may actually have given participants a way out of the self-regulatory feedback-loop. Specifically, Gapinski et al. (2003) exposed participants to a confederate complaining either about how bad they looked or about their computer. It is possible that such downward social comparison information was enough to reduce the perceived discrepancies from appearance standards and help participants exit the feedback loop (see Carver & Scheier, 1998, on the role of downward social comparisons in self-regulation).

We believe that prolonged self-regulation, in which women in a state of self-objectification remain intensely self-focused, is what ultimately interferes with performance. Carver and Scheier (1998) noted that the most disruptive effects of self-regulation occur when a person cannot mentally disengage from meeting the goal or standard, leading to repeated negative thoughts about the self. Thus, attention is continually directed back to the self and away from other tasks, ultimately leading to poorer task performance. These arguments are compatible with several different literatures, including research on test anxiety and cognitive interference (e.g., Sarason, Pierce, & Sarason, 1996; Wine, 1971). In short, when focus on the self is prolonged and evaluatively negative—as we believe occurs when women self-objectify—performance suffers.

IMPLICATIONS OF THE SELF-REGULATORY FRAMEWORK FOR SELF-OBJECTIFICATION RESEARCH

Whereas empirical interest in the consequences of self-objectification has exploded within the past decade, strikingly little attention has been paid to understanding the processes through which self-objectification can interfere with performance. As we have reviewed in this chapter, there is initial evidence that self-objectification can decrease flow states and impair cognitive and physical performance, primarily among women. Although trait and state forms of self-objectification both appear to have deleterious effects, the conditions under which chronic versus situational forms of self-objectification can most severely impair performance remain to be elucidated.

One major obstacle to the progression of this literature is its lack of a clear conceptualization of the potential mediating processes. How does self-objectification lead to these poor performance outcomes? We outlined a theoretical framework that brings together self-regulation and self-objectification. In doing so, we noted how many of the findings in the self-objectification literature can fit into this framework. We recognize, of course, that much more additional work needs to be done to test the utility of this perspective. We hope, however, that using the framework will raise a number of empirical questions that the next generation of self-objectification research can answer. For example, whereas researchers examining body image have long documented that the female beauty ideal is toned, large-chested and—most important—highly unattainable (Wolf, 1991), objectification researchers have not yet examined the types of appearance standards with which women may be comparing themselves in a state of self-objectification. What are women thinking about, either consciously or unconsciously, when they are in a state of self-objectification? If women are, in fact, comparing themselves with a highly unattainable ideal and feeling discrepant from this ideal, what are they doing to reduce it? Our data suggest that women may be generating intentions to change their physical body through either dieting or exercise behaviors. However, how might these discrepancies or negative self-conscious emotions elicit behaviors that are helpful or hurtful to women? Given the simultaneously burgeoning levels of both extreme dietary restriction (i.e., anorexia, bulimia) and obesity (Bray, 2005; Hoek, 2005), how might self-objectification processes feed into one or both of these behavioral extremes? Minimal research has addressed these issues (for an exception, see Strelan, Mehaffey, & Tiggemann, 2003).

Moreover, using the self-regulation framework gives researchers several new avenues for attempting to disrupt self-objectification's negative impact. For example, finding new ways to shift women from objective to subjective self-awareness may reduce the negative performance outcomes. Likewise, changing the content of appearance standards or finding ways to reduce perceived discrepancies may lead to more positive outcomes. In general, finding novel ways to help women become unstuck from the negative feedback loop may lead to a new understanding of how to reduce self-objectification.

Needless to say, objectification research is far from understanding the full range of effects of self-objectification processes. One important question for objectification researchers to answer concerns how pervasive and chronic forms of self-objectification can interfere with performance for a prolonged period of time and can create cumulative negative consequences for women. Researchers who have examined the effects of sexism demonstrate that sexism is quite pervasive; diary studies demonstrate that undergraduate women experience one to two sexist incidents each week (Swim et al., 2001). Further, researchers have substantiated that sexist behaviors (Dardenne, Dumont, & Bollier, 2007), exposure to gender-stereotypical content (Davies, Spencer, Quinn, & Gerhardstein, 2002), and even the mere possibility of encountering sexism (Adams, Garcia, Purdie-Vaughns, & Steele, 2006) can create deleterious performance effects. Chronic exposure to sexism can also have long-term outcomes in both personal and professional contexts, including lowered psychological well-being (Moradi & Funderburk, 2006) and career withdrawal (Chan, Lam, Chow, & Cheung, 2008; Magley, Hulin, Fitzgerald, & DeNardo, 1999).

Given that a significant proportion of all sexist events experienced come in the form of unwanted and sexually objectifying behaviors (Kozee et al., 2007; Swim et al., 2001), it is likely that self-objectification processes underlie a significant portion of the impact of sexism. That is, if subtle situational features such as the mere presence of a male gaze (Calogero, 2004) can lead women to become preoccupied with their appearance, self-objectification processes may be occurring quite frequently in their daily lives. However, to date, no research has examined the possibility of these cumulative effects of self-objectification across the life span. Understanding when self-objectification occurs and how cognitively disruptive it is remains a crucial goal in self-objectification research.

REFERENCES

Adams, G., Garcia, D. M., Purdie-Vaughns, V., & Steele, C. M. (2006). The detrimental effects of a suggestion of sexism in an instruction situation. *Journal of Experimental Social Psychology, 42*, 602–615. doi:10.1016/j.jesp.2005.10.004

Baumeister, R. F., Heatherton, T. F., & Tice, D. M. (1994). *Losing control: How and why people fail at self-regulation.* San Diego, CA: Academic Press.

Bray, G. A. (2005). A brief history of obesity. In C. G. Fairburns & K. D. Brownell (Eds.), *Eating disorders and obesity: A comprehensive handbook* (pp. 382–387). New York, NY: Guilford Press.

Breines, J. G., Crocker, J., & Garcia, J. A. (2008). Self-objectification and well-being in women's daily lives. *Personality and Social Psychology Bulletin, 34*, 583–598. doi:10.1177/0146167207313727

Calogero, R. M. (2004). A test of objectification theory: The effect of the male gaze on appearance concerns in college women. *Psychology of Women Quarterly, 28*, 16–21. doi:10.1111/j.1471-6402.2004.00118.x

Calogero, R. M., & Watson, N. (2009). Self-discrepancy and chronic social self-consciousness: Unique and interactive effects of gender and real–ought discrepancy. *Personality and Individual Differences, 46*, 642–647. doi:10.1016/j.paid.2009.01.008

Carver, C. S., & Scheier, M. F. (1981). *Attention and self-regulation: A control-theory approach to human behavior.* New York, NY: Springer-Verlag.

Carver, C. S., & Scheier, M. F. (1998). *On the self-regulation of behavior.* New York, NY: Cambridge University Press.

Cash, T. F., & Pruzinsky, T. (Eds.). (2004). *Body image: A handbook of theory, research, and clinical practice.* New York, NY: Guilford Press.

Chan, D. K.-S., Lam, C. B., Chow, S. Y., & Cheung, S. F. (2008). Examining the job-related, psychological, and physical outcomes of workplace sexual harassment: A meta-analytic review. *Psychology of Women Quarterly, 32*, 362–376. doi:10.1111/j.1471-6402.2008.00451.x

Csikszentmihalyi, M., & Csikszentmihalyi, I. S. (1988). *Optimal experience: Psychological studies of flow in consciousness.* New York, NY: Cambridge University Press.

Dardenne, B., Dumont, M., & Bollier, T. (2007). Insidious dangers of benevolent sexism: Consequences for women's performance. *Journal of Personality and Social Psychology, 93*, 764–779. doi:10.1037/0022-3514.93.5.764

Daubenmier, J. J. (2005). The relationship of yoga, body awareness, and body responsiveness to self-objectification and disordered eating. *Psychology of Women Quarterly, 29,* 207–219. doi:10.1111/j.1471-6402.2005.00183.x

Davies, P. G., Spencer, S. J., Quinn, D. M., & Gerhardstein, R. (2002). Consuming images: How television commercials that elicit stereotype threat can restrain women academically and professionally. *Personality and Social Psychology Bulletin, 28,* 1615–1628. doi:10.1177/014616702237644

de Beauvoir, S. (1952). *The second sex* (H. M. Parshley, Trans.). New York, NY: Vintage Books.

Duval, S., & Wicklund, R. A. (1972). *A theory of objective self awareness.* Oxford, England: Academic Press.

Earnshaw, V., Quinn, D. M., & Kenny, D. A. (2009). *Meta-accuracy of body-related judgments: Are self-objectifying women inaccurate?* Manuscript submitted for publication.

Engle, R. W. (2002). Working memory capacity as executive attention. *Current Directions in Psychological Science, 11,* 19–23. doi:10.1111/1467-8721.00160

Fredrickson, B. L., & Harrison, K. (2005). Throwing like a girl: Self-objectification predicts adolescent girls' motor performance. *Journal of Sport and Social Issues, 29,* 79–101. doi:10.1177/0193723504269878

Fredrickson, B. L., & Roberts, T.-A. (1997). Objectification theory: Toward understanding women's lived experiences and mental health risks. *Psychology of Women Quarterly, 21,* 173–206. doi:10.1111/j.1471-6402.1997.tb00108.x

Fredrickson, B. L., Roberts, T.-A., Noll, S. M., Quinn, D. M., & Twenge, J. M. (1998). That swimsuit becomes you: Sex differences in self-objectification, restrained eating, and math performance. *Journal of Personality and Social Psychology, 75,* 269–284. doi:10.1037/0022-3514.75.1.269

Galinsky, A. D., Magee, J. C., Inesi, M. E., & Gruenfeld, D. H. (2006). Power and perspectives not taken. *Psychological Science, 17,* 1068–1074. doi:10.1111/j.1467-9280.2006.01824.x

Gapinski, K. D., Brownell, K. D., & LaFrance, M. (2003). Body objectification and "fat talk": Effects on emotion, motivation, and cognitive performance. *Sex Roles, 48,* 377–388. doi:10.1023/A:1023516209973

Greenleaf, C. (2005). Self-objectification among physically active women. *Sex Roles, 52,* 51–62. doi:10.1007/s11199-005-1193-8

Greenleaf, C., & McGreer, R. (2006). Disordered eating attitudes and self-objectification among physically active and sedentary female college students. *Journal of Psychology, 140,* 187–198. doi:10.3200/JRLP.140.3.187-198

Hass, R. G. (1984). Perspective taking and self-awareness: Drawing an E on your forehead. *Journal of Personality and Social Psychology, 46,* 788–798. doi:10.1037/0022-3514.46.4.788

Hebl, M. R., King, E. B., & Lin, J. (2004). The swimsuit becomes us all: Ethnicity, gender, and vulnerability to self-objectification. *Personality and Social Psychology Bulletin, 30,* 1322–1331. doi:10.1177/0146167204264052

Higgins, E. T. (1987). Self-discrepancy: A theory relating self and affect. *Psychological Review, 94,* 319–340. doi:10.1037/0033-295X.94.3.319

Hoek, H. W. (2005). Distribution of eating disorders. In C. G. Fairburns & K. D. Brownell (Eds.), *Eating disorders and obesity: A comprehensive handbook* (pp. 233–237). New York, NY: Guilford Press.

Huebner, D. M., & Fredrickson, B. L. (1999). Gender differences in memory perspectives: Evidence for self-objectification in women. *Sex Roles, 41,* 459–467. doi:10.1023/A:1018831001880

Kane, M. J., & Engle, R. W. (2003). Working-memory capacity and the control of attention: The contributions of goal neglect, response competition, and task set to Stroop interference. *Journal of Experimental Psychology: General, 132,* 47–70. doi:10.1037/0096-3445.132.1.47

Kemeny, M. E., Gruenewald, T. L., & Dickerson, S. S. (2004). Shame as the emotional response to threat to the social self: Implications for behavior, physiology, and health. *Psychological Inquiry, 15,* 153–160.

Kozee, H. B., Tylka, T. L., Augustus-Horvath, C. L., & Denchik, A. (2007). Development and psychometric evaluation of the Interpersonal Sexual Objectification Scale. *Psychology of Women Quarterly, 31,* 176–189. doi:10.1111/j.1471-6402.2007.00351.x

Magley, V. J., Hulin, C. L., Fitzgerald, L. F., & DeNardo, M. (1999). Outcomes of self-labeling sexual harassment. *Journal of Applied Psychology, 84,* 390–402. doi:10.1037/0021-9010.84.3.390

MacLeod, C. (1991). Half a century of research on the Stroop effect: An integrative review. *Psychological Bulletin, 109,* 163–203. doi:10.1037/0033-2909.109.2.163

Moradi, B., & Funderburk, J. R. (2006). Roles of perceived sexist events and perceived social support in the mental health of women seeking counseling. *Journal of Counseling Psychology, 53,* 464–473. doi:10.1037/0022-0167.53.4.464

Moradi, B., & Huang, Y.-P. (2008). Objectification theory and psychology of women: A decade of advances and future directions. *Psychology of Women Quarterly, 32,* 377–398. doi:10.1111/j.1471-6402.2008.00452.x

Muraven, M., & Baumeister, R. F. (2000). Self-regulation and depletion of limited resources: Does self-control resemble a muscle? *Psychological Bulletin, 126,* 247–259. doi:10.1037/0033-2909.126.2.247

Quinn, D. M., & Chaudoir, S. R. (2009). *Self-objectification as self-regulation.* Unpublished manuscript, University of Connecticut.

Quinn, D. M., Kallen, R. W., & Cathey, C. (2006). Body on my mind: The lingering effect of state self-objectification. *Sex Roles, 55,* 869–874.

Quinn, D. M., Kallen, R. W., & Spencer, S. J. (in press). Stereotype threat. In J. F. Dovidio, M. Hewstone, P. Glick, & V. M. Esses (Eds.), *Handbook of prejudice, stereotyping, and discrimination.* London, England: Sage.

Quinn, D. M., Kallen, R. W., Twenge, J. M., & Fredrickson, B. L. (2006). The disruptive effect of self-objectification on performance. *Psychology of Women Quarterly, 30,* 59–64.

Rathunde, K. R., & Csikszentmihalyi, M. (1993). Undivided interest and the growth of talent: A longitudinal study of adolescents. *Journal of Youth and Adolescence*, *22*, 385–405.

Sarason, I. G., Pierce, G. R., & Sarason, B. R. (1996). *Cognitive interference: Theories, methods, and findings*. Hillsdale, NJ: Erlbaum.

Scheier, M. F., & Carver, C. S. (1983). Self-directed attention and the comparison of self with standards. *Journal of Experimental Social Psychology*, *19*, 205–222.

Schmeichel, B. J., Vohs, K. D., & Baumeister, R. F. (2003). Intellectual performance and ego depletion: Role of the self in logical reasoning and other information processing. *Journal of Personality and Social Psychology*, *85*, 33–46.

Strelan, P., Mehaffey, S. J., & Tiggemann, M. (2003). Self-objectification and esteem in young women: The mediating role of reasons for exercise. *Sex Roles*, *48*, 89–95.

Swim, J. K., Hyers, L. L., Cohen, L. L., & Ferguson, M. J. (2001). Everyday sexism: Evidence for its incidence, nature, and psychological impact from three daily diary studies. *Journal of Social Issues*, *57*, 31–53.

Szymanski, D. M., & Henning, S. L. (2007). The role of self-objectification in women's depression: A test of objectification theory. *Sex Roles*, *56*, 45–53.

Tangney, J. P., Miller, R. S., Flicker, L., & Barlow, D. H. (1996). Are shame, guilt, and embarrassment distinct emotions? *Journal of Personality and Social Psychology*, *70*, 1256–1269.

Tiggemann, M., & Boundy, M. (2008). Effect of environment and appearance compliment on college women's self-objectification, mood, body shame, and cognitive performance. *Psychology of Women Quarterly*, *32*, 399–405

Tiggemann, M., & Kuring, J. K. (2004). The role of body objectification in disordered eating and depressed mood. *British Journal of Clinical Psychology*, *43*, 299–311.

Tiggemann, M., & Slater, A. (2001). A test of objectification theory in former dancers and non-dancers. *Psychology of Women Quarterly*, *25*, 57–64.

Wine, J. (1971). Test anxiety and direction of attention. *Psychological Bulletin*, *76*, 92–104.

Wolf, N. (1991). *The beauty myth: How images of beauty are used against women*. New York, NY: William Morrow.

7

MENTAL HEALTH RISKS OF SELF-OBJECTIFICATION: A REVIEW OF THE EMPIRICAL EVIDENCE FOR DISORDERED EATING, DEPRESSED MOOD, AND SEXUAL DYSFUNCTION

MARIKA TIGGEMANN

This chapter sets out to review the existing empirical evidence demonstrating the mental health risks associated with self-objectification in women. In particular, it evaluates the research evidence for objectification theory's (Fredrickson & Roberts, 1997) contention that self-objectification leads to a number of negative behavioral and experiential consequences (increase in both shame and anxiety about the body and appearance, decrease in awareness of internal bodily states, and decrease in the experience of peak motivational states or flow), which in turn accumulate to put women at increased risk of three particular mental health disorders: eating disorders, depression, and sexual dysfunction. These serious clinical conditions are experienced disproportionately by women. It should be noted, however, that many women suffer milder forms of these conditions in negative body image, disordered eating, depressed mood, and low sexual satisfaction on a daily basis.

Most of the studies presented in this chapter take as their starting point the position that although all Western women exist in a society that sexually objectifies the female body, there will be differences among women in the degree to which they internalize an observer's perspective on their bodies. Hence, self-objectification is conceptualized as an individual difference or trait variable that is relatively stable over time (see Chapter 2, this volume).

In this chapter, I consider the role of self-objectification in disordered eating, depression, and sexual dysfunction. Then I present an overview of the smaller amount of research conducted using experimental and longitudinal methodologies, before concluding with some final remarks. In so doing, I attempt both to summarize what is known and to identify gaps in the literature for future research.

EVIDENCE CONCERNING DISORDERED EATING

To date, the majority of empirical research testing the predictions of objectification theory has focused on the outcome of disordered eating. This is perhaps the most obvious potential outcome in a society in which weight and shape are major concerns for many women. Disordered eating encompasses not only the clinical eating disorders of anorexia and bulimia nervosa but also more normative behaviors like skipping meals and trying faddish diets. Indeed, these studies have necessarily used continuous measures of disordered eating symptoms as is appropriate for nonclinical samples, and so do not speak directly to clinical eating disorders.

Evidence From Samples of Undergraduate Women

There is now a considerable body of correlational support for certain aspects of objectification theory as it relates to disordered eating. In particular, in samples of female undergraduate students, links have been demonstrated between self-objectification or self-surveillance and body shame (Calogero, 2009; McKinley, 1998; McKinley & Hyde, 1996; Moradi, Dirks, & Matteson, 2005; Muehlenkamp & Saris-Baglama, 2002; Muehlenkamp, Swanson, & Brausch, 2005; Noll & Fredrickson, 1998; Steer & Tiggemann, 2008; Tiggemann & Kuring, 2004; Tiggemann & Slater, 2001; Tylka & Hill, 2004), between self-objectification or self-surveillance and body dissatisfaction or body esteem (Daubenmier, 2005; McKinley, 1998; McKinley & Hyde, 1996; Strelan & Hargreaves, 2005), and between self-objectification or self-surveillance and measures of disordered eating (Calogero, 2009; Daubenmier, 2005; Moradi et al., 2005; Muehlenkamp & Saris-Baglama, 2002; Myers & Crowther, 2008; Noll & Fredrickson, 1998; Tiggemann & Slater, 2001; Tylka & Hill, 2004).

A few studies have attempted to more formally test the specific mediational pathway proposed by objectification theory, whereby body shame mediates the relationship between self-objectification and disordered eating. In the first such study, Noll and Fredrickson (1998) confirmed that self-objectification was related to greater body shame, which was in turn related to greater eating disorder symptomatology. Beyond this indirect relationship, there was also a direct positive relationship between self-objectification and disordered eating. This finding of either partial mediation (Moradi et al., 2005) or full mediation of the link between self-objectification or self-surveillance and disordered eating by body shame has since been replicated (Calogero, 2009; Hurt et al., 2007; Tiggemann & Slater, 2001).

Whereas the mediating role of body shame appears well supported, the role of the other postulated mediators of the relationship between self-objectification and disordered eating (appearance anxiety, decreased flow, lack of awareness of internal states) has been less investigated. In the first attempt to test the entire model of objectification theory as it applies to disordered eating, Tiggemann and Slater (2001) confirmed links between self-objectification and appearance anxiety, in addition to the previously established links between self-objectification and body shame and disordered eating. In their sample of undergraduate students, self-objectification was not related to either flow or awareness of internal states. Further, their data confirmed that specifically body shame (but not appearance anxiety, flow, or awareness of internal states) partially mediated the pathway between self-objectification and disordered eating. However, a larger later study by Tiggemann and Kuring (2004) supported a mediating role for appearance anxiety. In particular, they found that the relationship between self-objectification and disordered eating was fully mediated by body shame and appearance anxiety. They also found a relationship between self-objectification and decreased flow (but not awareness of internal states).

Some research has focused particularly on the role of internal awareness as a mediator. The findings to date are mixed and ambiguous. On the one hand, as indicated earlier, a number of studies have found no relationship between self-objectification and awareness of internal states (Daubenmier, 2005; Tiggemann & Kuring, 2004; Tiggemann & Slater, 2001). On the other hand, Muehlenkamp and Saris-Baglama (2002) did find a relationship between self-surveillance and internal awareness, although this construct did not mediate the relationship between self-surveillance and disordered eating. Similarly, Tylka and Hill (2004) showed that self-surveillance was related to interoceptive awareness, which refers to the awareness of stimuli originating from within the body. Finally, Myers and Crowther (2008) showed not only that self-objectification was related to interoceptive awareness but also that this construct partially mediated the relationship between self-objectification and eating disorder attitudes. The difference in results most likely lies in the particular measure of internal awareness. Myers and Crowther argued that it is the lack of awareness of internal states specific to hunger, satiety, and associated emotions (as measured by the interoceptive awareness subscale of the Eating Disorder Inventory; Garner, Olmsted & Polivy, 1983) that is pertinent, rather than awareness of general internal states.

Evidence From Other Samples of Women

Nearly all the early work investigating the predictions of objectification theory was conducted with college or university women. Consequently, the research has been confined to a very restricted sample in terms of age, education, socioeconomic status, and other demographic variables. However, there is now increasing evidence coming from a more varied set of samples of women.

Fredrickson and Roberts (1997) postulated that women will be most targeted for sexual objectification during their years of reproductive potential. Accordingly, as women age, they are less so targeted and start to become relatively less visible. One possible positive consequence is that older women might be able to gradually relinquish the observer's perspective on themselves and in that way experience improved well-being. This logically leads to the prediction that both self-objectification and its proposed negative consequences will decrease with age (see Chapter 5, this volume). In support, the middle-aged mothers of undergraduate students have been shown to have lower levels of self-surveillance and body shame than their daughters (McKinley, 1999; McKinley & Hyde, 1996). It is interesting that the relationship between self-surveillance and body shame was stronger for the young women than for the middle-aged women (McKinley, 2006a). More generally, increasing age is associated with lower self-objectification among women (Greenleaf, 2005; Roberts, 2004; Tiggemann & Lynch, 2001).

In a large community sample of women ranging in age from 20 to 84 years, Tiggemann and Lynch (2001) found that self-objectification, self-surveillance, appearance anxiety, and disordered eating all significantly reduced with age. Self-objectification and self-surveillance were related to body shame, appearance anxiety, and disordered eating across the entire age range, and body shame and appearance anxiety partially mediated the relationship between self-objectification and disordered eating, in accord with the proposed mediational steps. Thus, objectification theory seems applicable to women across a broad range of ages.

Even fewer studies have examined the components of objectification theory in samples younger than undergraduate students. Given that adolescence is a time of great physical maturation, as well as of increased self-awareness, self-consciousness, preoccupation with image, and concern with social acceptance (Harter, 1999), adolescence might present a critical period for the development of self-objectification. Thus, the self-monitoring and concern with external appearance intrinsic to self-objectification may be particularly salient for adolescent girls. Certainly, a number of studies have shown that the majority of adolescent girls suffer dissatisfaction with their bodies and wish to be thinner (e.g., Attie & Brooks-Gunn, 1989), with many engaging in dieting or other unhealthy weight loss behaviors (e.g., Stice, Killen, Hayward, & Taylor, 1998). The eating disorders of anorexia and bulimia nervosa also typically have their onset during late adolescence (Beumont & Touyz, 1985).

In the first study with adolescent girls (age range 12 to 16 years, mean age = 14.5 years), Slater and Tiggemann (2002) observed levels of self-objectification comparable with adult women. They found that just as is the case in undergraduate women, self-objectification was correlated with body shame, appearance anxiety, and disordered eating, and that the relationship between self-objectification and disordered eating was partially mediated by body shame. More recently, self-surveillance has been correlated with body shame in younger girls ages 10 to 12 years (mean age = 11.2; Grabe, Hyde, & Lindberg, 2007; Lindberg, Grabe, & Hyde, 2007). Among 6th to 12th graders (ages 10 to 19 years, mean age = 13.4), Harrison and Fredrickson (2003) found that self-objectification increased with grade. However, self-objectification was correlated with body shame and disordered eating across all grades. Thus, it appears that self-objectification and its consequences are already pertinent to girls as young as 11 years old.

The study by Harrison and Fredrickson (2003) is one of the few to explicitly test for ethnic or cultural differences. It is interesting to note that there were no significant differences found in levels of self-objectification, body shame, or disordered eating between White girls and girls of color (mostly African American). Nor was there any difference in the strength of observed relationships, indicating that objectification theory seems equally applicable to both groups. In contrast, the study by Frederick, Forbes, Grigorian, and Jarcho (2007) with a large sample of undergraduate women found that the relationship between self-surveillance and body dissatisfaction was stronger in minority (Asian and Hispanic) women than in White women. As yet, the steps of objectification theory have not been fully tested among different ethnic and cultural groups. More generally, the present research is restricted almost exclusively to samples of North American and Australian women.

A number of studies have investigated self-objectification among physically active and fit samples. For aerobic participants at fitness centers, self-objectification has been related to body dissatisfaction and disordered eating (Prichard & Tiggemann, 2005; Strelan, Mehaffey, & Tiggemann, 2003). Yoga participants have been shown to score lower on all these measures than aerobic participants (Daubenmier, 2005). In contrast, former dancers (having previously studied classical ballet) scored higher on self-objectification and disordered eating than nondancers (Tiggemann & Slater, 2001). Among physically active women, self-objectification was correlated with body shame, appearance anxiety, flow (negatively), and disordered eating (Greenleaf, 2005; Greenleaf & McGreer, 2006). Further, body shame and appearance anxiety (but not flow) mediated the relationship between self-objectification and disordered eating for these physically active women (Greenleaf & McGreer, 2006).

All the studies noted thus far carry the implicit assumption that participants are heterosexual women. Indeed, the very conceptualization of sexual objectification and accompanying self-objectification is based on a view of women as objects primarily for male pleasure. Hence, it is difficult to make predictions about women who do not aim to attract men. Kozee and Tylka (2006) investigated self-objectification in lesbian women as well as in a comparison group of heterosexual women. They found that the lesbians scored lower on disordered eating but paradoxically higher on self-surveillance. The authors concluded that the model provided a good fit for their heterosexual sample but not for the lesbian sample. In contrast, Haines et al. (2008) found self-surveillance to be related to body shame and disordered eating attitudes in their sample of lesbians. Further, body shame partially mediated the relationship between self-surveillance and disordered eating, and thus the authors concluded strong support for the model as applicable to lesbians.

In comparison with the many demonstrations of relationships between self-objectification, body shame, and disordered eating in samples of university students and other groups of women, only one study has examined these relationships in an actual clinical sample. In a sample of young women diagnosed with eating disorders who were receiving residential treatment at an eating disorders facility, Calogero, Davis, and Thompson (2005) found that self-objectification predicted disordered eating (drive for thinness) directly, as well as indirectly, through the effect of body shame. Thus, the partial mediation of the relationship between self-objectification and eating disorders by body shame replicated that generally shown in nonclinical samples.

In summary, there is now considerable support for the validity of objectification theory as it applies to disordered eating. A number of studies have now clearly established the link between trait self-objectification and disordered eating itself, as well as between self-objectification and the postulated mediator of body shame. These links have been demonstrated repeatedly in female undergraduate samples, as well as more sporadically in samples of older and younger women, physically active women, and women with clinical eating disorders. On balance, there is sufficient evidence to conclude that the relationship between self-objectification and disordered eating is at least partially mediated by body shame and appearance anxiety, as proposed in the theory. The other proposed mediators (flow and awareness of internal states) have yet to receive such confirmation. One conspicuous and important lack is the dearth of research investigating ethnic or cultural differences.

EVIDENCE CONCERNING DEPRESSED MOOD

In contrast to disordered eating, there has been relatively little research on the effect of self-objectification on depression or depressed mood. However, this smaller body of research has supported objectification theory as it applies to depression. Miner-Rubino, Twenge, and Fredrickson (2002) found self-objectification to be associated with body shame, neuroticism, negative affectivity, and depressive symptoms in female undergraduate students. The link between self-objectification and depressive symptoms has been replicated in other samples of undergraduate women (Grabe & Jackson, 2009; Muehlenkamp & Saris-Baglama, 2002; Muehlenkamp et al., 2005; Tiggemann & Kuring, 2004). Muehlenkamp and Saris-Baglama (2002) found both a direct relationship between self-surveillance and depressive symptoms and an indirect relationship mediated by lack of internal awareness.

Tiggemann and Kuring (2004) aimed to test the complete model of objectification theory as it applies to depression, in a way parallel to eating disorders. As reported earlier, self-objectification was positively correlated with body shame and appearance anxiety and negatively correlated with flow but not awareness of internal states. It was also correlated with depressed mood. The relationship between self-objectification and depressed mood was fully mediated by body shame and appearance anxiety (but not flow). Szymanski and Henning (2007) replicated this pattern of relationships with different measures of flow and depressed mood. In their study, the relationship between self-objectification and depressed mood was completely mediated by body shame, appearance anxiety, and flow. Similarly, Hurt et al. (2007) found self-surveillance to be related to body shame, depressive symptoms, and self-esteem (negatively). The relationships between self-surveillance and depressive symptoms and self-esteem were fully mediated by body shame. In their lesbian sample, Haines et al. (2008) likewise found the relationship between self-surveillance and depressive symptomatology to be fully mediated by body shame.

All of the studies mentioned here were conducted with young adult or undergraduate student samples. However, in their sample of young adolescent girls (10 to 12 years old), Grabe et al. (2007) also found self-surveillance to be related to depressive symptoms, both at the time of initial testing and 2 years later.

In summary, there is a small body of evidence demonstrating that self-objectification is related to depressive symptomatology and that this relationship is mediated by body shame. However, nearly all the research has been conducted with female undergraduate samples. In addition to the restriction in range of demographic variables this imposes, this represents a nonclinical sample for whom levels of depression may be relatively low. As a consequence, all studies investigate depressive symptoms or depressed mood rather than clinically diagnosable depression.

EVIDENCE CONCERNING SEXUAL FUNCTIONING

The third mental health risk that self-objectification is postulated to contribute to is sexual dysfunction. Here objectification theory focuses on self-conscious body monitoring, body shame and anxiety, and inattention to internal bodily states as factors that may inhibit sexual experiences for women. Indeed, it might be argued that objectification theory should be particularly relevant to the sexual domain. In contrast to eating disorders and depression, sexual activity by definition involves another person focusing attention on one's body. Therefore, self-objectification and its negative consequences are likely to be exacerbated in the particular context of sexual activity. However, to date, there has been surprisingly little research on the predictions of objectification theory in the domain of women's sexual functioning.

Although not using either of the measures of self-objectification, Wiederman (2000) observed that approximately one third of college women in his sample reported experiencing body image self-consciousness during physical intimacy. Such self-consciousness and negative thoughts about the appearance of one's body during sexual activity have in turn been shown to decrease women's sexual functioning (Cash, Maikkula, & Yamamiya, 2004; Dove & Wiederman, 2000). If a woman is distracted by thoughts about her body, she is less likely to be able to concentrate enough on her own sexual pleasure to gain maximum sexual satisfaction. Relatedly, Sanchez and Kiefer (2007) found that body shame was related to sexual self-consciousness, which was in turn related to decreased sexual arousability, difficulty in reaching orgasm, and less sexual pleasure.

Steer and Tiggemann (2008) attempted to specifically test the predictions of objectification theory as it applies to women's sexual functioning. They showed that both self-objectification and self-surveillance were related to body shame, appearance anxiety, and body image self-consciousness during sex, with these three variables in turn related to poorer general sexual functioning. In their final path analysis, the relationship between self-surveillance and body image self-consciousness during sex was partially mediated by body shame and appearance anxiety, and the relationship between these latter two and sexual functioning was fully mediated by body image self-consciousness during sex. Body image self-consciousness during sexual activity itself was lower among participants who were in an exclusive relationship than participants not currently in a relationship. These findings support Fredrickson and Roberts's (1997) suggestion that the shame and anxieties that a woman holds about her body do indeed carry over into the sexual context. Further, the study identifies the self-consciousness related to body image experienced by women during sexual activity as the mechanism by which their body shame and appearance anxiety affect their overall sexual functioning. Similarly, Calogero and Thompson (2009a) found that self-surveillance was related to body shame, lower sexual self-esteem, and lower sexual satisfaction. In their final path model, the influence of self-surveillance on sexual satisfaction was both direct and indirect, partially mediated by body shame. In summary, it appears that objectification theory provides a potentially very useful framework for examining women's sexual functioning and experience, one which at present remains surprisingly unexplored.

CONCLUSIONS FROM AND LIMITATIONS OF CORRELATIONAL STUDIES

The correlational studies in the preceding section show links between self-objectification and all of disordered eating, depressive symptoms, and sexual dysfunction at subclinical levels. In the main, the studies also show mediation by body shame and sometimes others of the postulated mediators. Future research should investigate these pathways more fully.

Almost always, however, the three outcome variables have been treated in isolation, separately from one another. This seems wasteful, both theoretically and in practice. Although objectification theory clearly makes no claim to explain all depression or all eating disorders or all sexual dysfunction (and should not be evaluated as such), it does offer a set of contributing factors for each. Eating disorders, depression, and sexual dysfunction are conceptualized as potential outcomes of the same underlying states arising from the experience of self-objectification, and thus the theory would predict some overlap. In fact, the *Diagnostic and Statistical Manual of Mental Disorders* (4th edition, Text Revision; American Psychiatric Association, 2000) explicitly states that eating disorders are often comorbid with depression. And poor sexual functioning is a typical characteristic of eating disorders and depression. To the extent that self-objectification is an underlying causal component of eating disorders, depression, and sexual dysfunction, a stronger test of the model would be provided if self-objectification (and its consequences) could account for the interrelationships between these conditions.

A few studies have simultaneously investigated disordered eating and depressive symptoms within the same sample (Haines et al., 2008; Hurt et al., 2007; Muehlenkamp & Saris-Baglama, 2002; Tiggemann & Kuring, 2004). These have generally found parallel relationships for disordered eating and depressed mood. Tiggemann and Kuring (2004) explicitly tested the overlap.

They found that the positive relationship between disordered eating and depressed mood was reduced to close to zero when self-objectification and its consequences (body shame, appearance anxiety, flow, and awareness of internal states) were partialed out. This indicates that self-objectification and its proposed consequences do indeed account for the bulk of the common variance between disordered eating and depressed mood. Future research might usefully explicitly examine the overlap with sexual functioning in the same way.

Relatedly, Calogero and Thompson (2009b) investigated sexual self-esteem and disordered eating in one sample. Specifically, self-surveillance was positively correlated with disordered eating and negatively correlated with sexual self-esteem and sexual self-competence. The relationship between self-surveillance and disordered eating was partially mediated by sexual self-esteem.

Objectification theory clearly puts forward a causal model in which self-objectification actually leads to mental health consequences. However, an important limitation in the correlational support described above is that all studies are cross-sectional in design and hence cannot unambiguously determine causality. Even path analysis and other structural modeling techniques that estimate the strength of connections assumed on the basis of a causal model are still in the end correlational techniques. So, although the evidence is consistent with the proposal that self-objectification leads to mental health consequences, the reverse causal sequence is equally plausible. For example, it is quite possible that women who experience disordered eating or depressed mood or poor sexual functioning might feel ashamed of their bodies and thereby come to be more aware of and self-conscious about them, resulting in increased self-objectification. More definitive causal conclusions require the use of more sophisticated and powerful designs. The following sections review the existing evidence based on experimental and longitudinal designs.

EXPERIMENTAL EVIDENCE ON THE ROLE OF SELF-OBJECTIFICATION IN MENTAL HEALTH

In addition to being a relatively stable individual difference or trait variable, objectification theory (Fredrickson & Roberts, 1997) proposes that self-objectification can also be triggered and magnified by certain situations, in particular those that accentuate an awareness of an observer's perspective of the body. Thus, self-objectification is conceptualized as both a property of the individual (trait self-objectification) and as a potential response to environmental contingencies that will fluctuate over time (state self-objectification; see Chapter 2, this volume). A number of studies have now used experimental methods to investigate the (causal) effects of state self-objectification.

These experimental designs are quite different from the correlational studies described earlier in two important ways. First, the correlational studies are designed to elucidate the relationships with naturally occurring self-objectification (i.e., trait self-objectification). In contrast, experimental manipulations are designed to actually evoke self-objectification across participants; that is, they are concerned with state self-objectification. Second, because clinical or even subclinical disordered eating and depression cannot be manipulated (ethically or in practice), experimental studies have relied on more normative measures of body dissatisfaction or restrained eating (both empirically demonstrated risk factors for eating disorders; Stice, 2002) or negative mood as a substitute for depression. In other words, outcomes represent much milder forms of disordered eating and depression.

A number of studies have now attempted to experimentally manipulate state self-objectification. In their seminal study, Fredrickson, Roberts, Noll, Quinn, and Twenge (1998) had participants try on and evaluate either a swimsuit or a sweater. The swimsuit condition produced greater body shame than the sweater condition (especially for women high on trait self-objectification), which in turn predicted symbolic restrained eating (eating most but not all of a chocolate chip cookie). Their second experiment confirmed that wearing the swimsuit produced self-objectification, greater body shame, and higher levels of negative emotions in general among women. Body shame (and trait self-objectification) also predicted the restrained eating of chocolate bars.

A number of other studies have now replicated the general findings using the swimsuit–sweater methodology. Specifically, Hebl, King, and Lin (2004) found that wearing the swimsuit produced increased body shame and poorer state self-esteem but no effect on eating behavior (candy). They also explicitly tested mediation and confirmed that the effect of condition on body shame and self-esteem was mediated by state self-objectification. Further, although there were mean differences in different ethnic groups, results held across ethnicity. That is, the same effects were observed in Caucasian, African American, Hispanic, and Asian American participants. Similarly, Gapinski, Brownell, and LaFrance (2003) showed that women in the swimsuit condition had higher state self-objectification and also were more anxious, more self-conscious, fearful, and humiliated than women in the sweater condition; in other words, they experienced more unpleasant emotional states. Quinn, Kallen, and Cathey (2006) replicated the finding of greater state self-objectification and shame for women in the swimsuit condition, as well as the mediation of the effect of condition on body-related thoughts by shame. They also showed that these body-related thoughts persisted at least for a short time, even when the women had redressed in their normal clothes. Collectively, these studies convincingly demonstrate that women's state self-objectification can be increased in situations in which attention is explicitly focused on the body by trying on a swimsuit and that this has negative consequences for their general mood and for their feelings about their bodies and themselves.

Clearly, trying on a swimsuit in front of a mirror is a reasonably intrusive method that forces attention quite directly on one's physical appearance. However, other studies have induced state self-objectification and demonstrated negative affective consequences by more subtle manipulations. For example, Calogero (2004) showed that the mere anticipation of male gaze increased state self-objectification in young women and led to greater body shame and social physique anxiety (but not intention to diet) when compared with participants who anticipated female gaze. Similarly, Roberts and Gettman (2004) demonstrated that state self-objectification could be elicited by subtle exposure to sexually objectifying words in a scrambled sentences task. This led to higher levels of shame, disgust, and appearance anxiety, and it lowered the appeal of physical sex for women, thereby illustrating the pervasiveness of the experience of self-objectification. More recently, Harper and Tiggemann (2008) showed that viewing thin idealized female magazine images in advertisements from women's magazines produced state self-objectification, weight-related appearance anxiety, body dissatisfaction, and negative mood.

To better understand the scope and reach of self-objectification and its consequences, research needs to continue to identify situational factors that can trigger state self-objectification. There may be many such potential triggers. In fact, Fredrickson and Roberts (1997) argued that every day women experience multiple contexts, and some of these protect them from objectification and others that do not. Tiggemann and Boundy (2008) aimed to experimentally examine the impact of an environment containing a number of incidental but potentially objectifying features, as well as the impact of an offhand appearance compliment on state self-objectification. These experimental manipulations address relatively subtle aspects of the physical and social environment and constitute ordinary situations that might readily be encountered in everyday life. Hence they involve minimal demand characteristics and enhance the external validity of the experiment. The results indicated that the incidental manipulation of the physical environment (via the presence of mirrors, scales, and magazine covers) did elicit state self-objectification (in women high on trait self-objectification). And perhaps unsurprisingly, the appearance compliment resulted in improved mood for everybody, as common sense would dictate. More interesting, however, for those women high on trait self-objectification, the improved mood was accompanied by an increase in state body shame. In some ways, this latter finding provides a very strong endorsement of objectification theory. A positive compliment about one's appearance, which made participants feel good in general, paradoxically led to increased body shame. This counterintuitive finding supports objectification theory's contention that anything that focuses on external appearance (even a compliment, as in the present case) can produce negative consequences.

In summary, a number of experimental studies have demonstrated that self-objectification can be triggered by certain situations. These include more obvious situations that draw awareness to the body (such as trying on a swimsuit), as well as more subtle, seemingly innocuous situations such as anticipating male gaze, reading objectifying words, or receiving an appearance compliment. The variety across these situations suggests that there may be many more.

Collectively, the studies suggest that aspects of the environment may pose more significant risks for women high on trait self-objectification. Given the ever-presence of media images and other appearance-focused messages in both the physical and social environment, contemporary women are likely to encounter such situations that have the potential to trigger self-objectification on a daily basis. If, as seems likely, women high on trait self-objectification respond to these situations with greater state self-objectification and body shame, then they may also be at greater risk for developing eating disorders, depression, and sexual dysfunction. Thus, the transient changes in state self-objectification and body shame experienced by women high on trait self-objectification provide a plausible mechanism for the link between trait self-objectification and the more serious mental health consequences outlined by Fredrickson and Roberts (1997).

This reasoning ties in with the findings of the one study with a very different methodology. Using experience sampling methodology to monitor self-objectification in the daily lives of college women (see Chapter 2, this volume), Breines, Crocker, and Garcia (2008) found that between-persons variance accounted for 38% of the total variance in state self-objectification, with the remaining 62% of variance occurring within persons. This large proportion of within-person variance suggests that self-objectification may explain variation in other aspects of women's experiences. Indeed, within-person increases in state self-objectification were associated with decreased vitality, poorer self-esteem, less positive affect, and less engagement in the present moment. Therefore, when participants self-objectified, they also experienced low levels of well-being (relative to their own average level of well-being across all of the reports). In other words, when participants were more aware of their appearance than usual, they were also likely to be feeling worse than usual.

Thus, there is a small but growing body of experimental evidence that state self-objectification can be evoked by certain situations and actually leads to body shame or negative affect. The causal direction in these experiments is clear: *from* the manipulation of state self-objectification *to* the outcomes of body shame or negative affect. However, this does not really speak to causality in naturalistic settings. In particular, it does not directly address the causal direction of the observed relationship between trait self-objectification and its postulated consequences. The latter necessarily develop over some time. For this, we need longitudinal studies that trace both self-objectification and its consequences over time.

LONGITUDINAL EVIDENCE FOR THE ROLE OF SELF-OBJECTIFICATION IN MENTAL HEALTH

In correlational studies, data are collected at one point in time. As a result, no claims can be made about the temporal sequencing of variables (even within path analyses or other structural models). Yet temporal precedence is a necessary, albeit not sufficient, condition for causality. That is, for one variable to be deemed a cause of another, changes in the first variable must minimally precede changes in the second variable in time. This can only be examined using longitudinal designs that measure variables over time.

A couple of longitudinal studies have presented evidence on changes in self-objectification over time (see Chapter 5, this volume). In particular, McKinley (2006a, 2006b) presented longitudinal analyses of 10-year follow-up data. She reported that over the 10 years, for young women (initially undergraduate students), self-surveillance and body shame scores had decreased, and body esteem scores had significantly increased, with less dieting and restricted eating. Corresponding rates were stable in the middle-aged group (mothers of the students) over the 10 years (McKinley, 2006a). Although McKinley reported that the within-time relationship between self-surveillance and body shame remained relatively consistent at both time points, she did not explicitly examine temporal aspects across time. Thus, the results as they stand do not speak to the question of temporal precedence.

To my knowledge, the only study to do so is that of Grabe et al. (2007). In their sample of adolescent girls (initially ages 10 to 12, mean age = 11.2 years) over 2 years, self-surveillance was related to depressive symptoms at both time points. More important, self-surveillance at Time 1 actually predicted body shame and depressive symptoms 2 years later (at Time 2). Prior values (Time 1) on depression were controlled when predicting subsequent depression. Further, Time 2 body shame (and rumination) mediated the relationship between Time 1 self-surveillance and Time 2 depressive symptoms. Thus the study shows that self-surveillance was temporally antecedent to body shame and depressive symptoms, consistent with its postulated causal role. This is the very first such evidence.

Grabe et al.'s (2007) study also incorporated boys. At Time 1 there was a significant gender difference on self-surveillance and body shame, whereby girls scored higher than boys, but it is interesting that there was no gender difference on depressive symptoms. Two years later at Time 2, there was also a gender difference in depressive symptoms. Thus, developmentally, the gender difference in self-surveillance (age 11) appears before the gender difference in depression (at age 13), again supporting the temporal precedence of self-surveillance.

CONCLUDING REMARKS

There is now a large body of evidence that self-objectification and self-surveillance are related to disordered eating and other associated phenomena, such as body shame and body dissatisfaction. Although most of this evidence comes from samples of undergraduate women, an increasing amount of research has confirmed aspects of the model with more diverse samples, in particular older women, physically active women, and women diagnosed with eating disorders. We surely now have enough correlational research on disordered eating, with two exceptions. First, aspects of race and ethnicity have not yet been properly explored. Second, there is insufficient research on younger samples.

A smaller body of research has demonstrated links between trait self-objectification and depression, as well as other indices of subjective well-being, such as negative affect. And research is only just beginning to address the third proposed mental health consequence of sexual dysfunction. Here nearly all the existing research has been conducted with undergraduate samples. Thus, the potential for objectification theory to contribute to the understanding of these phenomena has not yet been fully investigated. More research with more varied samples of women is required. Further, our understanding is liable to be advanced more quickly if these potential consequences are considered together rather than separately. As indicated earlier, self-objectification may help explain the comorbidity of eating disorders, depression, and sexual dysfunction.

One group that warrants particular and urgent attention is young girls. Although a little work has been directed at adolescents, there is reason to think that the consequences of objectification may play out at even a younger age. The American Psychological Association (2007) released its report on the sexualization of girls and women in February 2007. The task force concluded that the objectification and sexualization of young women and girls has increased over time, as indicated by the content of mainstream teen magazines, music videos, and music lyrics, and by the trend toward provocatively dressed dolls and sexy clothing marketed to young girls, the so-called tweens (usually defined as between 8 and 12 years old; see Chapter 3, this volume). However, to date, we do not have any data on the potential psychological and other effects of this increasing objectification of younger and younger girls. The American Psychological Association report noted that little research has focused specifically on girls rather than adult women. In fact, the need for such future studies focusing on girls forms part of their very first recommendation. Young girls may be particularly vulnerable to the effects of objectification.

The existing correlational evidence is supported by a small body of experimental research that demonstrates that certain situations can trigger state self-objectification and actually (causally) lead to negative consequences such as body shame and negative affect. These include the more obvious situations that draw attention to the body (e.g., trying on a swimsuit), as well as more subtle, seemingly innocuous situations such as anticipating male gaze, reading objectifying words, or receiving an appearance compliment. The variety of these situations attests to the likelihood that women will encounter potentially objectifying situations every day of their lives. These experimental results support the direction of causation proposed in objectification theory for state self-objectification. However, they do not speak directly to the causal connections with trait self-objectification. For this, longitudinal studies are required. The results of the single longitudinal study to assess relationships across time (Grabe et al., 2007) indicated that self-surveillance actually preceded depressive symptoms in a sample of 10- to 12-year-old girls (the youngest sample in any of the studies), consistent with its proposed causal role.

Although the results are clearly patchy in some areas, as indicated above, and individual studies cannot offer more than a single piece in the puzzle, the total body of evidence converges to provide strong support for objectification theory. Taken together, the correlational, experimental, and longitudinal studies all point to the same conclusion: Self-objectification plays a significant role in women's mental health. Given the ubiquitous presence of the media and other appearance-focused influences, contemporary women are likely to encounter potentially objectifying conditions on a daily basis. These are liable to trigger state self-objectification (especially in women high on trait self-objectification), which leads to immediate increases in state body shame and negative mood. Over time, these may accumulate to increase the risk of developing eating disorders, depression, and sexual dysfunction.

One potential limitation that goes across all forms of methodology is that in the main, outcome variables have been relatively mild forms of body shame, depressed mood, or negative affect rather than actual clinical eating disorders or depression. With the exception of the study by Calogero et al. (2005), all have used nonclinical samples. However, this can also be viewed as an advantage. Disordered eating and depressed mood (as well as sexual dysfunction) can be conceptualized as on a continuum, ranging from zero at one end to clinical disorders of the utmost severity at the other. Whereas relatively few women (although greater numbers than men) suffer from clinical eating disorders or depression, many women in our society suffer some degree of body concern, disordered eating, depressed mood, or sexual difficulties. In fact, the list of specific experiences for which evidence exists for an association with self-objectification is now very long and includes all of body shame, body dissatisfaction, lower body esteem, disordered eating symptoms and attitudes, dietary restraint, eating disorders, appearance anxiety, decreased flow, lack of interoceptive awareness, decreased vitality, neuroticism, negative affect, depressive symptoms, self-consciousness, feelings of humiliation and disgust, low self-esteem, body-related self-consciousness during sex, poor sexual functioning, low sexual self-esteem, and low sexual self-competence. None of these are exotic pathologies; rather, they are common everyday experiences for many women, all potentially underpinned by self-objectification.

We have demonstrated that self-objectification is related not only to potentially very serious mental health disorders but also to less serious but more normative conditions. Hence, self-objectification may have a profound and far-reaching effect on women's lived day-to-day experience. Together, the evidence confirms that self-objectification is an important explanatory concept in the mental health of contemporary women.

REFERENCES

American Psychiatric Association. (2000). *Diagnostic and statistical manual of mental disorders* (4th edition, Text Revision). Washington, DC: American Psychiatric Press.

American Psychological Association. (2007). *Report of the APA Task Force on the Sexualization of Girls*. Washington, DC: Author.

Attie, I., & Brooks-Gunn, J. (1989). Development of eating problems in adolescent girls: A longitudinal study. *Developmental Psychology, 25*, 70–79. doi:10.1037/0012-1649.25.1.70

Beumont, P. J. V., & Touyz, S. W. (1985). The syndrome of anorexia nervosa. In S. W. Touyz & P. J. V. Beumont (Eds.), *Eating disorders: Prevalence and treatment* (pp. 1–10). Sydney, Australia: Williams & Wilkins.

Breines, J. G., Crocker, J., & Garcia, J. A. (2008). Self-objectification and well-being in women's daily lives. *Personality and Social Psychology Bulletin, 34*, 583–598. doi:10.1177/0146167207313727

Calogero, R. M. (2004). A test of objectification theory: The effect of the male gaze on appearance concerns in college women. *Psychology of Women Quarterly, 28*, 16–21. doi:10.1111/j.1471-6402.2004.00118.x

Calogero, R. M. (2009). Objectification processes and disordered eating in British women and men. *Journal of Health Psychology, 14,* 394–402. doi:10.1177/1359105309102192

Calogero, R. M., Davis, W. N., & Thompson, J. K. (2005). The role of self-objectification in the experience of women with eating disorders. *Sex Roles, 52,* 43–50. doi:10.1007/s11199-005-1192-9

Calogero, R. M., & Thompson, J. K. (2009a). Potential implications of the objectification of women's bodies for women's sexual satisfaction. *Body Image, 6,* 145–148. doi:10.1016/j.bodyim.2009.01.001

Calogero, R. M., & Thompson, J. K. (2009b). Sexual self-esteem in American and British college women: Relations with self-objectification and eating problems. *Sex Roles, 60,* 160–173. doi:10.1007/s11199-008-9517-0

Cash, T. F., Maikkula, C. L., & Yamamiya, Y. (2004). Baring the body in the bedroom: Body image, sexual self-schemas, and sexual functioning among college women and men. *Electronic Journal of Human Sexuality, 7.* Retrieved from http://www.ejhs.org.

Daubenmier, J. J. (2005). The relationship of yoga, body awareness, and body responsiveness to self-objectification and disordered eating. *Psychology of Women Quarterly, 29,* 207–219. doi:10.1111/j.1471-6402.2005.00183.x

Dove, N. L., & Wiederman, M. W. (2000). Cognitive distraction and women's sexual functioning. *Journal of Sex & Marital Therapy, 26,* 67–78. doi:10.1080/009262300278650

Frederick, D. A., Forbes, G. B., Grigorian, K. E., & Jarcho, J. M. (2007). The UCLA Body Project I: Gender and ethnic differences in self-objectification and body satisfaction among 2,206 undergraduates. *Sex Roles, 57,* 317–327. doi:10.1007/s11199-007-9251-z

Fredrickson, B. L., & Roberts, T. (1997). Objectification theory: Toward understanding women's lived experiences and mental health risks. *Psychology of Women Quarterly, 21,* 173–206. doi:10.1111/j.1471-6402.1997.tb00108.x

Fredrickson, B. L., Roberts, T. A., Noll, S. M., Quinn, D. M., & Twenge, J. M. (1998). That swimsuit becomes you: Sex differences in self-objectification, restrained eating, and math performance. *Journal of Personality and Social Psychology, 75,* 269–284. doi:10.1037/0022-3514.75.1.269

Gapinski, K. D., Brownell, K. D., & LaFrance, M. (2003). Body objectification and "fat talk": Effects on emotion, motivation, and cognitive performance. *Sex Roles, 48,* 377–388. doi:10.1023/A:1023516209973

Garner, D. M., Olmsted, M. P., & Polivy, J. (1983). Development and validation of a multidimensional eating disorder inventory for anorexia nervosa and bulimia. *International Journal of Eating Disorders, 2,* 15–34. doi:10.1002/1098-108X(198321)2:2<15::AID-EAT2260020203>3.0.CO;2-6

Grabe, S., Hyde, J. S., & Lindberg, S. M. (2007). Body objectification and depression in adolescents: The role of gender, shame, and rumination. *Psychology of Women Quarterly, 31,* 164–175. doi:10.1111/j.1471-6402.2007.00350.x

Grabe, S., & Jackson, B. (2009). Self-objectification and depressive symptoms: Does their association vary among Asian American and White American men and women? *Body Image, 6*, 141–144. doi:10.1016/j.bodyim.2009.02.001

Greenleaf, C. (2005). Self-objectification among physically active women. *Sex Roles, 52*, 51–62. doi:10.1007/s11199-005-1193-8

Greenleaf, C., & McGreer, R. (2006). Disordered eating attitudes and self-objectification among physically active and sedentary female college students. *Journal of Psychology, 140*, 187–198. doi:10.3200/JRLP.140.3.187-198

Haines, M. E., Erchull, M. J., Liss, M., Turner, D. L., Nelson, J. A., Ramsey, L. R., & Hurt, M. M. (2008). Predictors and effects of self-objectification in lesbians. *Psychology of Women Quarterly, 32*, 181–187. doi:10.1111/j.1471-6402.2008.00422.x

Harper, B., & Tiggemann, M. (2008). The effect of thin ideal media images on women's self-objectification, mood, and body image. *Sex Roles, 58*, 649–657. doi:10.1007/s11199-007-9379-x

Harrison, K., & Fredrickson, B. L. (2003). Women's sports media, self-objectification, and mental health in black and white adolescent females. *Journal of Communication, 53*, 216–232. doi:10.1111/j.1460-2466.2003.tb02587.x

Harter, S. (1999). *The construction of the self: A developmental perspective*. New York, NY: Guilford Press.

Hebl, M. R., King, E. B., & Lin, J. (2004). The swimsuit becomes us all: Ethnicity, gender, and vulnerability to self-objectification. *Personality and Social Psychology Bulletin, 30*, 1322–1331. doi:10.1177/0146167204264052

Hurt, M. M., Nelson, J. A., Turner, D. L., Haines, M. E., Ramsey, L. R., Erchull, M. J., & Liss, M. (2007). Feminism: What is it good for? Feminine norms and objectification as the link between feminist identity and clinically relevant outcomes. *Sex Roles, 57*, 355–363. doi:10.1007/s11199-007-9272-7

Kozee, H. B., & Tylka, T. L. (2006). A test of objectification theory with lesbian women. *Psychology of Women Quarterly, 30*, 348–357. doi:10.1111/j.1471-6402.2006.00310.x

Lindberg, S. M., Grabe, S., & Hyde, J. S. (2007). Gender, pubertal development, and peer sexual harassment predict objectified body consciousness in early adolescence. *Journal of Research on Adolescence, 17*, 723–742.

McKinley, N. M. (1998). Gender differences in undergraduates' body esteem: The mediating effect of objectified body consciousness and actual/ideal weight discrepancy. *Sex Roles, 39*, 113–123. doi:10.1023/A:1018834001203

McKinley, N. M. (1999). Women and objectified body consciousness: Mothers' and daughters body experience in cultural, developmental, and familial context. *Developmental Psychology, 35*, 760–769. doi:10.1037/0012-1649.35.3.760

McKinley, N. M. (2006a). The developmental and cultural contexts of objectified body consciousness: A longitudinal analysis of two cohorts of women. *Developmental Psychology, 42*, 679–687. doi:10.1037/0012-1649.42.4.679

McKinley, N. M. (2006b). Longitudinal gender differences in objectified body consciousness and weight-related attitudes and behaviors: Cultural and developmental contexts in the transition from college. *Sex Roles*, *54*, 159–173. doi:10.1007/s11199-006-9335-1

McKinley, N. M., & Hyde, J. S. (1996). The Objectified Body Consciousness Scale: Development and validation. *Psychology of Women Quarterly*, *20*, 181–215. doi:10.1111/j.1471-6402.1996.tb00467.x

Miner-Rubino, K., Twenge, J. M., & Fredrickson, B. L. (2002). Trait self-objectification in women: Affective and personality correlates. *Journal of Research in Personality*, *36*, 147–172. doi:10.1006/jrpe.2001.2343

Moradi, B., Dirks, D., & Matteson, A. V. (2005). Roles of sexual objectification experiences and internalization of standards of beauty in eating disorder symptomatology: A test and extension of objectification theory. *Journal of Counseling Psychology*, *52*, 420–428. doi:10.1037/0022-0167.52.3.420

Muehlenkamp, J. J., & Saris-Baglama, R. N. (2002). Self-objectification and its psychological outcomes for college women. *Psychology of Women Quarterly*, *26*, 371–379. doi:10.1111/1471-6402.t01-1-00076

Muehlenkamp, J. J., Swanson, J. D., & Brausch, A. M. (2005). Self-objectification, risk taking, and self-harm in college women. *Psychology of Women Quarterly*, *29*, 24–32. doi:10.1111/j.1471-6402.2005.00164.x

Myers, T. A., & Crowther, J. H. (2008). Is self objectification related to interoceptive awareness? An examination of potential mediating pathways to disordered eating attitudes. *Psychology of Women Quarterly*, *32*, 172–180. doi:10.1111/j.1471-6402.2008.00421.x

Noll, S. M., & Fredrickson, B. L. (1998). A mediational model linking self-objectification, body shame, and disordered eating. *Psychology of Women Quarterly*, *22*, 623–636. doi:10.1111/j.1471-6402.1998.tb00181.x

Prichard, I., & Tiggemann, M. (2005). Objectification in fitness centers: Self-objectification, body dissatisfaction, and disordered eating in aerobic instructors and aerobic participants. *Sex Roles*, *53*, 19–28. doi:10.1007/s11199-005-4270-0

Quinn, D. M., Kallen, R. W., & Cathey, C. (2006). Body on my mind: The lingering effect of state self-objectification. *Sex Roles*, *55*, 869–874. doi:10.1007/s11199-006-9140-x

Roberts, T.-A. (2004). Female trouble: The menstrual self-evaluation scale and women's self-objectification. *Psychology of Women Quarterly*, *28*, 22–26. doi:10.1111/j.1471-6402.2004.00119.x

Roberts, T.-A., & Gettman, J. Y. (2004). Mere exposure: Gender differences in the negative effects of priming a state of self-objectification. *Sex Roles*, *51*, 17–27. doi:10.1023/B:SERS.0000032306.20462.22

Sanchez, D. T., & Kiefer, A. K. (2007). Body concerns in and out of the bedroom: Implications for sexual pleasure and problems. *Archives of Sexual Behavior*, *36*, 808–820. doi:10.1007/s10508-007-9205-0

Slater, A., & Tiggemann, M. (2002). A test of objectification theory in adolescent girls. *Sex Roles, 46*, 343–349. doi:10.1023/A:1020232714705

Steer, A., & Tiggemann, M. (2008). The role of self-objectification in women's sexual functioning. *Journal of Social and Clinical Psychology, 27*, 205–225. doi:10.1521/jscp.2008.27.3.205

Stice, E. (2002). Risk and maintenance factors for eating pathology: A meta-analytic review. *Psychological Bulletin, 128*, 825–848. doi:10.1037/0033-2909.128.5.825

Stice, E., Killen, J. D., Hayward, C., & Taylor, C. B. (1998). Age of onset for binge eating and purging during adolescence: A four-year survival analysis. *Journal of Abnormal Psychology, 107*, 671–675. doi:10.1037/0021-843X.107.4.671

Strelan, P., & Hargreaves, D. (2005). Women who objectify other women: The vicious circle of objectification. *Sex Roles, 52*, 707–712. doi:10.1007/s11199-005-3737-3

Strelan, P., Mehaffey, S. J., & Tiggemann, M. (2003). Self-objectification and esteem in young women: The mediating role of reasons for exercise. *Sex Roles, 48*, 89–95. doi:10.1023/A:1022300930307

Szymanski, D. M., & Henning, S. L. (2007). The role of self-objectification in women's depression: A test of objectification theory. *Sex Roles, 56*, 45–53. doi:10.1007/s11199-006-9147-3

Tiggemann, M., & Boundy, M. (2008). Effect of environment and appearance compliment on college women's self-objectification, mood, body shame, and cognitive performance. *Psychology of Women Quarterly, 32*, 399–405. doi:10.1111/j.1471-6402.2008.00453.x

Tiggemann, M., & Kuring, J. K. (2004). The role of body objectification in disordered eating and depressed mood. *British Journal of Clinical Psychology, 43*, 299–311. doi:10.1348/0144665031752925

Tiggemann, M., & Lynch, J. E. (2001). Body image across the life span in adult women: The role of self-objectification. *Developmental Psychology, 37*, 243–253. doi:10.1037/0012-1649.37.2.243

Tiggemann, M., & Slater, A. (2001). A test of objectification theory in former dancers and non-dancers. *Psychology of Women Quarterly, 25*, 57–64. doi:10.1111/1471-6402.00007

Tylka, T. L., & Hill, M. S. (2004). Objectification theory as it relates to disordered eating among college women. *Sex Roles, 51*, 719–730. doi:10.1007/s11199-004-0721-2

Wiederman, M. W. (2000). Women's body image self-consciousness during physical intimacy with a partner. *Journal of Sex Research, 37*, 60–68. doi:10.1080/00224490009552021

IV

PREVENTION AND DISRUPTION OF SEXUAL AND SELF-OBJECTIFICATION

8

EMBODYING EXPERIENCES AND THE PROMOTION OF POSITIVE BODY IMAGE: THE EXAMPLE OF COMPETITIVE ATHLETICS

JESSIE E. MENZEL AND MICHAEL P. LEVINE

As Fredrickson and Roberts (1997) posited, and as the research in this volume confirms, sexually objectifying experiences tend to activate processes of self-surveillance and body control that constitute self-objectification, which in turn increases the risk of body shame and other components of negative body image, disordered eating, and unhealthy forms of weight and shape management. Furthermore, studies of the determinants of self-objectification and its negative effects have illuminated the interplay between various cultural contexts (e.g., mass media, peer behavior in school), the socialization processes for males and females, and personality variables that moderate vulnerability to objectification. Various sexually objectifying conditions promote self-objectification in females (and to an extent in males), and those psychological processes by which sexually objectifying conditions become self-objectification mediate the resulting severity of negative body image and disordered eating.

Given the importance of understanding, assessing, and promoting positive body image and not just reducing negative body image (e.g., Levine &

The authors extend their thanks to Nora Erickson (Kenyon College 2010) for guiding us to the Beals (2004) categorization of "lean" (thin-build) sports.

Piran, 2004; Levine & Smolak, 2006; Smolak & Murnen, 2004), this chapter addresses the possibility of an important analogy and antidote to the pathway of sexually objectifying experiences. In this chapter, we consider whether social and environmental conditions that establish and activate psychophysical processes promoting positive body image can help to prevent, in a primary fashion, risk factors for development of disordered eating, depression, and other conditions influenced by self-objectification. We follow the work of Piran (2001, 2002; Piran Carter, Thompson, & Pajouhandeh, 2002; see also Levine & Piran, 2004) in referring to the positive social and environmental conditions, as well as to the related and desirable psychological and physical processes, as *embodying*.

Researchers interested in prevention, health promotion, and feminist developmental theory have recently begun to investigate, from several perspectives, components of the following proposition: Embodying conditions and experiences lead to embodiment and positive body image, which lead to less exposure to objectifying experiences and less consolidation and expansion of self-objectification processes, which lead to greater health and well-being and less risk for negative body image and disordered eating. The principal goal of this chapter is to review theories and studies on this newly proposed embodiment pathway. We clarify the nature of positive body image, the types of experiences that are embodying, and the subjective experience of embodiment. Following a consideration of the nature and assessment of positive body image, we address the relationship of this construct to the experience of embodiment. Then we analyze competitive athletics as an example of a source of embodying experiences that may moderate the impact of objectifying experiences inside and outside sports. We conclude by considering various other contexts that do or could promote embodiment and how this might be applied to prevention of negative body image and disordered eating.

THE NATURE AND ASSESSMENT OF POSITIVE BODY IMAGE

Most experts acknowledge that the construct (and phenomenology) of body image is multifaceted, but there is precious little agreement on the number of fundamental dimensions or facets (Cash & Pruzinsky, 2002; Thompson, Heinberg, Altabe, & Tantleff-Dunn, 1999). The existence of affective, cognitive, perceptual, or behavioral components has been supported by prominent research-based definitions, such as those provided by Cash and Pruzinsky (2002), the *Diagnostic and Statistical Manual of Mental Disorders* (4th ed., Text Revision; American Psychiatric Association, 2000) in its diagnostic criteria for body image and eating disorders, and Fisher's (1986) classic review of the body image literature.

For example, Cash and Pruzinsky's (2002) useful definition of body image goes well beyond the cognitive–affective appraisals of appearance and weight captured in the "Am I good looking in comparison with cultural standards?" question so commonly emphasized in body image research. Cash and Pruzinsky's definition encompasses how people experience the sensorimotor functioning (e.g., perception of sensation) and the competence of their bodies (e.g., strength, coordination). A person's body image, while intensely personal and private in most respects, also has an important interpersonal dimension. Moreover, just as emotion has an expressive, communicative component, body image is also manifest through self-expression and interpersonal behavior that in turn influence the ways in which people respond to the person. This dynamic is typically acknowledged in transactional developmental models, in the reciprocal determinism emphasized by social cognitive theory, and in a number of other paradigms (Levine & Smolak, 2006). Thus, according to Cash and Pruzinsky (see also Thompson et al., 1999), environmental influences (e.g., mass media, peer teasing, obesity stigmatization, and reactions of parents and siblings to the onset of puberty) transact with neuropsychological tendencies, physiology, self-concept and self-evaluation, and a person's cognitive schemas (e.g., thin ideal internalization) to construct a complex, multidimensional body image.

Body Image: Conceptualizing the Positive

Although the majority of research in the body image field has focused primarily on negative body image and body image disturbance (Avalos, Tylka, & Wood-Barcalow, 2005; Grogan, 2008), Cash and Pruzinsky's (2002) comprehensive description of body image applies to positive as well as negative body image. In the relatively sparse research on positive body image, there are two models of the relationship between positive and negative aspects of body image. Using the language of Costa and McCrae (1992) in their factor-analytic model of the Big Five personality characteristics, the first approach postulates one super factor or domain. In this model, positive and negative body image are conceptualized as being on a single continuum, such that positive body image is the opposite of, or clear lack of, body image disturbance; in other words, each person may be placed between extremely high body satisfaction and extremely low body dissatisfaction. This approach can be seen in Neumark-Stzeiner's longitudinal Project EAT (e.g., Eisenberg, Neumark-Sztainer, & Paxton, 2006) and in McVey's development of programs designed to promote positive body image (e.g., McVey & Davis, 2002).

The second approach is essentially a Big Two model, although the two super factors are not orthogonal. Rather, analogous to the current thinking about positive and negative affect, the domains of positive body image and negative body image can be understood as distinct but inversely correlated continua (see, e.g., Crawford & Henry, 2004; Terracciano, McCrae, & Costa, 2003).

Components of Positive Body Image

The specific components of the positive body image domain from the Big Two model have not been identified, but we and others assume that (a) positive body image is multifaceted, that is, multidimensional; (b) its facets will be positive in and of themselves, and each will have a clear connection with increased physical and mental health; and (c) positive body image is best examined using three facets (dimensional constructs) that are, to some extent, relevant to understanding body image disturbance but also include features unique to a positive body image construct (Avalos et al., 2005; Menzel & Levine, 2007; Piran et al., 2002). These dimensions are (a) appreciation of appearance and function, (b) awareness of and attentiveness to body experiences, and (c) positive cognitions for coping with interpersonal challenges to a healthy body image.

Appreciation of appearance and function refers to favorable opinions and positive affective components captured by descriptors such as liking, pride, happiness, respect, and interest. Appreciation of appearance, or *body satisfaction,* is the component of positive body image that has the most empirical support (Eisenberg et al., 2006; Kelly, Wall, Eisenberg, Story, & Neumark-Sztainer, 2005; McVey & Davis, 2002). Body satisfaction has a variety of meanings, reflected in a variety of corresponding measures. The Body Shape Satisfaction Scale (Pingitore, Spring, & Garfield, 1997) assesses on a satisfaction–dissatisfaction continuum 10 different body parts or attributes (e.g., build, waist, thighs, face). Other researchers have used the Body Image subscale of the Self-Image Questionnaire for Young Adolescents (Petersen, Shulenberg, Abramowitz, Offer, & Jarcho, 1984) and the Body Esteem Scale (Mendelson, Mendelson, & White, 2001). These two scales tap affective and social comparison aspects of body image indicative of positive feelings toward the body (e.g., "I am proud of my body," Petersen et al., 1984; "I'm as nice looking as most people," Mendelson et al., 2001). Note that assessment of body satisfaction can include either satisfaction or dissatisfaction with the body as a whole or with specific body areas, and the focus of evaluation may or may not have anything to do with weight or slenderness (Thompson et al., 1999).

Studies of the correlates of appearance appreciation and body satisfaction confirm the positive implications of having a positive body image. People who say that, in general, they like and appreciate their bodies tend to report, for example, the following correlates, which are reasonably interpreted as benefits: increased levels of caring about being healthy and fit, fewer unhealthy weight control practices, fewer episodes of binge eating, greater satisfaction with sexual functioning, and greater physical activity (Fredrickson & Roberts, 1997; Kelly et al., 2005; McVey & Davis, 2002; Neumark-Sztainer, Paxton, Hannah, Haines, & Story, 2006; Smolak & Murnen, 2004; Weaver & Byers, 2006).

Studies of appreciation of appearance and of positive body image overlap substantially with the investigation of body dissatisfaction. These studies typically adopt a one-domain model, in that body satisfaction is almost always discussed and measured (as described earlier) as a bipolar contrast or counterpoint to negative body image. Consequently, it is reasonable to conclude that some of the same variables that predict body dissatisfaction may also predict body satisfaction. A telling example is the negative correlation between body mass index (BMI = [weight in kg]/[height in m]^2) and body satisfaction (Eisenberg et al., 2006). This association between thinness and body satisfaction suggests that body satisfaction may be highly dependent on the proximity of a person's appearance to sociocultural ideals that are not ultimately healthy or "positive" (Babio, Arija, Sancho, & Canals, 2008; Thompson et al., 1999). Therefore, in considering the role of cognitions, feelings, evaluations, and motives regarding bodily attributes, it is important to recognize other sources of body appreciation. These include the body's ability to demonstrate strength, power, and flexibility; to be physically fit; to learn new movements; and to perform skillfully and effectively in everyday contexts. One's appreciation of the body does not have to be limited to how it appears but can also develop out of—and be expressed through—how the body functions in the world and how this physicality feels. Objectification theory emphasizes the benefits of appreciating strength, stamina, physical fitness, coordination, health, and other more competence-based attributes of one's physical self-concept (Fredrickson & Roberts, 1997; Noll & Fredrickson, 1998). Fredrickson and Roberts (1997) proposed that valuing one's body in terms of competence (as opposed to engaging in self-surveillance, which maintains and extends the focus on external appearance) could serve as a protective factor against disordered eating, depression, and sexual dysfunction.

A second important dimension of positive body image is *awareness of and attentiveness to the body*. This refers to how connected or attuned an individual is to his or her bodily experiences, including emotions, hunger, sex drive, pain, and fatigue. Being able to listen to and correctly ascertain what is happening in one's own body is theoretically related to how an individual is able to respond and care for the body (Daubenmier, 2005). Caring for the body, or good body responsiveness, is manifest in a variety of healthy behaviors, including sleeping, eating patterns, and both avoiding and taking seriously illness and injury. Body responsiveness and body awareness are moderately to highly correlated constructs (Daubenmier, 2005), especially in relation to self-care, and body responsiveness is strongly and negatively associated with disordered eating behaviors, self-objectification, and BMI (Daubenmier, 2005; Impett, Daubenmier, & Hirschman, 2006).

The third fundamental component of a positive body image is a *set of adaptive cognitions* that enable the person to resist or dilute the strength of the multitude of interpersonal and cultural challenges to developing and sustaining a healthy body image. According to several well-established cognitive models (Cash & Pruzinsky, 2002; Fairburn, Schafran, & Cooper, 1999), at the nucleus of negative body image is a self-schema in which appearance, weight, and shape are central to self-concept and thus exert an undue influence on psychological functioning (see also American Psychiatric Association, 2000, pp. 589, 594). In stark contrast, feminist-empowerment-relational theory (Piran, 2001; Piran et al., 2002; see also Levine & Smolak, 2006, Chapter 8) and, interestingly, existential theory (Maddi, 1996) coincide in proposing that individuals with a positive (vital, embodied, resilient) body image are likely to have a schema in which the body is paramount to experiencing, understanding, expressing, and defining the self. Over time, and with practice and encouragement, people have the potential to know, trust, find meaning in, and even construct their bodies as part of themselves (Maddi, 1996; Piran et al., 2002). The summation of positive body experiences and the ability for self-expression through the body should lead to lower appearance investment and lower levels of appearance- and gender-based self-surveillance, and therefore to fewer and less intense negative evaluations of the self (e.g., body shame) as a result of failing to meet culturally accepted ideals of beauty (Fredrickson & Roberts, 1997; Piran, 2001; Smolak & Murnen, 2004). Conditions that foster the development and consolidation of these positive body-self connections will likely encourage development of the attentiveness and appreciation components of positive body image. The integration of attentiveness, appreciation, and beliefs about vitality and function might best be characterized as "respect," that is, seeing one's body as an integral part and expression of one's self.

The specific beliefs composing the cognitive component of positive body image have not been completely outlined or elaborated. Nevertheless, it is likely that beliefs such as "I play and I exercise for fun, fitness, and friendship" (Burgard & Lyons, 1994) are prominent, leaving no room for harsh, all-or-none convictions such as "I must work out as much as possible if I want to keep my weight under control and not 'let myself go' like my mother did." Psychometric research (Cash, Santos, & Williams, 2005), clinical experience (Cash, 2008), and prevention theory (Levine & Smolak, 2006, Chapter 6) suggest that the cognitive component of positive body image includes appraisal and coping processes that help maintain positive feelings toward the body by buffering, contradicting, and challenging or combating the seemingly ubiquitous situations or experiences that pose a threat to body image. Research by Cash et al. (2005) highlights the importance of a cognitive strategy called *positive rational acceptance*. This is characterized by thoughts and behaviors that enable the individual to accept a threatening situation (e.g., "I tell myself that I feel self-conscious in new social situations, as do many people"), attend to and magnify positive aspects of the self (e.g., "I remind myself of my good qualities"), or engage in rational self-talk about appearance (e.g., "I tell myself that I probably look better than I feel I do"). Use of positive rational acceptance was found not only to be negatively correlated with disordered eating attitudes but also to be positively associated with global self-esteem and with the positive influence of body image on everyday functioning, such as on mood, sex life, and interpersonal relationships (Cash et al., 2005).

Body Appreciation Scale

The Body Appreciation Scale (BAS; Avalos et al., 2005) is currently the most comprehensive measure of positive body image. The theoretical basis for the instrument reflects the two-domain approach (see earlier) to body image in that the BAS was constructed in response to the inability of traditional measures of negative body image to capture, by negative contrast, characteristics of positive body image. The 13-item BAS assesses four facets or components of the domain of positive body image: (a) favorable opinions of the body; (b) acceptance of the body in spite of weight, body shape, and imperfections; (c) respect for the body by attending to its needs and engaging in healthy behaviors; and (d) protection of the body by rejecting unrealistic media ideals. As predicted, women who scored high on the BAS also exhibited lower levels of body preoccupation, body dissatisfaction, appearance evaluation, and disordered eating attitudes and behaviors (Avalos et al., 2005). The BAS was also associated with greater psychological well-being, above and beyond the variance accounted for by other measures of body image. Furthermore, the BAS is uncorrelated with BMI (Swami, Hadji-Michael, & Furnham, 2008), which supports the idea that positive body image extends beyond the appearance satisfaction that could be due to thinness in accordance with normative but unhealthy cultural standards (Babio et al., 2008; Eisenberg et al., 2006). One potentially significant limitation of the BAS, though, is that it does not address appreciation of competence-based aspects of the body. In addition, recent BAS data obtained from Malay and Chinese women living in Malaysia revealed the presence of two factors (labeled General Body Appreciation and Body Image Investment), as compared with the single, latent Body Appreciation factor obtained in the United States by Avalos et al. (2005, Studies 1 and 2). This suggests the presence of significant cross-cultural (and thus, perhaps, subcultural) differences in the nature of positive body image (Swami & Chamorro-Premuzic, 2008).

EMBODIMENT

In determining what kinds of behaviors, contexts, and interactions would be instrumental in promoting a positive body image, an important but slippery construct to consider is *embodiment*. To define embodiment as a positive, healthy, and highly desirable state and trait, that is, as more than just "not disembodiment," we initially consulted the online *Oxford English Dictionary* (n.d.). The fourth of seven definitions of *em-body* is "to cause to become part of a body; to unite into one body; to incorporate . . . [particular elements] in a system or complex unity." We then combined this emphasis on integration and unity with both Avalos et al.'s (2005) model, as described earlier, and with Piran's empowerment-relational model of positive body image, as described in the next section. The result is the following working definition: Embodiment refers to an integrated set of connections in which a person experiences her or his body as comfortable, trustworthy, and deserving of respect and care because the person experiences her or his body as a key aspect of—and expresses through her or his physicality—competence, interpersonal relatedness, power, self-expression, and well-being (Menzel & Levine, 2007).

Piran's Empowerment-Relational Theory

Empowerment-relational theory is a feminist approach to prevention that emphasizes how important it is for girls and women to have positive experiences "in" their bodies and to develop the ability to voice and act on their physical and personal needs (Levine & Smolak, 2006). Piran's multidimensional theory of embodiment incorporates positive body experiences such as bodily awareness, respect, control, instrumentality, mind–body connection, and biopsychosocial empowerment. As a result, an embodied woman experiences—and expresses to others—physical freedom; body functionality and power; a commitment to caring for one's body; a relative lack of externally oriented self-consciousness about her body; and awareness, seen in the ability to know and voice her bodily experience and needs (Piran, 2001, 2002; Piran et al., 2002; see also Levine & Smolak, 2006, Chapter 7). In terms of empowerment-relational theory, an embodied woman has numerous positive experiences and attributes. These result from a close, connected, intimate relationship with her body that enables her to act effectively on and in the world and to express herself to others.

In keeping with the theme of vital integration, an embodied woman accepts and respects her body as an inextricable part of her being in the physical, social, and psychological realms (Maddi, 1996; Piran, 2001, 2002). Her body becomes a source of her lived experience and useful, meaningful feelings, both of which augment her ability to be instrumental (independent and agentic) and expressive (interdependent and receptive; Impett, Schooler, & Tolman, 2006); Piran, 2001, 2002; Piran et al., 2002; Van Wolputte, 2004). This combination of instrumentality and expressiveness in a harmonious body–self integration enables the embodied person to develop the interpersonal connections, the social competencies, and the collective sense of efficacy necessary to support the embodiment of others by fostering individual and social change (Levine & Piran, 2004; Levine & Smolak, 2006; Maine, 2000; Piran, 2001).

Thus, Piran agrees with Avalos et al. (2005), Daubenmier and colleagues (Daubenmier, 2005; Impett, Daubenmier, & Hirschman, 2006), and Parsons and Betz (2001) that embodiment is a potentially uplifting, empowering, and beneficial state of being for women. Conversely, Piran's theory argues that the characteristic (chronic) absence or loss of embodiment—the state of *dis-embodiment*, which includes self-objectification—sets the stage for a spectrum of unhealthy behaviors in women, such as disordered eating, self-injury (e.g., cutting), substance abuse, depression, and risky sexual behavior (Levine & Piran, 2004; Piran et al., 2002).

Embodiment and Instrumentality

On a less abstract level, it is noteworthy that Piran et al.'s (2002) construct of embodiment incorporates characteristics that Parsons and Betz (2001; see also Daubenmier, 2005) found to be inversely related to self-objectification. One of several definitions of *instrumentality* used by Parsons and Betz focused on the perceived ability to take care of one's self (including one's body) and to take action (including physical action) on one's own behalf, and thus to experience and enact a sense of authentic, problem-oriented control of one's life. Piran's construct of embodiment is also consistent with a broader, more traditional definition of instrumentality that "encompasses traits that predispose toward action, assertiveness, desire to master, and willingness to take risks" (Bozionelos, 2001, p. 958). This experience and exertion of embodied control contrasts sharply with the narrow, neurotic, and often illusory control that feeds the disembodied state(s) of anorexia nervosa. Indeed, it is well established that self-reported instrumentality is a major contributor to psychological well-being (see, e.g., Saunders & Kashubeck-West, 2006), and it has a small but significant inverse relationship with eating disorders in particular (Murnen & Smolak, 1997).

Embodiment as a Significant Contributor to Positive Body Image

Further investigation of the experience and correlates of embodiment, along with identification of conditions that are embodying, would be significant contributions to understanding and promoting positive body image. We propose that there is considerable overlap between the constructs of embodiment and positive body image. The more opportunities that a woman (or man) has for forming a close, connected, and intimate relationship with her body, the better she would be able to know and be comfortable with voicing her bodily needs, with responding to and taking care of her bodily needs, and with appreciating all aspects of her body. Furthermore, an embodied person would consider her (or his) body to be a key part of who she is and how she relates to the world. Self-esteem would be based not in large part on what the body looks like in a mirror illuminated by the harsh light of narrow cultural standards, but rather to a reasonable degree on what the body can do and how it contributes to and represents self-expression and individual style. Consequently, the embodied person will tend to be protected from and better able to cope with challenges to body image.

ATHLETICS AS A SOURCE OF EMBODYING EXPERIENCES AND POSITIVE BODY IMAGE

Athletics have received attention in both the objectification and body image literature because sports offer girls and women numerous opportunities to experience their bodies in nonobjectified ways (Fredrickson & Roberts, 1997; Rubin, Nemeroff, & Russo, 2004).

Athletics and Embodiment

In terms of embodying experiences and their subsequent consolidation as embodiment, athletics could theoretically help women build the following features of embodiment: more frequent states of mind–body integration, increased body awareness, increased body responsiveness, an increased sense of physical empowerment, and an overall sense of physical competence.

Mind–Body Integration

The first potential link between athletics and embodiment is the opportunity for experiencing more frequent and pronounced states of mind–body integration, a major element of embodiment. One specific type of mind–body integration frequently observed in athletes is *flow*, or what some athletes call "being in the zone" (Fredrickson & Roberts, 1997). Flow is a specific, time-limited, but very positive and enlivening state of mind–body integration that sometimes occurs when one is engaged in deep, unself-conscious concentration on a certain activity or task whose demands are almost perfectly matched to one's level of skill and commitment (Csikszentmihalyi, 1990). Jackson, Kimiecik, Ford, and Marsh (1998) argued that athletics are an ideal arena in which to experience flow because of the balance between challenge and skill, the establishment of clear goals, and the receiving of unambiguous feedback (e.g., finish time, points, assists, how high one jumped or vaulted). Competitive athletics offer many opportunities for experiencing flow, both in competition and in practice; it may well be that success at the higher levels requires the capacity for frequent experiences of this positive state. Jackson et al. (1998) found that feeling in tune with and in control of one's movements, the ability to block out irrelevant and distracting thoughts about the environment to focus on what one needs to do (i.e., appropriate focus), and being mentally and physically relaxed are among the many factors influencing the likelihood of experiencing flow in sport. Each of these factors is characteristic of an internally oriented sense of the physical self.

Conversely, objectifying aspects of sporting events (e.g., spectators, video and photography, judging, tight-fitting uniforms, a perfectionist emphasis on "my look" or "my looks") may negatively affect an athlete's level of arousal and focus of attention. However, although objectification theory would predict appearance-focused sports (e.g., gymnastics, figure skating) to be the least conducive to the experience of flow (Parsons & Betz, 2001), preliminary research suggests that athletes participating in non-appearance-focused sports are no more likely to experience flow than athletes in appearance-focused sports (Dorland, 2006; Russell, 2001). As noted previously, in contrast to pursuing and maintaining an external, appearance-focused perspective regarding their bodies, athletes in most sports need to do—and trust their bodies to be able to do automatically—a great many things so the athlete can focus on competing with other athletes and/or with objective performance standards such as time, height vaulted, or weight in kilogram lifted. This means that all athletes, including those in sports with aesthetic standards overseen by judges, are encouraged to devote considerable time and attention to developing, refining, and applying skills, strength, stamina, coordination, and other physical and psychological attributes that promote an internally oriented experience of one's body. Therefore, the ability to experience flow, a mind–body integration state, may be indicative of an embodied sense of self because of the internal orientation and shutting out of external distractions that are required for the experience.

Body Awareness and Body Responsiveness

Two other constituents of embodying experience, body awareness and body responsiveness (i.e., the desire to care for the body), have been shown to be higher in women who regularly participate in physical activities that actively promote mind–body integration. Daubenmier (2005) found higher levels of body awareness and responsiveness in women who regularly participated in yoga but not in aerobic exercise. No direct comparisons have been made between girls or women who regularly participate in yoga and girls or women who participate in athletics. As noted earlier, the experience of flow in athletics might be a type of mind–body experience that would foster increased body awareness and responsiveness. An important factor in this regard is being physically prepared for competition. Making sure the body is physically prepared is a correlate of achieving flow (Russell, 2001). Being physically prepared is in large part a reflection of the athlete's ability to take care of his or her body by preventing injury (e.g., by warming up, cooling down, and stretching), taking in adequate and appropriate foods for muscle recovery, and getting sufficient rest and sleep. Knowing how far to push the body in terms of testing its physical limits (without inducing injury or excessive pain) is also a kind of an awareness an athlete must have to reach new levels of performance (Menzel & Levine, 2007).

Physical Empowerment and Physical Competence

Last, sport is an area that allows women to readily defy—or at the very least "problematize"—the sexual objectification, objectlike passivity, and ineffectiveness that surrounds women's bodies, clothing, and poses (see Chapter 3, this volume; Smolak & Murnen, 2004). It is important, therefore, to acknowledge that female collegiate athletes report that the benefits of their sport arise from the physical nature of athletic competition (Krane, Choi, Baird, Aimar, & Kauer, 2004). Three major themes that emerged from Krane et al.'s (2004) qualitative study of athletics, femininity, and muscularity were function, pride, and empowerment. Function related to the fact that women felt stronger and more powerful, giving them the competitive edge in their sports. The women also expressed pride in their athletic achievements because of the hard work that they put into training and competition and because of the respect they felt they had earned from others. Being athletic also made women feel empowered through increased self-esteem, confidence, independence, and self-respect. In addition, Blinde, Taub, and Han (2001) described three related empowering qualities that college-age women gain from athletics: a sense of body competence, a belief in the self as competent, and a proactive approach to life. This sense of physical competence and physical empowerment is characteristic of Piran's (2001, 2002; Piran et al., 2002) definition of embodiment in that these features enable a person to be instrumental and expressive.

Athletics, Positive Body Image, and Protection From Self-Objectification

By participating in an environment that lends itself to the development of embodiment, girls and women (and men) may develop a more positive body image and be protected against self-objectification. If it is the case that having embodying experiences can help to foster positive body image, then athletics should also be an area in which the key aspects of positive body image are also observed: appreciation of appearance and function, attentiveness and awareness, and positive, protective cognitions. Meta-analytic reviews (e.g., Hausenblas & Downs, 2001; Smolak, Murnen, & Ruble, 2000) indicate that, in general, female athletes ages 14 through 30 are more satisfied with their appearance than female nonathletes. In terms of embodiment and its links with positive body image, other studies have found that female athletes tend to have a greater appreciation for the function of their bodies and to feel empowered as the result of the unique physical experiences that athletics have to offer (Blinde et al., 2001; Krane et al., 2004). It is also noteworthy that, for older adolescents at least, female athletes have significantly higher self-esteem than nonathletes when their sports participation is associated with a positive body image, a sense of physical competence, and development of "traditionally masculine" characteristics, such as agency, assertion, and self-reliance (Richman & Shaffer, 2000). These themes of physical empowerment and competence have helped female athletes to negotiate (or cope with) the fact that their bodies tend to differ significantly from, that is, may not comply with, hegemonic ideals of slender, willowy feminine beauty (Krane et al., 2004).

Furthermore, athletics have been found to be associated with lower levels of self-objectification. The few extant studies of athletes and objectification lend some support to Fredrickson and Roberts's (1997) contention that athletic participation could be one way to prevent girls and women from internalizing a passive, object-oriented sense of self (see also Bissell, 2004). Indeed, the competence-based items of the Self-Objectification Questionnaire (Noll & Fredrickson, 1998) are strongly connected to various dimensions of athletic performance, and athletes devote considerable time and attention to developing and applying strength, stamina, coordination, and other physical attributes that promote an internally oriented experience of their body in competence-based terms. In support of this theory, studies have shown that participation in certain sports (i.e., nonweight-focused sports) and mere exposure to sports media are negatively associated with reported self-objectification, eating symptomatology, and body shame (Daniels, 2006; Harrison & Fredrickson, 2003). In two experimental studies, women ages 18 through 87 who regularly participated in yoga exhibited lower levels of self-objectification and higher levels of other mental health benefits compared with control women (Daubenmier, 2005; Impett, Daubenmier, & Hirschman, 2006).[1]

Athletic Bodily Experiences Scale

Using a survey instrument designed specifically to measure embodying experiences that occur as a result of participating in athletics, Menzel and Levine (2007) examined the quantitative relationships among athletic participation, embodiment, and self-objectification. The Athletic Body Experiences (ABE) scale was administered to over 100 NCAA Division III varsity athletes. As predicted, women with high ABE scale scores also exhibited lower levels of body dissatisfaction, along with better body awareness, lower body shame, and fewer disordered eating attitudes and behaviors. Menzel and Levine's findings support the proposition that embodiment, as measured by the ABE scale and defined by Piran et al. (2002), may have at least two benefits. First, embodiment contributes to fewer negative evaluations of the self, that is, to less body shame as a result of failing to meet culturally accepted ideals of beauty. Second, embodiment also facilitates a greater connection with internal feelings and experiences (body awareness). However, this study is only the first to use the ABE scale to measure positive aspects of body image in the context of competitive athletics, and the scale itself is still under construction. Future studies are needed to determine whether embodiment and embodying experiences are quantitatively related to other aspects of athletic participation, self-objectification, and positive body image.

LIMITATIONS OF THE ATHLETICS EXAMPLE

Although athletics for girls and women have been hailed as an unparalleled opportunity for females to empower themselves by experiencing and valuing the active, instrumental, and competence-based aspects of their bodies,

---

[1]It is important to note that a study of 1st-year college students comparing those who had participated in sports in high school (i.e., former athletes) with nonathletes found no differences in self-objectification as measured by the Self-Objectification Questionnaire. Moreover, in contrast to objectification theory, the former athletes exhibited higher levels of body shame, a construct related to higher, not lower, levels of self-objectification (Parsons & Betz, 2001). The latter finding is perplexing because the former high school athletes also reported higher levels of body instrumentality and internal locus of control, both of which were negatively associated with self-objectification within the sample.

sports are also one of the high-risk contexts receiving a lot of attention in the body image and disordered eating literature (Johnson, Powers, & Dick, 1999; Powers & Thompson, 2008; Smolak et al., 2000). Certain sports in particular seem to place girls and women at greater risk of body image disturbance, self-objectification, and disordered eating. In general, athletes participating in elite or weight-focused sports tend to have greater rates of disordered eating, lower levels of body satisfaction, and greater pressure (either perceived or real) to be lean in order to succeed in their sport (Smolak et al., 2000).[2] Examples of lean or weight-focused sports include gymnastics, figure skating, swimming, cycling, wrestling, and long-distance running. Given our society's current glorification of slenderness and its vilification of fat as the antithesis of being fit and in control (Brownell, Puhl, Schwartz, & Rudd, 2005), weight-focused and thin-build sports inevitably focus the attention of the coaches, parents, judges, and other audiences—and thus the athletes—on thinness and leanness. The substantial direct pressure that some female competitive athletes face to conform to a certain size or shape (see Ginsberg & Gray, 2006) is probably intensified by the fact that athletics remain an area in which women are still pictured and viewed (and enjoyed by men) as heterosexual objects who should somehow combine great skill and dedication with a commitment to being stylish, feminine, and "looking hot" (Buysse & Embser-Herbert, 2004; Shugart, 2003).

Therefore, although athletic participation appears to be one way to prevent girls and women from internalizing a passive, object-oriented sense of self (Bissell, 2004; Fredrickson & Roberts, 1997), we also know that there are many aspects of the athletic experience that remain problematic. However, by using the theories of embodiment and positive body image that were developed on the basis of feminist-empowerment-relational models, we may be better able to target the potential benefits of athletics when it comes to body image and combating self-objectification and to understand why differences in these outcomes are observed depending on the athletic context. Moreover, some research does suggest that the core psychopathology of body dissatisfaction and disordered eating is different in female athletes than nonathletes. For example, it appears that athletes can exhibit disordered eating behavior

---

[2]Elite athletes compete at a top national (e.g., in the United States, NCAA Division I athletics), international (e.g., at the Olympics), and/or professional level (Cobb, 2006; Smolak et al., 2000). Beals (2004) characterized weight-focused sports as "lean" or "thin-build" sports. There are three subcategories of such sports in which there is an actual or perceived competitive advantage to having low body weight: (a) *judged or aesthetic* sports, in which an emphasis on physical appearance and thinness actually confers a competitive advantage because judges use scoring systems that emphasize aesthetic performance and "presentation" in addition to competitive physical competence; (b) *endurance* sports, in which low body weight is believed to increase speed or movement; and (c) *weight class* sports, in which an inability to meet a specific weight requirement may result in termination from competition or placement in another competition category where one's chances of winning are significantly reduced.

and elevated weight preoccupation despite having high levels of body satisfaction, self-esteem, and effectiveness compared with nonathlete controls (Byrne & McLean, 2002; Hinton & Kubas, 2005). The theories of positive body image and embodiment presented here are useful because they guide us away from unidimensional models of body image and toward a consideration of nonaesthetic components of body image, including active prevention efforts by women to protect themselves against harmful, idealized images.

CONCLUSIONS AND FUTURE DIRECTIONS

We believe it is time for those committed to understanding and eradicating sexual objectification to devote a substantial amount of effort to articulating and establishing a healthy replacement for widespread self-objectification and its many negative concomitants. Specifically, there is a clear need to continue researching the nature, assessment, and development of positive body image. This conclusion drives our current conviction that several intersecting theories and lines of research should be applied to an understanding of the potential social and environmental contexts for fostering a positive body image that can help deflect and resist the many cultural forces that openly promote unhealthy levels of drive for thinness, fear of fat, mistrust of the body, and the undue influence of weight and shape on self-concept. These theories and the important overlapping components are shown in Table 8.1.

Table 8.1 clearly reflects a convergence of ideas about the components of positive body image and embodiment. Preliminary evidence, reviewed in this chapter, supports the necessary assumption that these components are indeed positive. Substantial evidence exists for the proposition that negative body image and disordered eating can be prevented when girls and young women are given opportunities for consciousness-raising, connection with each other and with mentors, the development of mental and physical competencies, and the experience of choice and control in promoting changes in group norms and in their various communities (Levine & Piran, 2004; Levine & Smolak, 2006, 2009; Piran, 1999, 2001). However, beyond these facts, a great many questions and unexplored areas remain.

In our opinion, here are the principal questions that require research attention before the potentially positive impact of embodying experiences on body image, healthy eating, and self-care can be better understood:

- What is the best way to conceptualize and assess positive and negative body image (see Table 8.1)?
- Is embodiment a productive way to conceptualize and promote positive body image (see Table 8.1)?

TABLE 8.1
Positive Body Image

Dimension	Avalos et al. (2005) Body Appreciation Scale	Piran (2001, 2002)[a] An Embodied Woman	Daubenmier (2005) Mind–Body Integration	Menzel and Levine (2007)[a] Embodied Athlete
Appreciation of appearance and function	Favorable opinions	Physical freedom Functionality Power(ful)	Mind–body integration	Source of competence, joy, personal growth, well-being
Awareness of and attentiveness to body experiences	Respect Attention to needs Healthy (self-care) behaviors	Commitment to caring Lack of self-consciousness Knowing/voicing needs	Awareness Lack of self-consciousness Responsiveness Self-care	Respect Attention to needs Healthy self-care
Positive cognitions for coping with challenges to healthy body image	Acceptance in spite of imperfections Rejection of unrealistic media ideals	Critical social perspective[b] Connected to women	Acceptance	Proud Confident Self-concept favors strength and function

Note. All characteristics, for example, "favorable opinions" and "respect," apply to the body.
[a]Embodied women, including embodied female athletes, experience and express these "characteristics."
[b]See Piran (2001); see also Levine and Piran (2004).

- Combining the first two questions, what is the relationship between embodiment and self-objectification?
- In what ways is positive body image (and embodiment) "positive"? And, in particular, does it function as a source of resilience, that is, as a protective factor during early adolescence and other high-risk periods for negative body image, disordered eating, depression, and social anxiety?

If these questions can be answered in reliable and valid ways, then we would have a solid foundation for testing the hypotheses that form one major theme of this chapter and our work together: Compared with nonathletes, girls and women participating in competitive athletics will tend to have a more positive body image in part (at least) because they have more embodying experiences, both in the context of athletics and in general (e.g., in relation to sexuality). However, an even bigger task ahead is using theories of embodiment to identify contexts other than athletics that could help women to form more empowered, connected, caring, and competent relationships with their bodies. Good candidates for embodying activities lend themselves to the same level of physical activity, determination, enjoyment, and challenge (in terms of skill development and personal goal setting) that characterize athletics. Examples include hiking, scuba diving, rock climbing, martial arts, riding and working with horses, and yoga. In addition, contexts or environments that enable women to comfortably and safely voice their bodily concerns or narratives and feelings related to physical development (e.g., women's groups or consciousness-raising events) might also help to form more intimate relationships with the body (Piran, 1999, 2001). As corollaries of our hypothesis concerning athletics and other embodying contexts, we also predict that (a) the path from competitive athletics (and other embodying contexts) to embodying experiences to positive body image will be partially mediated by a reduction in self-objectification (see Figure 8.1), and (b) those girls and women participating in elite and/or lean sports who report higher levels of positive body image and lower levels of disordered eating (i.e., are more resilient) will also report more embodying experiences.

As a final observation and future direction, it is noteworthy that out of the approximately 100 published and unpublished outcome studies for prevention programs related to body image, only a few have addressed athletes (Levine & Smolak, 2006). However, two of the most sophisticated, successful, and nationally recognized interventions in history, the ATLAS (Athletes Training and Learning to Avoid Steroids) and ATHENA (Athletes Targeting Healthy Exercise and Nutrition Alternatives) programs (http://www.ohsu.edu/hpsm/atlas.cfm), are designed by researchers at the Oregon Health Sciences University as selective prevention for high school male and female athletes, respectively (Elliot & Goldberg, 2008; Goldberg et al., 2000). It is

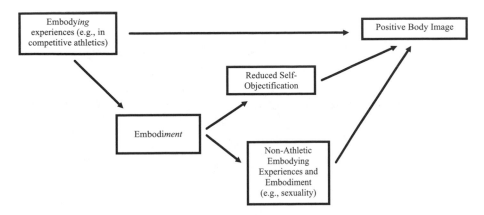

Figure 8.1. Preliminary model for the relationship between embodying experiences and positive body image.

our hope and expectation that as research progresses on the relationship among self-objectification, embodiment, and positive body image, researchers will follow Piran's (1999, 2001, 2002) lead in turning their attention to the ways in which research, prevention, and advocacy can help identify and make potentially beneficial environments (like athletics) more embodying for girls and women and less objectifying in terms of weight, shape, and appearance.

REFERENCES

American Psychiatric Association. (2000). *Diagnostic and statistical manual of mental disorders* (4th ed., Text Revision). Washington, DC: Author.

Avalos, L., Tylka, T. L., & Wood-Barcalow, N. (2005). The Body Appreciation Scale: Development and psychometric evaluation. *Body Image, 2,* 285–297. doi:10.1016/j.bodyim.2005.06.002

Babio, N., Arija, V., Sancho, C., & Canals, J. (2008). Factors associated with non-clinical adolescents at risk of eating disorders. *Journal of Public Health, 16,* 107–115. doi:10.1007/s10389-007-0133-1

Beals, K. A. (2004). *Disordered eating among athletes: A comprehensive guide for health professionals.* Champaign, IL: Human Kinetics.

Bissell, K. (2004). What do these messages really mean? Sports media exposure, sports participation, and body image distortion in women between the ages of 18 and 75. *Journalism & Mass Communication Quarterly, 81,* 108–123.

Blinde, E. M., Taub, D. E., & Han, L. (2001). Sport participation and women's personal empowerment: Experiences of the collegiate athlete. In A. Yiannakis & M. J. Melnick (Eds.), *Contemporary issues in sociology of sport* (pp. 159–168). Champaign, IL: Human Kinetics.

Bozionelos, N. (2001). The relationship of instrumental and expressive traits with computer anxiety. *Personality and Individual Differences, 31,* 955–974.

Brownell, K. D., Puhl, R. M., Schwartz, M. B., & Rudd, L. (Eds.). (2005). *Weight bias: Nature, consequences, and remedies.* New York, NY: Guilford Press.

Burgard, D., & Lyons, P. (1994). Alternatives in obesity treatment: Focusing on health for fat women. In P. Fallon, M. A. Katzman, & S. C. Wooley (Eds.), *Feminist perspectives on eating disorders* (pp. 212–230). New York, NY: Guilford Press.

Buysse, J. A. M., & Embser-Herbert, M. S. (2004). Constructions of gender in sport: An analysis of intercollegiate media guide cover photographs. *Gender & Society, 18,* 66–81. doi:10.1177/0891243203257914

Byrne, S., & McLean, N. (2002). Elite athletes: Effects of the pressure to be thin. *Journal of Science and Medicine in Sport, 5,* 80–94. doi:10.1016/S1440-2440(02)80029-9

Cash, T. F. (2008). *The body image workbook: An 8-step program for learning to like your looks* (2nd ed.). Oakland, CA: New Harbinger.

Cash, T. F., & Pruzinsky, T. (Eds.). (2002). *Body image: A handbook of theory, research, and clinical practice.* New York, NY: Guilford Press.

Cash, T. F., Santos, M. T., & Williams, E. F. (2005). Coping with body-image threats and challenges: Validation of the Body Image Coping Strategies Inventory. *Journal of Psychosomatic Research, 58,* 191–199. doi:10.1016/j.jpsychores.2004.07.008

Cobb, K. L. (2006). Eating disorders in athletes: A review of the literature. In P. I. Swain (Ed.), *Eating disorders: New research* (pp. 65–98). Hauppauge, NY: Nova Science.

Costa, P. T., & McCrae, R. R. (1992). *NEO-PI-R: Professional manual for the Revised NEO Personality Inventory and NEO Five-Factor Inventory.* Odessa, FL: Psychological Assessment Resources.

Crawford, J. R., & Henry, J. D. (2004). The Positive and Negative Affect Schedule (PANAS): Construct validity, measurement properties and normative data in a large non-clinical sample. *British Journal of Clinical Psychology, 43,* 245–265. doi:10.1348/0144665031752934

Csikszentmihalyi, M. (1990). *Flow: The psychology of optimal experience.* New York, NY: Harper & Row.

Daniels, E. A. (2006). Media representations of active women: What are girls seeing and does it affect their self-concept? *Dissertation Abstracts International, 67*(5-B), 2858. Retrieved from PsycINFO Database Record.

Daubenmier, J. (2005). The relationship of yoga, body awareness, and body responsiveness to self-objectification and disordered eating. *Psychology of Women Quarterly, 29,* 207–219. doi:10.1111/j.1471-6402.2005.00183.x

Dorland, J. M. (2006). *Objectification theory: Examining the relation between self-objectification and flow for college-aged women athletes.* Unpublished doctoral dissertation, University of Akron, OH. Retrieved from http://www.ohiolink.edu/etd/view.cgi?acc_num=akron1163634310

Elliot, D. L., & Goldberg, L. (2008). The ATHENA (Athletes Targeting Healthy Exercise & Nutrition Alternatives) harm reduction/health promotion program for female high school athletes. In C. LeCroy & J. E. Mann (Eds.), *Handbook of prevention and intervention programs for adolescent girls* (pp. 205–239). Hoboken, NJ: Wiley.

Eisenberg, M. E., Neumark-Sztainer, D., & Paxton, S. J. (2006). Five-year change in body satisfaction among adolescents. *Journal of Psychosomatic Research, 61,* 521–527. doi:10.1016/j.jpsychores.2006.05.007

Fairburn, C. G., Schafran, R., & Cooper, Z. (1999). A cognitive behavioural theory of anorexia nervosa. *Behaviour Research and Therapy, 37,* 1–13. doi:10.1016/S0005-7967(98)00102-8

Fisher, S. (1986). *Development and structure of body image* (Vol. 1). Hillsdale, NJ: Erlbaum.

Fredrickson, B., & Roberts, T. (1997). Objectification theory: Toward understanding women's lived experiences and mental health risks. *Psychology of Women Quarterly, 21,* 173–206. doi:10.1111/j.1471-6402.1997.tb00108.x

Ginsberg, R. L., & Gray, J. J. (2006). The differential depiction of female athletes in judged and non-judged sport magazines. *Body Image, 3,* 365–373. doi:10.1016/j.bodyim.2006.05.003

Goldberg, L., MacKinnon, D. P., Elliot, D. L., Moe, E. L., Clarke, G., & Cheong, J. W. (2000). The Adolescents Training and Learning to Avoid Steroids Program: Preventing drug use and promoting health behaviors. *Archives of Pediatrics & Adolescent Medicine, 154,* 332–338.

Grogan, S. (2008). *Body image: Understanding body dissatisfaction in men, women, and children.* London, England: Routledge.

Harrison, K., & Fredrickson, B. (2003). Women's sports media, self-objectification, and mental health in black and white adolescent females. *Journal of Communication, 53,* 216–232. doi:10.1111/j.1460-2466.2003.tb02587.x

Hausenblas, H., & Downs, D. (2001). Comparison of body image between athletes and nonathletes: A meta-analytic review. *Journal of Applied Sport Psychology, 13,* 323–339. doi:10.1080/104132001753144437

Hinton, P. S., & Kubas, K. (2005). Psychosocial correlates of disordered eating in female collegiate athletes: Validation of the ATHLETE Questionnaire. *Journal of American College Health, 54,* 149–156. doi:10.3200/JACH.54.3.149-156

Impett, E. A., Daubenmier, J. J., & Hirschman, A. L. (2006). Minding the body: Yoga, embodiment, and well-being. *Sexuality Research & Social Policy, 3,* 39–48. doi:10.1525/srsp.2006.3.4.39

Impett, E. A., Schooler, D., & Tolman, D. L. (2006). To be seen and not heard: Feminist ideology and adolescent girls' sexual health. *Archives of Sexual Behavior, 35,* 129–142. doi:10.1007/s10508-005-9016-0

Jackson, S., Kimiecik, J., Ford, S., & Marsh, H. (1998). Psychological correlates of flow in sport. *Journal of Sport & Exercise Psychology, 20,* 358–378.

Johnson, C., Powers, P. S., & Dick, R. (1999). Athletes and eating disorders: The National Collegiate Athletic Association Study. *International Journal of Eating Disorders, 26,* 179–188. doi:10.1002/(SICI)1098-108X(199909)26:2<179::AID-EAT7>3.0.CO;2-Z

Kelly, A. M., Wall, M., Eisenberg, M. E., Story, M., & Neumark-Sztainer, D. (2005). Adolescent girls with high body satisfaction: Who are they and what can they teach us? *Journal of Adolescent Health, 37,* 391–396. doi:10.1016/j.jadohealth.2004.08.008

Krane, V., Choi, P. Y. L., Baird, S. M., Aimar, C. M., & Kauer, K. J. (2004). Living the paradox: Female athletes negotiate femininity and muscularity. *Sex Roles, 50,* 315–329. doi:10.1023/B:SERS.0000018888.48437.4f

Levine, M. P., & Piran, N. (2004). The role of body image in the prevention of eating disorders. *Body Image, 1,* 57–70. doi:10.1016/S1740-1445(03)00006-8

Levine, M. P., & Smolak, L. (2006). *The prevention of eating problems and eating disorders: Theory, research, and practice.* Mahwah, NJ: Erlbaum.

Levine, M. P., & Smolak, L. (2009). Recent developments and promising directions in the prevention of negative body image and disordered eating in children and adolescents. In L. Smolak & J. K. Thompson (Eds.), *Body image, eating disorders, and obesity in youth: Assessment, prevention, and treatment* (pp. 215–239). Washington, DC: American Psychological Association. doi:10.1037/11860-011

Maddi, S. R. (1996). *Personality theories: A comparative analysis* (6th ed.). Pacific Grove, CA: Brooks/Cole.

Maine, M. (2000). *Body wars: Making peace with women's bodies.* Carlsbad, CA: Gurze Books.

McVey, G., & Davis, R. (2002). A program to promote positive body image: A 1-year follow-up evaluation. *Journal of Early Adolescence, 22,* 96–108. doi:10.1177/0272431602022001005

Mendelson, B. K., Mendelson, M. J., & White, D. R. (2001). Body-Esteem Scale for Adolescents and Adults. *Journal of Personality Assessment, 76,* 90–106. doi:10.1207/S15327752JPA7601_6

Menzel, J., & Levine, M. P. (2007, August). *Female athletes and embodiment: Development and validation of the Athlete Body Experiences Questionnaire.* Poster presented at the 115th Annual Convention of the American Psychological Association, San Francisco, CA.

Murnen, S. K., & Smolak, L. (1997). Femininity, masculinity, and disordered eating: A meta-analytic review. *International Journal of Eating Disorders, 22,* 231–242. doi:10.1002/(SICI)1098-108X(199711)22:3<231::AID-EAT2>3.0.CO;2-O

Neumark-Sztainer, D., Paxton, S. J., Hannan, P. J., Haines, J., & Story, M. (2006). Does body satisfaction matter? Five-year longitudinal associations between body satisfaction and health behaviors in adolescent females and males. *Journal of Adolescent Health, 39,* 244–251. doi:10.1016/j.jadohealth.2005.12.001

Noll, S., & Fredrickson, B. (1998). A mediational model linking self-objectification, body shame, and disordered eating. *Psychology of Women Quarterly, 22,* 623–636. doi:10.1111/j.1471-6402.1998.tb00181.x

Oxford English Dictionary [OED Online]. (n.d.). Retrieved from http://dictionary.oed.com/cgi/entry/50073710?single=1&query_type=word&queryword=embody

Parsons, E., & Betz, N. (2001). The relationship of participation in sports and physical activity to body objectification, instrumentality, and locus of control among young women. *Psychology of Women Quarterly, 25,* 209–222. doi:10.1111/1471-6402.00022

Petersen, A. C., Shulenberg, J. E., Abramowitz, R. H., Offer, D., & Jarcho, H. D. (1984). A Self-Image Questionnaire for Young Adults (SIQYA): Reliability and validity studies. *Journal of Youth and Adolescence, 13,* 93–111. doi:10.1007/BF02089104

Pingitore, R., Spring, B., & Garfield, D. (1997). Gender differences in body satisfaction. *Obesity Research, 5,* 402–409.

Piran, N. (1999). The reduction of preoccupation with body weight and shape in schools: A feminist approach. In N. Piran, M. P. Levine, & C. Steiner-Adair (Eds.), *Preventing eating disorders: A handbook of interventions and special challenges* (pp. 148–159). Philadelphia, PA: Brunner/Mazel.

Piran, N. (2001). Re-inhabiting the body from the inside out: Girls transform their school environment. In D. L. Tolman & M. Brydon-Miller (Eds.), *From subjects to subjectivities: A handbook of interpretative and participatory methods* (pp. 218–238). New York, NY: New York University Press.

Piran, N. (2002). Embodiment: A mosaic of inquiries in the area of body weight and shape preoccupation. In S. M. Abbey (Ed.), *Ways of knowing in and through the body: Diverse perspectives on embodiment* (pp. 211–214). Welland, Ontario, Canada: Soleil.

Piran, N., Carter, W., Thompson, S., & Pajouhandeh, P. (2002). Powerful girls: A contradiction in terms? Young women speak about the experience of growing up in a girl's body. In S. Abbey (Ed.), *Ways of knowing in and through the body: Diverse perspectives on embodiment* (pp. 206–210). Welland, Ontario, Canada: Soleil.

Powers, P., & Thompson, R. (2008). *The exercise balance.* Carlsbad, CA: Gürze Books.

Richman, E., & Shaffer, D. (2000). "If you let me play sports": How might sport participation influence the self-esteem of adolescent females? *Psychology of Women Quarterly, 24,* 189–199. doi:10.1111/j.1471-6402.2000.tb00200.x

Rubin, L. R., Nemeroff, C. J., & Russo, N. F. (2004). Exploring feminist women's body consciousness. *Psychology of Women Quarterly, 28,* 27–37. doi:10.1111/j.1471-6402.2004.00120.x

Russell, W. D. (2001). An examination of flow state occurrence in college athletes. *Journal of Sport Behavior, 24,* 83–107.

Saunders, K. J., & Kashubeck-West, S. (2006). The relations among feminist identity, development gender-role orientation, and psychological well-being in women. *Psychology of Women Quarterly, 30,* 199–211. doi:10.1111/j.1471-6402.2006.00282.x

Shugart, H. A. (2003). She shoots, she scores: Mediated constructions of contemporary female athletes in coverage of the 1999 US Women's Soccer Team. *Western Journal of Communication, 67,* 1–31.

Smolak, L., & Murnen, S. K. (2004). A feminist approach to eating disorders. In J. K. Thompson (Ed.), *Handbook of eating disorders and obesity* (pp. 590–605). Hoboken, NJ: Wiley.

Smolak, L., Murnen, S. K., & Ruble, A. (2000). Female athletes and eating problems: A meta-analysis. *International Journal of Eating Disorders, 27,* 371–380. doi:10.1002/(SICI)1098-108X(200005)27:4<371::AID-EAT1>3.0.CO;2-Y

Swami, V., & Chamorro-Premuzic, T. (2008). Factor structure of the Body Appreciation Scale among Malaysian women. *Body Image, 5,* 409–413. doi:10.1016/j.bodyim.2008.04.005

Swami, V., Hadji-Michael, M., & Furnham, A. (2008). Personality and individual difference correlates of positive body image. *Body Image, 5,* 322–325. doi:10.1016/j.bodyim.2008.03.007

Terracciano, A., McCrae, R. R., & Costa, P. T. (2003). Factorial and construct validity of the Italian Positive and Negative Affect Schedule (PANAS). *European Journal of Psychological Assessment, 19,* 131–141. doi:10.1027//1015-5759.19.2.131

Thompson, J. K., Heinberg, L. J., Altabe, M., & Tantleff-Dunn, S. (1999). *Exacting beauty: Theory, assessment, and treatment of body image disturbance.* Washington, DC: American Psychological Association. doi:10.1037/10312-000

Van Wolputte, S. (2004). Hang on to your self: Of bodies, embodiment, and selves. *Annual Review of Anthropology, 33,* 251–269. doi:10.1146/annurev.anthro.33.070203.143749

Weaver, A. D., & Byers, E. S. (2006). The relationships among body image, body mass index, exercise, and sexual functioning in heterosexual women. *Psychology of Women Quarterly, 30,* 333–339. doi:10.1111/j.1471-6402.2006.00308.x

9

FIGHTING SELF-OBJECTIFICATION IN PREVENTION AND INTERVENTION CONTEXTS

TRACY L. TYLKA AND CASEY L. AUGUSTUS-HORVATH

Preventing and treating self-objectification in girls and women is a colossal challenge. Part of this challenge stems from its connection to the ubiquitous, recurrent, persistent, and permissible sexual objectification that is part of the daily lives of so many girls and women (see Chapter 3, this volume). Because sexual objectification is a deeply rooted form of sexism, it will take time and extensive effort to overturn it. Self-objectification is also challenging to prevent and treat because girls and women are taught that being vigilant about their physical appearance will lead to increased societal rewards and social power (Breines, Crocker, & Garcia, 2008; Unger, 1979). These perceived benefits may prevent women from understanding the long-term deleterious consequences self-objectification has for their well-being. Despite these challenges, however, psychologists can work to prevent self-objectification and, once it has occurred, treat it to ameliorate its maladaptive consequences. These efforts, at their core, should raise consciousness using interventions grounded in feminist, gestalt, cognitive–behavioral, and interpersonal theory. In this chapter, we discuss (a) intrapersonal strategies to reduce the likelihood of self-objectifying, (b) therapeutic interventions to treat high levels of self-objectification, and (c) interpersonal and societal-level interventions to reduce the prevalence and cultural acceptance of sexual objectification. These strategies and interventions are outlined in Table 9.1.

TABLE 9.1
Strategies to Fight Self-Objectification in Girls and Women

Type of strategy	Specific strategies
Prevention	Promote a contextualization schema. • Articulate and discuss the ill effects of sexual objectification. • Discuss how sexual objectification results from a maladaptive society, not personal inadequacy. • Help girls identify and label instances of sexual objectification (criticisms and compliments). • Create and practice personalized scripts to be able to respond to objectifying comments. Define assertiveness and practice communicating in this manner. • Encourage girls to practice and maintain appropriate boundaries in interpersonal relationships. Raise awareness that engaging in body comparison is harmful. • Practice strategies to relate to same-sex peers in non-appearance-oriented ways. • Instruct girls to "catch themselves" when they engage in body comparison and commit to avoiding this behavior. Promote media literacy. • Explore how body size is portrayed in the media. • Collaborate to actively protest offensive media images and messages. • Encourage girls to advocate for positive body images by the media and retailers. • Provide guidelines for writing letters and e-mails to offensive companies and companies that promote a positive message. • Help parents limit time children spend viewing media emphasizing the thin ideal, discuss the impossibility of the thin ideal with their children, promote healthy eating in lieu of rigid dieting. Emphasize women's internal qualities. • Use the Tree of Strength exercise (Full of Ourselves program; Steiner-Adair & Sjostrom, 2006). • Help girls generate personal affirmations that honor their intellect, personality, and character. Provide embodied experiences. • Promote a functional view of the body and body appreciation (Full of Ourselves program). • Use guided meditation and body scan activities (Full of Ourselves program). • Use bioenergetic punches (Full of Ourselves program). • Offer Hatha yoga to increase embodiment and empowerment. Promote a schema for exercise that honors the body by focusing on functionality and pleasure.

TABLE 9.1
Strategies to Fight Self-Objectification in Girls and Women   *(Continued)*

Type of strategy	Specific strategies
Intervention	Place self-objectification in context. • Address the positive benefits clients have received for engaging in self-objectification (yet emphasize that these benefits are short-lived and superficial). • Address harmful effects clients have experienced from engaging in self-objectification. • Conduct an environmental analysis of objectifying situations in which clients are exposed. Help clients manage triggers to self-objectification. • Find ways to decrease the amount of time they spend in objectifying situations. Help clients brainstorm methods for decreasing social comparison opportunities. Help clients replace maladaptive body-related thoughts with adaptive thoughts. Implement cognitive dissonance interventions in group format (e.g., Stice et al., 2001). • Have clients actively critique the thin ideal (e.g., name costs associated with the thin ideal, resist peer pressure to adopt the thin ideal, dissuade others from adopting the thin ideal). • Reframe body hatred statements to body appreciation and respect statements. • Use sensate enhancement interventions to connect clients to pleasures and functions of their body. • Provide grounding techniques to enhance embodiment and empowerment. • Offer structured eating opportunities (if clients are disconnected from hunger and satiety cues). • Employ intuitive eating (if clients are at least somewhat connected to hunger and satiety cues). • Use mindfulness and emotion regulation (dialectical behavioral therapy; Linehan, 1993). • Explain to clients the physiological and biological aspects of anxiety. • Help clients formulate and cultivate social support networks that are not appearance based.
Society level	Communicate to the media research findings on the deleterious effects of sexual and self-objectification via press releases. Help schools and communities develop peer networks focused on embodiment, intellectual concentration, and ways to contextualize sexual objectification. Help design and implement community workshops/programs for caregivers (e.g., discuss the harm in sexual objectification, how to prevent socializing daughters to focus on appearance).

(continues)

TABLE 9.1

Strategies to Fight Self-Objectification in Girls and Women   *(Continued)*

Type of strategy	Specific strategies
	Develop programs for men (similar to The Men's Program; Foubert 2000) that focus on lowering their tendency to engage in sexual objectification.
	Exert persistent effort and collaborate with other professionals to promote awareness and accountability in media outlets for their role in perpetuating weightism and sexual objectification.
	Inform media that average-sized models are just as effective as thin models to sell products.
	Inform media representatives of the harm that stems from pairing weight loss messages with articles on positive body image or adaptive eating.
	Inform families and communities of the ill effects caused when attention is focused on women's body shape/weight and instead emphasize the functionality and strength of women's bodies.
	Use Fat Talk Free Week to raise awareness of harm from engaging in fat talk and encourage people to commit to eliminating this negative discourse around fat.
	Protest advertising companies' (and other media outlets') use of fat talk and dieting talk.

PREVENTING SELF-OBJECTIFICATION

Women who self-objectify experience more negative emotions and fewer positive emotions, report diminished feelings of authenticity, and are less able to focus on tasks that demand cognitive attention (Breines et al., 2008; Quinn, Kallen, Twenge, & Fredrickson, 2006; Szymanski & Henning, 2007). They experience high levels of body shame (e.g., Moradi, Dirks, & Matteson, 2005; Tiggemann & Slater, 2001; Tylka & Hill, 2004), frequently compare their bodies with other women's bodies (e.g., Grabe, Hyde, & Lindberg, 2007; Strelan & Hargreaves, 2005), dissociate from their hunger and satiety cues (Tylka & Hill, 2004), engage in disordered eating (e.g., Moradi et al., 2005; Tiggemann & Slater, 2001), hold negative attitudes toward their menses (Roberts, 2004; Roberts & Waters, 2004), and are more likely to smoke (Harrell, Fredrickson, Pomerleau, & Nolen-Hoeksema, 2006). If girls and women have high relationship contingency (i.e., connecting their self-worth to obtaining and maintaining a romantic relationship) alongside high self-objectification, they may further sacrifice their physical health to achieve and maintain beauty (e.g., getting cosmetic surgery, rigidly dieting) and endure unhealthy relationships as they fear that the relationship will dissolve if they assert their rights, opinions, and ideas (Sanchez & Kwang, 2007).

Whereas reducing the prevalence of sexual objectification in Western culture is likely to decrease girls' and women's tendency to self-objectify, it will likely take time and will be met with much resistance from individuals who profit from sexually objectifying women's bodies (e.g., the pornography industry, advertisers of beauty products marketed to women, the dieting industry), boys and men who feel entitled (via sexism) to gaze at women's bodies, and girls and women who have internalized society's messages to use their sexuality to acquire power. Thus, individual-level strategies aimed at preventing girls and women from engaging in self-objectification are imperative.

Promoting a Contexualization Schema

We must teach girls in early childhood to contextualize sexual objectification by identifying objectification as a problem within society. Drawing from Freeman's (1979) concept of the null environment, if we do not actively help girls and women to (a) articulate and discuss the ill effects of sexual objectification and (b) develop a schema to contextualize it, then they are more likely to internalize a view of themselves as a sexual object, or self-objectify. Experiencing sexual objectification may leave women feeling powerless against being targets of frequent unrealistic appearance-based evaluations; therefore, they may rigidly diet or change their body via other means (e.g., cosmetic surgery) as a way to assert control (Peterson, Grippo, & Tantleff-Dunn, 2008). However, adopting a contextualization schema would help girls and women buffer this feeling of powerlessness because appropriate blame would be placed on the objectifiers (e.g., "It is a reflection of the person objectifying me rather than an indication of my worth"). Girls and women should be encouraged to contextualize sexual objectification, even when appearance-based comments directed at them are meant to be complimentary (Calogero, Herbozo, & Thompson, 2009). Therefore, their self-worth would be less contingent on another's evaluation of their appearance, whether it is positive or negative. Girls' and women's self-worth would remain intact and they would feel empowered knowing that they have the skills to deflect sexual objectification.

The development of a contextualization schema would first require educating girls and women about sexual objectification. Included would be a discussion about how sexual objectification is a result of a maladaptive society, one that evaluates people on their appearance rather than on their inner qualities, and not a result of their adequacy or inadequacy as a person. Then, girls and women could be helped to identify and label instances of sexual objectification (both criticisms and compliments), such as catcalls, being whistled at, others' gazes, being told that they look great, being told to lose weight, being told to change their appearance, their partners' gazes at other women's bodies, and comparing their body with other girls' and women's bodies.

Often, girls and women are not taught how to respond or react to sexually objectifying comments, so they are essentially forced to just accept these comments and swallow their associated feelings. Metaphorically, this is another way they internalize objectification. Sexual objectification often occurs in unstructured and public contexts, and girls and women may find it difficult to respond powerfully and effectively in these moments. Having scripts in place and well practiced would help them form a contextualization schema and articulate to others that the comments and behaviors made in reference to their body are neither appreciated nor appropriate. Professionals should encourage girls' and women's ideas while creating scripts. In doing so, this allows them to (a) become involved in the process, (b) personalize the scripts so they are a genuine reflection of their personality and thus are more natural for them to say, and (c) observe and mirror the process of creating scripts so they can implement this strategy when needed for future occurrences. Also, they need to be prepared for open dialogue with the objectifier and know how to effectively manage their emotions during this dialogue. This will allow them to accurately articulate and communicate their reactions while remaining a constructive learning opportunity for the objectifier.

In each script, girls and women should label the behavior and provide a specific request while placing appropriate responsibility on the objectifier. Some example scripts may include "Hey, look at my face and not my breasts"; "You hurt me when you stare at women's bodies. Plus, you are treating them like objects. To respect both me and them, please don't do that"; "It's not cool to make jokes or say negative things about women's bodies—it's actually cruel"; "Focus on how we are inside rather than how we look"; and "Your comment hurt me. Please do not focus on my appearance—it's insulting. It's only one part of who I am."

Situations in which girls and women receive appearance-related compliments may be trickier, given that they are socialized to accept appearance-related positive feedback and respond with "thank you." Yet, because these comments are also harmful to women's body image and encourage self-objectification (Calogero et al., 2009), they need to be challenged. Scripts may include "I want you to value me for who I am on the inside"; "I know you meant it in a good way, but it objectifies women to focus on how they look"; and "Your comment that I look good because I lost weight makes me wonder how you felt about how I looked before. I don't want my attention or your attention to be focused on my weight." Girls and women should be given opportunities to practice these scripts and shape them to fit interactions with significant others, acquaintances, and strangers.

Assertiveness is necessary to be able to effectively challenge others' objectifying comments and behaviors. Because girls are often socialized to be passive, it is imperative that professionals help them articulate and practice how they can communicate that standing their ground is their right, is a form of self-protection, and will contribute to their strength. Professionals should define assertiveness (e.g., when a girl or woman has "power over her own attitudes, actions, and decisions" and "doesn't let other people—or images in magazines or peer pressure—define her"; Steiner-Adair & Sjostrom, 2006, p. 30) because many negative misconceptions exist about assertive women. A resource professionals could suggest for adolescent girls and women is the book *Back Off: How to Confront and Stop Sexual Harassment* (Langelan, 1993). Because sexual harassment and sexual objectification, as forms of sexism, are closely linked, women could use the strategies mentioned to confront objectification. These strategies involve nonviolent yet assertive personal confrontation techniques that leave women feeling empowered because they do not passively accept being objectified but do behave in a manner to reduce future occurrences of objectification. For instance, a woman who is whistled at by a stranger might state, "Whistling at women when they walk by is disrespectful. No one likes it. Please don't ever whistle at another woman you don't know again" or "Stop harassing women; no one likes it."

Professionals also can encourage girls and women to practice developing and maintaining appropriate boundaries in their relationships that demonstrate respect for themselves while remaining empathic to others. They could engage in group role-plays in which they practice speaking in a strong assertive voice and the group leader and members could give them constructive feedback. The fact that they will be better able to care for themselves and others if they claim their time rather than let others dictate how they spend their time should be addressed. Such interventions would promote their authenticity, both within themselves and in their relationships.

Avoiding Body Comparison

It is important to raise girls' and women's awareness of the harmful nature of body comparison. If a woman perceives that another woman is evaluating her appearance, it can direct her attention to her body and to speculate on the meaning of this observer's evaluative gaze (e.g., "Why is she looking at my stomach; is it larger than hers?"). The onlooker conjointly experiences shifts in her own body image as she makes upward and downward social comparisons (Strelan & Hargreaves, 2005). Not surprisingly, these types of body comparisons can negatively affect women's relationships with each other. When college women compared themselves with thin-ideal media images, their overall hostility toward other women increased significantly (Loya, Cowan, & Walters, 2006). Moreover, women who reported higher body shame also reported greater hostility toward women. Here again, having girls and women contextualize sexual objectification and practice strategies in which they relate to their same-sex peers in nonappearance-oriented ways may discourage them from objectifying their peers as well as preserve the quality of their same-sex relationships. Once girls and women are aware that they are perpetuating sexual objectification by engaging in body comparison, they can be instructed to catch themselves in this behavior, remind themselves that this is a form of objectification, and reaffirm their commitment to not engage in this behavior.

Understanding, Confronting, and Regulating Exposure to Sexually Objectifying Media

Media images and messages that sexually objectify girls and women are both abundant and repetitive (see Chapter 3, this volume; Harper & Tiggemann, 2008; Harrison & Fredrickson, 2003; Kilbourne, 1994; Levy, 2005; Prichard & Tiggemann, 2005) and likely linger in women's minds (Quinn, Kallen, & Cathey, 2006). For a woman who is confronted daily by these media images and messages, the "big picture of her life is one of chronic, day-to-day self-objectification" (Harrison & Fredrickson, 2003, p. 229). Professionals must work with girls and women to actively protest offensive media images and messages and to educate marketers about the deleterious effects of sexual objectification.

We suggest that programs targeting how the thin ideal and body size are portrayed in the media could be adapted specifically to target sexual objectification in the media. For example, some prevention programs, such as GO GIRLS! (Piran, Levine, & Irving, 2000), include girls working together to explore how body size is portrayed in the media and to promote responsible advertising and advocate for positive body images by the media and major retailers. Girls often identify (a) the emotions attached to thin models and actresses (e.g., happiness), (b) the representation of body size (e.g., fat women are represented less than thin women), (c) the number of articles focused on appearance, (d) messages to get attention from boys or men, (e) the extent women bond together to engage in negative body talk and facilitate positive change, and (f) the number of articles or messages promoting self-acceptance.

Girls who have negative or positive reactions to media content are encouraged to write letters or send e-mails to representatives of the outlets. For instance, girls could write to companies who exclude and sexualize female athletes rather than value their skill (Harrison & Fredrickson, 2003). Girls are given guidelines on what to include in the letter or e-mail, such as statements of the issue/problem, how they feel about the issue/problem, and what they would like the representative to do differently. These letters and e-mails foster a sense of social activism against objectification, and research has supported their efficacy in reducing body dissatisfaction (Piran, 2001; Yamamiya,

Cash, Melnyk, Posavac, & Posavac, 2005). In addition, these programs buffer the impact of sexual objectification on disordered eating (McKinley & Wojszwilo, 1999).

Parents have an important role to play in regulating girls' exposure to the thin-ideal image. Existing resources designed to protect children from aggression in the media could offer guidance in this area. Although violent television, movies, and video games encourage aggression in children (Anderson et al., 2003), when parents limit the amount of time and types of games their children play, children show fewer aggressive behaviors (Gentile, Lynch, Linder, & Walsh, 2004). Active parental involvement in children's media usage, such as discussing the inappropriateness of violent solutions to real-life conflicts and generating alternative nonviolent solutions to problems, additionally reduces the impact of media violence on children (Anderson et al., 2003). In a similar vein, parents can limit the time spent watching or looking at media (the *E!* or *Entertainment* channel, fashion magazines) that emphasize the thin ideal, discuss the impossibility of the thin-ideal body type, and promote healthy (intuitive) eating rather than rigid dieting to reduce the impact of media standards of beauty on girls (Neumark-Sztainer, Eisenberg, Fulkerson, Story, & Larson, 2008). School curricula have been developed to teach children how to reduce the time and types of aggressive programs and violent games watched or played. These curricula show many positive effects, such as a reduction in aggressive behaviors on playgrounds (Robinson, Wilde, Navracruz, Haydel, & Varady, 2001). Perhaps educators can tailor these curricula to media images, offering practical strategies that children can use to reduce their exposure to the societal-ideal image.

Emphasizing Women's Internal Qualities

The Full of Ourselves prevention program (Steiner-Adair & Sjostrom, 2006) was specifically designed to enhance feelings of empowerment in girls (Grades 4–8) via positive strength-building group activities that help prevent self-objectification. After engaging in the program, which consists of eight 45- to 60-min sessions, the girls in 6th through 8th grades become peer leaders for the girls in 4th through 5th grades. Two adult leaders are needed to guide the sessions; these adult leaders are often teachers, guidance counselors, and school nurses.

One example of an activity to prevent self-objectification in the Full of Ourselves program is the Tree of Strength exercise. Girls are instructed to write the names of each important, admired, and respected woman in their lives on construction paper leaves. The girls then share the valued characteristics of each woman with other participants, while honoring her by placing her leaf on a large paper tree. Once each girl has participated, program facilitators reflect the inner characteristics mentioned by the girls and underscore the notion that these characteristics are more valuable than their external appearance.

Providing Embodying Experiences

Professionals can help schools and communities develop networks of positive peer groups for girls and women that do not focus on appearance or engage in fat/diet talk but that incorporate activities that promote connection with the body, intellectual concentration, and ways to contextualize sexual objectification. Program facilitators can help draw participants' awareness to how their body helps them perform daily activities and experience pleasures. Then, participants can reflect their appreciation for these gifts by promising that they will treat themselves with love, respect, and care. Professionals can also assist girls and women in generating and practicing their own affirmations that are individualized and honor their intellect, personality, and character. They can help girls and women practice these affirmations, perhaps in a flashcard format.

The Full of Ourselves program articulates guided meditation activities that help girls get in touch with the miraculous nature and the functionality of their bodies. For instance, in a body scan exercise, girls are guided to imagine that they are breathing through every pore of their skin, with every inhalation bringing "positive golden light" into their body and mind, which soaks up the light "like a sponge" and fills them with inner confidence and power (Steiner-Adair & Sjostrom, 2006, p. 8). An additional body scan activity teaches girls to be aware of their body as a source of power and life by having them pause and focus their awareness on one body part or function at a time, such as their breathing, posture, toes, feet, hands, feelings, temperature, and energy level.

Also, bioenergetic punches are practiced in Full of Ourselves. These punches are not a method to fight but a metaphor of girls' power to stand up for themselves and be confident. Girls are told to shake out their hands and feet, jog in place to get their energy moving, and then imagine themselves anchored to the ground with their knees bent and punch out into the air in front of them, one arm at a time (Steiner-Adair & Sjostrom, 2006).

Exercising to Honor the Body

Professionals need to promote a schema that centers on exercising for functionality and pleasure (e.g., health, enjoyment, mood, fitness) as this form of exercise is related to lower self-objectification, higher body satisfaction, and higher self-esteem (Prichard & Tiggemann, 2005; Strelan, Mehaffey, & Tiggemann, 2003). In contrast, exercising for appearance (e.g., weight control, body tone, increased attractiveness) is associated with the opposite trend. Girls need to be encouraged to participate in sports in which appearance, body shape, and weight are less important for success (e.g., basketball, soccer) because they promote a positive, connected, and functional orientation toward the body (Parsons & Betz, 2001; Petrie, 1996). It is imperative to help girls and women change their negative perceptions about exercise. Honoring the body's need for movement should be fun and pleasurable rather than overly intense, painful, strenuous, and militant. Examples may include playing games, gardening, hiking, Pilates, dance, and yoga. Girls and women should be discouraged from exercising in fitness centers that contain large mirrors and posters featuring sexualized and idealized female bodies, and where they may be subject to leering gazes and where women wear revealing clothing that trigger self-objectification and body comparison (Calogero & Pedrotty, 2007; Strelan et al., 2003). Instead, professionals may suggest exercising at home or outside with friends.

TREATING SELF-OBJECTIFICATION

Self-objectification is maintained by (a) disruptive cognitions internalized about the body, (b) shameful and nonappreciative attitudes toward the body, (c) maladaptive behaviors geared to alter the body, and (d) a lack of connection with the body. It is important to recognize that girls internalize appearance-related commentary and gender roles before they are cognitively able to contexualize this objectification. The strategies already covered acknowledge that girls have some preexisting degree of internalization and therefore can be included within prevention and therapy settings. In this section, we reveal additional techniques aimed at reducing girls' and women's tendency to continue their self-objectification patterns in more structured therapeutic contexts.

Placing Self-Objectification in Context

Clinicians and clients need to have a dialogue about the positive, yet short-lived and superficial, benefits awarded to those in society who engage in self-objectification. Acknowledging these societal rewards allows girls and women to externalize the blame for when they have engaged in self-objectification. Otherwise, they could possibly blame themselves once they are cognizant that they self-objectify.

Clinicians also need to address the harmful effects of sexual and self-objectification and help clients articulate specific ways in which objectification has limited their authenticity, development, relationships, body, mind, and spirit. Clients can be advised that because they are now aware and informed of its harmful effects, they have the ability to contextualize sexual objectification and not allow these instances to affect their self-worth. Such a balanced approach allows girls and women to focus efforts on developing inner character and a positive, connected stance with their bodies.

Managing Triggers to Self-Objectification

Because a contextualization schema cannot provide foolproof protection against diminished self-worth given the incessant societal pressures to self-objectify and the constant reminders of the societal benefits of engaging in self-objectification, clinicians must assist girls and women with recognizing and managing triggers of their self-objectification. For example, clinicians can help clients conduct an environmental or ecological analysis of objectifying circumstances. Clients record situations they are exposed to in their daily lives. Clinicians look objectively at this record and help clients pinpoint specific contexts (e.g., settings, groups of people, and/or individuals) that prompt their self-objectification. Clinicians could then work with clients to decrease the amount of time they spend in these situations (e.g., bars, fitness centers). Sometimes these situations cannot be avoided or arise unexpectedly (e.g., family gatherings). Then, clinicians could help clients develop individualized scripts and coping strategies that they can use to feel more empowered and retain their sense of self in these situations. Together, clinicians and clients can brainstorm methods for decreasing other social comparison opportunities (e.g., replacing fashion magazine subscriptions with magazine subscriptions of their favorite hobby) and work to replace maladaptive body-comparison thoughts (e.g., "I wish I had her body") with adaptive thoughts (e.g., "Inner qualities make people beautiful" and "Different body shapes add spice to life").

Actively Critiquing the Thin Ideal

Treatment programs can integrate cognitive dissonance interventions that require clients to actively critique the thin-ideal media image (adopting the thin ideal as the most desirable body type is a relevant aspect of self-objectification). Clients are encouraged to act contrary to a previously held attitude, which causes dissonance, and they are likely to change their attitudes to fit their behavior (Stice, Chase, Stormer, & Appel, 2001). To be effective, clients must believe that they voluntarily assume the counterattitudinal stance.

For instance, Stice et al. (2001) had young adult women who had internalized the thin ideal voluntarily take a stance against it. To induce women into adopting an anti-thin-ideal position, they were told that "research suggests that when women discuss ways to help younger girls avoid body image problems, the women often improve their own body satisfaction and related factors" (Stice et al., 2001, p. 249). Participants then performed verbal, written, and behavioral exercises such as (a) writing a one-page statement about the costs associated with the pursuit of the thin ideal that was later discussed by the group, (b) performing role-plays in which they had to resist peer pressure to adopt the thin ideal and dissuade chronic dieters from pursuing the thin ideal, (c) examining their reflection in a full-length mirror at home and recording their positive aspects, (d) articulating as a group how difficulties challenging the thin ideal could be surmounted, and (e) generating as a group recommendations that could help younger girls accept their bodies and avoid pursuing the thin ideal. Women experienced a reduction in thin-ideal internalization, dieting, body dissatisfaction, negative affect, and bulimic symptoms at a 4-week follow-up (Stice et al., 2001) and maintained their outcomes at a 2- to 3-year follow-up (Stice, Marti, Spoor, Presnell, & Shaw, 2008).

Cognitive dissonance prevention programs have been repeatedly studied with various samples of college women and adolescent girls (e.g., Stice, Shaw, Burton, & Wade, 2006). In fact, these programs meet the American Psychological Association (1995) criteria for an efficacious intervention and can be delivered at low cost by sororities (Becker, Ciao, & Smith, 2008). The Sorority Body Image Program, which is based on Stice et al.'s (2001) cognitive dissonance program, recruits sorority members who have already completed the SBIP to run the program as peer leaders, and 90 to 120 women complete the program annually (http://www.bodyimageprogram.org/program/). The Sorority Body Image Program offers guidelines for others who want to begin such programs at their schools, universities, or sororities (Becker et al., 2008).

Respecting the Body

Clinicians need to direct clients to appreciate their body (even though it may be inconsistent with the thin ideal) and honor it by engaging in healthy behaviors (Avalos, Tylka, & Wood-Barcalow, 2005). Clinicians could help clients heal their body hatred by reframing statements such as "My body betrayed me" to "I am betraying my body by hating how I look, taking for granted what it does for me and the pleasures it brings to me, and not providing the nourishment that it requires and deserves" and "I will respect my body by taking care of its needs." Clinicians could help clients identify negative, private appearance-focused body talk (e.g., "My thighs are huge and disgusting" and "I hate my flabby stomach") and replace them with positive functionality-focused statements (e.g., "My thighs are strong and allow me to enjoy dancing" and "My stomach allows me to carry children").

Sensate enhancement interventions, wherein clients focus on their senses when performing activities (e.g., cooking a nutritious meal, going on a nature hike, sitting in front of a crackling fire, moving rhythmically to music, stroking a pet), may be used to facilitate a connection with the pleasures and functions of the body. Clinicians may urge clients to create "comfort kits" by gathering soothing objects for all senses (e.g., comforting music, a calming picture, scented lotions, soft blanket) to enhance respect and appreciation for the functioning of the body.

Working to enhance embodiment (i.e., body awareness and responsiveness) can also help clients have a more positive and connected stance toward their bodies (Soth, 2006). Disembodiment occurs when individuals lose a sense of identification with their body by internalizing an observer's perspective, ignoring hunger and satiety cues, requiring the body to perform when it is injured or sick, abusing the body by rigidly dieting, misusing laxatives, exercising excessively, self-mutilation, and treating it as a substitute for the total person (Soth, 2006). One intervention that could encourage embodiment is Hatha yoga, a movement-based form of relaxation and meditation that combines physical postures, exercises, and breathing techniques. Women who completed a 2-month Hatha yoga immersion program reported decreased self-objectification and increased body awareness, positive affect, and life satisfaction (Impett, Daubenmier, & Hirschman, 2006). Embodiment also could be fostered by grounding techniques (e.g., imagery exercises such that they are a sturdy "oak tree") that orient clients to experience their body as strong and assertive and as a present inhabitant rather than an observer (Reichert, 1994). It should be noted to clients that grounding techniques promote empowerment, whereas rigid dieting promotes disempowerment by making them feel weak and fragile from hunger.

Eating to Honor the Body

Body appreciation and embodiment translate into nourishing the body (Avalos & Tylka, 2006). Clients need to be instructed that they are more likely to engage in healthy and balanced eating (a stated goal of many girls and women) if they initially respect and appreciate their body rather than abuse it or feel shameful toward it (Avalos & Tylka, 2006). Clinicians can inform clients that intuitive eating is an adaptive eating style that involves eating in response to internal hunger and satiety cues rather than situational or emotional triggers (Tylka, 2006). To follow intuitive eating, clients could be encouraged to give themselves unconditional permission to eat when they are physically hungry and what food they are hungry for, providing that they stop eating when they are physically satisfied.

Interventions exist that teach intuitive eating principles (Tribole & Resch, 2003), and they can be used to effectively treat clients with various levels of self-objectification and eating disturbance. The Center for Change in Orem, Utah, is an inpatient and outpatient treatment center for eating disorders that integrates intuitive eating principles into its program. Clients' hunger and satiety cues, however, may have been substantially weakened from prolonged attempts to suppress them. Before intuitive eating is incorporated, then, it often is necessary to have structured regular eating opportunities that reacquaint clients to what it feels like to be hungry and satisfied. Clients may benefit from reviewing physiological signals of hunger (e.g., stomach growling, difficulty concentrating, feeling weak, and headaches) and monitoring these signals throughout the day. Once reacquainted with hunger and satiety sensations, clients can be directed to map their hunger level on a scale from 1 (*starving*) to 10 (*completely stuffed*) and stay within the 3 (*moderately hungry*) to 6 (*slightly full*) range. Helping clients identify emotional triggers (e.g., boredom, loneliness, sadness, anxiety, joy) and situational triggers (e.g., having a jar of candy on their desk) that disrupt their tendency to intuitively eat is important. Differentiating emotions from physical hunger may be difficult. Clients can be instructed that if sensations of hunger come on suddenly, soon after a meal, or only experienced in the mouth, then they may reflect an emotional need rather than physical hunger.

Identifying and Coping With Emotions

Because self-objectification also suppresses internal awareness, clients may have difficulty identifying and appropriately expressing their emotions and needs. Mindfulness and emotion regulation techniques embedded in dialectical behavioral therapy (Linehan, 1993) would help clients connect with themselves by describing their emotional and physical experiences while remaining rational, and using various adaptive coping skills to deal effectively with emotions without eating (if not physically hungry) or avoiding to eat (if physically hungry). Clinicians could explain the physiological and biological aspects of anxiety and stress, such that clients with a hyperactive stress response may identify a nonthreatening situation as a potential threat and interpret everything through a negative cognitive filter (Beck, 1967). Instead, clients can learn to challenge the content of their irrational beliefs and replace these beliefs with rational ones. This process can help them (a) identify their negative emotions and thoughts, (b) determine the appropriateness of these emotions and thoughts from a more objective standpoint, and (c) cope in an active manner by attempting to directly alter the stress or reframe how they think about the stress (Holahan & Moos, 1987).

It is interesting to note that women are physiologically primed to deal with stress through the tend-and-befriend response, which involves nurturing activities that promote safety and reduce stress in the self and others and the need to create and maintain social support networks that aid in stress reduction (Taylor et al., 2000). When women engage in the tend-and-befriend response, oxytocin is believed to interact with estrogen to more greatly reduce the biological stress response. This reinforces the need for clinicians to help their female clients formulate and cultivate strong social support networks that are not appearance focused.

REDUCING THE CULTURAL ACCEPTANCE OF SEXUAL OBJECTIFICATION

In keeping with feminist theory, professionals must not place the burden of change solely on girls and women to fight against their own self-objectification. Girls can internalize sexual objectification before they have the cognitive capacity to challenge it. It is imperative that professionals also engage in social action: They must fight to reduce sexual objectification within society.

Publicizing Research on Sexual Objectification

Professionals need to disseminate their findings on the detrimental impact of sexual objectification. These findings would be of interest to members of their university or hospital research communications department who write press releases of new research for print and broadcast reporters. Press releases are an important tool for communicating information about sexual and self-objectification to national and international media outlets, including magazines, newspapers, radio, and television news and talk shows. Professionals must then be available to answer questions and clarify their findings to assure that they are presented accurately to the public.

Constructing Primary Prevention Programs for Caregivers

Professionals could design and implement community workshops and curriculum programs for parents or caregivers that are advertised and promoted at elementary and secondary schools. Ideally, professionals could obtain grants to evaluate these programs for their effectiveness, which would also increase funding agencies' awareness of the damage of sexual objectification and the pressing need for such programs.

Facilitators of such programs could help caregivers to (a) become aware of the toxic nature of sexual objectification, (b) appreciate differences in the content of messages that girls and boys receive regarding self-worth, and (c) recognize ways that they disproportionately perpetuate the link between girls' self-worth and their attractiveness and the link between boys' self-worth and their inner qualities and abilities. Facilitators can help caregivers identify how gender roles and sexism have shaped and constrained their daughters' and sons' development, as well as help caregivers articulate ways to promote gender equality in their children. Facilitators could also address how caregivers directly and indirectly encourage their sons to objectify girls and women (e.g., "Tell me what your new girlfriend looks like") and generate alternative socialization patterns with boys (e.g., "Tell me what your new girlfriend likes to do"). In a similar vein, facilitators could show caregivers how to reward and recognize girls for their internal qualities, such as behaving assertively and engaging in behaviors that hone their talents and educational efforts. Caregivers should have opportunities to identify specific instances whereby they encourage their daughters to self-objectify (e.g., "You look fat in that outfit," "Your friend is thinner than you," and "Makeup can help hide your flaws") and then help them generate statements and practice behaviors to use in place of the ones that are appearance focused (e.g., "You are amazing because of your sense of humor," "Pay attention to how you feel when playing your favorite sport," "You need to eat so you can focus on what you need to do"). These positive messages also need to be promoted within community-oriented interventions so that girls feel less appearance-related pressures from acquaintances and strangers as well as have social networks in which they feel unconditionally accepted.

Preventing Boys and Men From Sexually Objectifying Women

Prevention efforts need to be directed at lowering the frequency of which boys and men engage in sexual objectification. However, boys may actively resist curtailing their sexually objectifying behaviors, perhaps because they adopted the societal message that sexual objectification is innocuous, lack empathy toward women, feel entitled to objectify women, or view it as a means of affirming their masculinity (Good, Sherrod, & Dillon, 2000; Vandello, Bosson, Cohen, Burnaford, & Weaver, 2008). These sexist attitudes impede the process of reducing their sexual objectification, suggesting that change may be lengthy and difficult.

However, prevention programs that are successful in reducing another type of behavior stemming from sexism—sexual assault—could be used as a template for structuring programs to reduce sexual objectification. Drawing on belief system theory (Grube, Mayton, & Ball-Rokeach, 1994) and the elaboration likelihood model (Petty & Cacioppo, 1986), these programs are designed to increase men's motivation to hear a message and their ability to understand the message and perceive that it is relevant to them, without increasing defensiveness (Foubert, 2000).

One such program is The Men's Program. In this program, male facilitators show the One in Four (2000) training video to a group of men, which depicts a scenario of a male-on-male rape. The assailant is identified as heterosexual to debunk the myth that male-on-male rapes are perpetrated by gay men and to understand how heterosexual perpetrators use rape as a means of exerting power and control over another. Facilitators then link this scenario to situations of male-on-female rape to facilitate men's empathy toward rape survivors and to teach men how to support a rape survivor, confront jokes about rape, and reduce sexist behaviors toward women. To further facilitate the lesson, facilitators use guided imagery by having men imagine that a woman close to them is raped while a bystander watches and does nothing. The men then brainstorm ways that they could intervene in such a situation. This program has been shown to produce a variety of attitudinal and behavioral changes (e.g., increasing empathy for rape survivors, understanding the gravity of rape, confronting rather than laughing at rape jokes, helping actual sexual assault survivors, and reducing sexist behavior) in college men, fraternity men, high school boys, male athletes, men in the military, men who have committed sexual assault, and men of various ethnic identities (Foubert, 2000, 2005; Foubert & Cremedy, 2007; Foubert & Perry, 2007).

We suggest that programs targeting sexual objectification could incorporate similar features, such as male presenters, an all-male audience, and showing men being sexually objectified or assaulted. One important instructional tool that could be incorporated in these efforts is the film *Tough Guise: Violence, Media and the Crisis in Masculinity*, narrated by writer and filmmaker Jackson Katz (Jhally, 1999). Because Katz is a knowledgeable male authority figure, boys and men may be more likely to internalize his message. This film reveals how media promote masculine ideology, the destructiveness of adopting such an ideology, and strategies for men to adopt more effective relationships. Direct negative consequences for men are revealed in this video, which increases the relevance of the message to them (Petty & Cacioppo, 1986). After showing the film, male facilitators could dialogue with the group about appropriate ways to support girls and women in their attempts to contextualize sexual objectification and how to become active in teaching other boys and men ways of relating to women without sexually objectifying them. For example, boys and men could work alongside women and other marginalized groups to speak out against objectification, violence, sexism, and heterosexism. They can also model less rigid male roles by articulating and showing emotions and affection within relationships, committing to nonviolence while still acting in a courageous manner, not looking at pornography or partaking in activities that demean and/or sexualize women, and treating women with respect.

Combating Weightism

To tackle self-objectification fully, we must also recognize that the objectification of women is inextricably tied with *weightism*, that is, a prejudice or bias against people whose bodies carry more fat and/or represent the fatter end of the weight spectrum. The belief that "fat is bad" and "thin is good" is perpetuated at almost every level of society. The media's portrayal of an ultra-thin body type as the only attractive shape for women is harmful to women for many reasons. First, and most strikingly, the images are not real—this beauty ideal is impossible to achieve as women cannot airbrush their bodies in real time in real life. Second, even though this beauty ideal is impossible, it is projected as achievable, as long as girls and women buy and use certain products that are paired with it. Third, weightist beliefs and images foster greater internalization of the thin ideal among girls and women, as they are paired with glamour, wealth, happiness, confidence, and popularity (Engeln-Maddox, 2006; Evans, 2003; Grabe, Ward, & Hyde, 2008). Fourth, these narrowly defined images of beauty are viewed as a normative comparison group against which girls and women should be compared and judged.

We encourage professionals to be more proactive in raising awareness among media outlets about their role in perpetuating these toxic weightist beliefs and images that harm girls and women, thereby holding them more accountable for the negative consequences of these media. To be sure, this would be no small task but would require numerous phone calls, e-mails, and letters over an extended period of time. In these efforts, we would suggest that professionals form or join networks (e.g., Listservs) that could work collectively to target weightism in such outlets. Two resources that do confront the objectification of women in the media include Ms. Magazine, which targets specific advertisements, and Media Watch, which informs people of sexist displays.

In considering the role of media outlets, one should not assume that all companies disregard the negative impact of weightist messages and images on girls and women; however, they may present the thin-ideal image because they believe that this image is most effective for selling products. Given their business motives, media representatives could be informed about research that has tested this belief. For example, Dittmar and Howard (2004) found that average-size models are just as effective at selling products as thin models but do not contribute to girls' and women's negative body image. Indeed, the Dove campaign has reported increased sales by using a much wider range of images that represent women across the weight and age spectrum to promote their products. Their website (http://www.campaignforrealbeauty.com/) offers practical interventions for promoting positive body image that target girls and mothers. The campaign offers workshops (i.e., Body Talk) across the United States, and its online materials suggest ways for mothers to build healthy relationships with—and encourage a healthy body image among—their daughters. These workshops can be organized by anyone in their hometown (for more information, see http://www.campaignforrealbeauty.com/dsef/pdfs/BodyTalk_Excerpt.pdf).

It is encouraging to see such fundamental shifts in the representation of women, especially by such influential organizations. Yet, good intentions by media outlets can still perpetuate mixed or harmful messages about women's bodies if they fail to consider the context in which the messages of positive body image will be communicated. Many magazines and other media outlets incorporate stories and articles that promote body acceptance and admonish disordered eating. For example, in the May 2008 issue of *Self* magazine, an article was published that highlighted chronic dieting and other maladaptive eating behaviors as being just as harmful as bona fide clinical eating disorders. However, this article was not headlined on the cover of the magazine. Instead, many of the cover's headlines and images showcased the very messages about appearance and weight loss that the article on disordered eating was trying to challenge. Thus, we would underscore the importance of highlighting not only the direct negative messages themselves but also the negative consequences that stem from pairing weight loss messages with articles on positive body image and adaptive eating (Kilbourne, 1994).

Similarly, professionals must underscore to family, partners, and friends the harm caused when attention is called to girls' and women's body shape and weight. Comments about appearance, especially about weight and shape, constitute a form of sexual objectification (Fredrickson & Roberts, 1997; Kozee, Tylka, Augustus-Horvath, & Denchik, 2007). These comments, regardless of whether they are positive or negative, do not facilitate positive body image but instead contribute to higher levels of self-surveillance, body dissatisfaction, shame, and disordered eating in girls and women (Calogero et al., 2009; Tylka & Hill, 2004). People may erroneously think that being described as "cute," "pretty," "thin," or "adorable" bolsters girls' and women's self-esteem and body image, but the opposite is also likely to occur, especially over time. To counter this myth, we suggest that professionals share research findings that demonstrate that even when girls and women feel good about being complimented on their appearance, they still report higher levels of chronic body monitoring and body dissatisfaction (Calogero et al., 2009). We can instruct family, friends, and partners on how to promote girls' and women's body acceptance and body esteem by deemphasizing physical appearance and emphasizing the functionality and strength of women's bodies (Avalos & Tylka, 2006).

Combating weightism also requires a focus on reducing the incidence and cultural acceptance of fat talk and dieting talk (Gapinski, Brownell, & LaFrance, 2003; Nichter & Vuckovic, 1994). *Fat talk* consists of individuals, often thin or average weight, voicing to others that they are fat in a self-deprecating manner (e.g., "I look so fat and hideous in this outfit," "I can't believe how much weight I've gained," "You're a lot thinner than me"). Fat talk allows girls and women to be the first surveyor or critic of their appearance, as they assume that others will be objectifying their body by evaluating it according to its semblance to the thin ideal. Girls and women also use fat talk to gain reassurance from friends and others that they are not fat, to facilitate body comparisons, and to bond with other women, as the shared value of thinness offers them a sense of solidarity and group affiliation (Gapinski et al., 2003). Similarly, *dieting talk* occurs when women discuss their diets or intentions to diet, for the same purposes as fat talk. Dieting talk also reinforces social connections by soliciting encouragement and fostering a sense of being united against fat. It is often portrayed within mainstream media advertisements such as Lean Cuisine and Progresso soup commercials that portray women, who are often thin, in an office setting or a party talking about the type of diet they are on, their struggles with finding a tasty diet food, how many calories their meals have, and how much weight they want to lose.

Fat talk and dieting talk need to be addressed at a cultural level. The Tri Delta sorority has organized an international Fat Talk Free Week in October that promotes a moratorium against this style of interaction. Community programs and campuses could use this week as a springboard to raise individuals' consciousness about this insidious form of bonding and commit to eliminating this type of talk among friends. Professionals could work with girls and women to critique media portrayals of women engaged in fat and/or dieting talk and construct more positive interactions (Piran, Levine, & Steiner-Adair, 1999). In addition, professionals could work toward dissuading advertising companies from using these types of scenarios to sell products and suggest alternative interactions that portray authentic and adaptive social relationships. Consequently, girls and women may feel less compelled to criticize and change their bodies.

CONCLUSION AND FUTURE DIRECTIONS

In this chapter, we drew from feminist, gestalt, cognitive–behavioral, and interpersonal theory and research to review strategies aimed at fighting self-objectification from prevention and treatment standpoints. We consider it imperative that professionals work to lower the incidence of sexual objectification within Western culture, raise girls' and women's consciousness of sexual objectification and the construction of media images, help them develop a contextualization schema to combat objectifying societal messages, foster and maintain their awareness and appreciation of their bodies, challenge their unrealistic beliefs associated with tying their self-worth to their appearance, and respect themselves by nourishing their bodies and asserting their rights.

We note gaps in this literature as well as avenues for future research. First, most of the findings on self-objectification have been based on samples of predominantly White and heterosexual high school or college women. There is very limited research on ethnicity and sexual orientation, and no research on socioeconomic status, to provide any definitive therapeutic strategies for diverse women. The therapeutic implications discussed here, then, should be considered tentative until further support is accrued. However, clinicians should be prepared to discuss the effects of sexual objectification with clients regardless of their ethnic background. In addition, sexual objectification contributes to the self-surveillance of both lesbian and heterosexual women; therefore, clinicians must not assume that a lesbian identity protects women from internalizing sexual objectification and focusing on their appearance (Haines et al., 2008; Hill & Fischer, 2008; Kozee & Tylka, 2006). Clients who struggle financially and the unique instances of sexual objectification they may face need to be investigated.

Second, it is necessary to create and evaluate programs to lower the frequency to which boys and men sexually objectify girls and women and endorse gender roles and masculine ideology. These programs could include strategies in The Men's Program (Foubert, 2005) and cognitive dissonance–based interventions (Stice et al., 2001). Specifically, male program leaders could have boys and men perform verbal, written, and behavioral exercises in which they take a stance against sexual objectification and masculine ideology. For example, boys and men could write a statement about the costs (to themselves and women) associated with sexual objectification (which is then discussed as a group), perform role-plays in which they had to individually dissuade other boys and men who acted in objectifying or gender role–specific ways, practice resisting pressure from other boys and men to objectify women in various situations and to view pornography, participate in group discussion about how difficulties challenging sexual objectification could be surmounted, and generate recommendations that could help other boys and men from engaging in gender role–specific behaviors and sexual objectification.

Third, sexual objectification is one limited aspect of sexism. Although many interventions discussed in this chapter may reduce sexist attitudes and behaviors, they do not combat all dimensions of sexism that overtly and covertly control women. The patriarchal status quo works to maintain women's self-objectification, with men benefiting in many ways from women being preoccupied with their appearance (Calogero & Jost, 2010). Therefore, much theoretical and empirical attention needs to be directed at how the broader construct of sexism contributes to self-objectification and how to effectively combat sexism within the prevention and treatment of self-objectification.

REFERENCES

American Psychological Association Task Force on Psychological Intervention Guidelines. (1995). *Template for developing guidelines: Interventions for mental dis-*

orders and psychological aspects of physical disorders. Washington, DC: American Psychological Association.

Anderson, C. A., Berkowitz, L., Donnerstein, E., Huesmann, L. R., Johnson, J., Linz, D., . . . Wartella, E. (2003). The influence of media violence on youth. *Psychological Science in the Public Interest, 4,* 81–110.

Avalos, L. C., & Tylka, T. L. (2006). Exploring a model of intuitive eating with college women. *Journal of Counseling Psychology, 53,* 486–497. doi:10.1037/0022-0167.53.4.486

Avalos, L. C., Tylka, T. L., & Wood-Barcalow, N. (2005). The Body Appreciation Scale: Development and psychometric evaluation. *Body Image, 2,* 285–297. doi:10.1016/j.bodyim.2005.06.002

Beck, A. T. (1967). *Depression: Clinical, experimental, and theoretical aspects.* New York, NY: Harper & Row.

Becker, C. B., Ciao, A. C., & Smith, L. M. (2008). Moving from efficacy to effectiveness in eating disorders prevention: The Sorority Body Image Program. *Cognitive and Behavioral Practice, 15,* 18–27. doi:10.1016/j.cbpra.2006.07.006

Breines, J. G., Crocker, J., & Garcia, J. A. (2008). Self-objectification and well-being in women's daily lives. *Personality and Social Psychology Bulletin, 34,* 583–598. doi:10.1177/0146167207313727

Calogero, R. M., Herbozo, S., & Thompson, J. K. (2009). Complementary weightism: The potential costs of appearance-related commentary for women's self-objectification. *Psychology of Women Quarterly, 33,* 120–132. doi:10.1111/j.1471-6402.2008.01479.x

Calogero, R. M., & Jost, J. T. (2010). *Self-subjugation among women: Stereotype exposure, self-objectification, and the buffering function of the need to avoid closure.* Manuscript submitted for publication.

Calogero, R. M., & Pedrotty, K. N. (2007). Daily practices for mindful exercise. In L. L'Abate, D. Embry, & M. Baggett (Eds.), *Handbook of low-cost preventive interventions for physical and mental health: Theory, research, and practice* (pp. 141–160). New York, NY: Springer-Verlag.

Dittmar, H., & Howard, S. (2004). Professional hazards? The impact of models' body size on advertising effectiveness and women's body-focused anxiety in professions that do and do not emphasize the cultural ideal of thinness. *British Journal of Social Psychology, 43,* 477–497. doi:10.1348/0144666042565407

Engeln-Maddox, R. (2006). Buying a beauty standard or dreaming of a new life? Expectations associated with media ideals. *Psychology of Women Quarterly, 30,* 258–266. doi:10.1111/j.1471-6402.2006.00294.x

Evans, P. C. (2003). "If only I were thin like her, maybe I could be happy like her": The self-implications of associating a thin female ideal with life success. *Psychology of Women Quarterly, 27,* 209–214. doi:10.1111/1471-6402.00100

Foubert, J. D. (2000). The longitudinal effects of a rape-prevention program on fraternity men's attitudes, behavioral intent and behavior. *Journal of American College Health, 48,* 158–163. doi:10.1080/07448480009595691

Foubert, J. D. (2005). *The Men's Program: A peer education guide to rape prevention* (3rd ed.). New York, NY: Routledge.

Foubert, J. D., & Cremedy, B. J. (2007). Reactions of men of color to a commonly used rape prevention program: Attitude and predicted behavior changes. *Sex Roles, 57,* 137–144. doi:10.1007/s11199-007-9216-2

Foubert, J. D., & Perry, B. C. (2007). Creating lasting attitude and behavior change in fraternity members and male student athletes: The qualitative impact of an empathy-based rape prevention program. *Violence Against Women, 13,* 70–86. doi:10.1177/1077801206295125

Fredrickson, B. L., & Roberts, T.-A. (1997). Objectification theory: Toward understanding women's lived experiences and mental health risks. *Psychology of Women Quarterly, 21,* 173–206. doi:10.1111/j.1471-6402.1997.tb00108.x

Freeman, J. (1979). How to discriminate among women without really trying. In J. Freeman (Ed.), *Women: A feminist perspective* (2nd ed., pp. 194–208). Palo Alto, CA: Mayfield.

Gapinski, K. D., Brownell, K. D., & LaFrance, M. (2003). Body objectification and "fat talk": Effects on emotion, motivation, and cognitive performance. *Sex Roles, 48,* 377–388. doi:10.1023/A:1023516209973

Gentile, D. A., Lynch, P. J., Linder, J. R., & Walsh, D. A. (2004). The effects of violent video game habits on adolescent aggressive attitudes and behaviors. *Journal of Adolescence, 27,* 5–22. doi:10.1016/j.adolescence.2003.10.002

Good, G. E., Sherrod, N. B., & Dillon, M. G. (2000). Masculine gender role stressors and men's health. In R. M. Eisler & M. Hersen (Eds.), *Handbook of gender, culture, and health* (pp. 63–81). Mahwah, NJ: Erlbaum.

Grabe, S., Hyde, J. S., & Lindberg, S. M. (2007). Body objectification and depression in adolescents: The role of gender, shame, and rumination. *Psychology of Women Quarterly, 31,* 164–175. doi:10.1111/j.1471-6402.2007.00350.x

Grabe, S., Ward, L. M., & Hyde, J. S. (2008). The role of the media in body image concerns among women: A meta-analysis of experimental and correlational studies. *Psychological Bulletin, 134,* 460–476. doi:10.1037/0033-2909.134.3.460

Grube, J. W., Mayton, D. M., & Ball-Rokeach, S. J. (1994). Inducing change in values, attitudes, and behaviors: Belief system theory and the method of value self-confrontation. *Journal of Social Issues, 50,* 153–173.

Haines, M. E., Erchull, M. J., Liss, M., Turner, D. L., Nelson, J. A., Ramsey, L. R., & Hurt, M. M. (2008). Predictors and effects of self-objectification in lesbians. *Psychology of Women Quarterly, 32,* 181–187. doi:10.1111/j.1471-6402.2008.00422.x

Harper, B., & Tiggemann, M. (2008). The effect of thin ideal media images on women's self-objectification, mood, and body image. *Sex Roles, 58,* 649–657. doi:10.1007/s11199-007-9379-x

Harrell, Z. A. T., Fredrickson, B. L., Pomerleau, C. S., & Nolen-Hoeksema, S. (2006). The role of trait self-objectification in smoking among college women. *Sex Roles, 54,* 735–743. doi:10.1007/s11199-006-9041-z

Harrison, K., & Fredrickson, B. L. (2003). Women's sports media, self-objectification, and mental health in Black and White adolescent females. *Journal of Communication, 53,* 216–232. doi:10.1111/j.1460-2466.2003.tb02587.x

Hill, M. S., & Fischer, A. R. (2008). Examining objectification theory: Lesbian and heterosexual women's experiences with sexual- and self-objectification. *Counseling Psychologist, 36,* 745–776. doi:10.1177/0011000007301669

Holahan, C. J., & Moos, R. H. (1987). Risk, resistance, and psychological distress: A longitudinal analysis with adults and children. *Journal of Abnormal Psychology, 96,* 3–13. doi:10.1037/0021-843X.96.1.3

Impett, E. A., Daubenmier, J. J., & Hirschman, A. L. (2006). Minding the body: Yoga, embodiment, and well-being. *Sexuality Research & Social Policy, 3,* 39–48.

Jhally, S. (Executive Producer and Director). (1999). *Tough guise (unabridged): Violence, media, & the crisis in masculinity* [Motion picture]. Available from Media Education Foundation, http://www.mediaed.org

Kilbourne, J. (1994). Still killing us softly: Advertising and the obsession with thinness. In P. Fallon, M. A. Katzman, & S. C. Wooley (Eds.), *Feminist perspectives on eating disorders* (pp. 395–418). New York, NY: Guilford Press.

Kozee, H. B., & Tylka, T. L. (2006). A test of objectification theory with lesbian women. *Psychology of Women Quarterly, 30,* 348–357. doi:10.1111/j.1471-6402. 2006.00310.x

Kozee, H. B., Tylka, T. L., Augustus-Horvath, C. L., & Denchik, A. L. (2007). Development and psychometric evaluation of the Interpersonal Sexual Objectification Scale. *Psychology of Women Quarterly, 31,* 176–189. doi:10.1111/j.1471-6402. 2007.00351.x

Langelan, M. J. (1993). *Back off: How to confront and stop sexual harassment and harassers.* New York, NY: Simon & Shuster.

Levy, A. (2005). *Feminist chauvinist pigs: Women and the rise of raunch culture.* New York, NY: Free Press.

Linehan, M. (1993). *Skills training manual for treating borderline personality disorder.* New York, NY: Guilford Press.

Loya, B. N., Cowan, G., & Walters, C. (2006). The role of social comparison and body consciousness in women's hostility toward women. *Sex Roles, 54,* 575–583. doi:10.1007/s11199-006-9024-0

McKinley, N. M., & Wojszwilo, A. (1999, March). *Feminism, political activism, and women's body consciousness.* Paper presented at the annual meeting of the Association of Women in Psychology, Providence, RI.

Moradi, B., Dirks, D., & Matteson, A. V. (2005). Roles of sexual objectification experiences and internalization of standards of beauty in eating disorder symptomatology: A test and extension of objectification theory. *Journal of Counseling Psychology, 52,* 420–428. doi:10.1037/0022-0167.52.3.420

Neumark-Sztainer, D., Eisenberg, M. E., Fulkerson, J. A., Story, M., & Larson, N. I. (2008). Family meals and disordered eating in adolescents: Longitudinal findings from Project EAT. *Archives of Pediatrics & Adolescent Medicine, 162,* 17–22. doi:10.1001/archpediatrics.2007.9

Nichter, M., & Vuckovic, N. (1994). Fat talk: Body image among adolescent girls. In N. Sault (Ed.), *Many mirrors: Body image and social relations* (pp. 109–131). New Brunswick, NJ: Rutgers University Press.

One in Four, Inc. (Producer). (2000). *The police rape training video* [Motion picture]. Available from One in Four, Inc., William and Mary School of Education, Jones 320, P.O. Box 8795, Williamsburg, VA 23187-8795.

Parsons, E. M., & Betz, N. E. (2001). The relationship of participation in sports and physical activity to body objectification, instrumentality, and locus of control among young women. *Psychology of Women Quarterly, 25,* 209–222. doi:10.1111/1471-6402.00022

Peterson, R. D., Grippo, K. P., & Tantleff-Dunn, S. (2008). Empowerment and powerlessness: A closer look at the relationship between feminism, body image, and eating disturbance. *Sex Roles, 58,* 639–648. doi:10.1007/s11199-007-9377-z

Petrie, T. A. (1996). Differences between male and female college lean sports athletes, nonlean sports athletes, and nonathletes on behavioral and psychological indices of eating disorders. *Journal of Applied Sport Psychology, 8,* 218–230. doi:10.1080/10413209608406478

Petty, R. E., & Cacioppo, J. T. (1986). *Communication and persuasion: Central and peripheral routes to attitude change.* New York, NY: Springer.

Piran, N. (2001). Reinhabiting the body. *Feminism & Psychology, 11,* 172–176. doi:10.1177/0959353501011002006

Piran, N., Levine, M. P., & Irving, L. M. (2000). GO GIRLS! Media literacy, activism, and advocacy project. *Healthy Weight Journal, 14,* 89–90.

Piran, N., Levine, M. P., & Steiner-Adair, C. (Eds.). (1999). *Preventing eating disorders: A handbook of interventions and special challenges.* Philadelphia, PA: Brunner/Mazel.

Prichard, I., & Tiggemann, M. (2005). Objectification in fitness centers: Self-objectification, body dissatisfaction, and disordered eating in aerobic instructors and aerobic participants. *Sex Roles, 53,* 19–28. doi:10.1007/s11199-005-4270-0

Quinn, D. M., Kallen, R. W., & Cathey, C. (2006). Body on my mind: The lingering effect of state self-objectification. *Sex Roles, 55,* 869–874. doi:10.1007/s11199-006-9140-x

Quinn, D. M., Kallen, R. W., Twenge, J. M., & Fredrickson, B. L. (2006). The disruptive effect of self-objectification on performance. *Psychology of Women Quarterly, 30,* 59–64. doi:10.1111/j.1471-6402.2006.00262.x

Reichert, E. (1994). Expressive group therapy with adult survivors of sexual abuse. *Family Therapy, 21,* 99–105.

Roberts, T.-A. (2004). Female trouble: The Menstrual Self-Evaluation Scale and women's self-objectification. *Psychology of Women Quarterly, 28,* 22–26. doi:10.1111/j.1471-6402.2004.00119.x

Roberts, T.-A., & Waters, P. L. (2004). Self-objectification and that "not so fresh feeling": Feminist therapeutic interventions for healthy female embodiment. In J. C. Chrisler (Ed.), *From menarche to menopause: The female body in feminist therapy* (pp. 5–21). New York, NY: Haworth Press.

Robinson, T. N., Wilde, M. L., Navracruz, L. C., Haydel, K. F., & Varady, A. (2001). Effects of reducing children's television and video game use on aggressive behavior: A randomized controlled trial. *Archives of Pediatrics & Adolescent Medicine, 155,* 17–23.

Sanchez, D. T., & Kwang, T. (2007). When the relationship becomes her: Revisiting women's body concerns from a relationship contingency perspective. *Psychology of Women Quarterly, 31,* 401–414. doi:10.1111/j.1471-6402.2007.00389.x

Soth, M. (2006). What therapeutic hope for a subjective mind in an objectified body? *Body, Movement and Dance in Psychotherapy, 1,* 43–56. doi:10.1080/17432970500418385

Steiner-Adair, C., & Sjostrom, L. (2006). *Full of Ourselves: A wellness program to advance girl power, health, and leadership.* New York, NY: Teachers College Press.

Stice, E., Chase, A., Stormer, S., & Appel, A. (2001). A randomized trial of a dissonance-based eating disorder prevention program. *International Journal of Eating Disorders, 29,* 247–262. doi:10.1002/eat.1016

Stice, E., Marti, C. N., Spoor, S., Presnell, K., & Shaw, H. (2008). Dissonance and healthy weight eating disorder prevention programs: Long-term effects from a randomized efficacy trial. *Journal of Consulting and Clinical Psychology, 76,* 329–340. doi:10.1037/0022-006X.76.2.329

Stice, E., Shaw, H., Burton, E., & Wade, E. (2006). Dissonance and healthy weight eating disorder prevention programs: A randomized efficacy trial. *Journal of Consulting and Clinical Psychology, 74,* 263–275. doi:10.1037/0022-006X.74.2.263

Strelan, P., & Hargreaves, D. (2005). Women who objectify other women: The vicious circle of objectification? *Sex Roles, 52,* 707–712. doi:10.1007/s11199-005-3737-3

Strelan, P., Mehaffey, S. J., & Tiggemann, M. (2003). Self-objectification and esteem in young women: The mediating role of reasons for exercise. *Sex Roles, 48,* 89–95. doi:10.1023/A:1022300930307

Szymanski, D. M., & Henning, S. L. (2007). The role of self-objectification in women's depression: A test of objectification theory. *Sex Roles, 56,* 45–53. doi:10.1007/s11199-006-9147-3

Taylor, S. E., Klein, L. C., Lewis, B. P., Gruenewald, T. L., Gurung, R. A. R., & Updegraff, J. A. (2000). Biobehavioral response to stress in females: Tend-and-befriend, not fight-or-flight. *Psychological Review, 107,* 411–429. doi:10.1037/0033-295X.107.3.411

Tiggemann, M., & Slater, A. (2001). A test of objectification theory in former dancers and non-dancers. *Psychology of Women Quarterly, 25,* 57–64. doi:10.1111/1471-6402.00007

Tribole, E., & Resch, E. (2003). *Intuitive eating: A revolutionary program that works.* New York, NY: St. Martin's Griffin.

Tylka, T. L. (2006). Development and psychometric evaluation of a measure of intuitive eating. *Journal of Counseling Psychology, 53,* 226–240. doi:10.1037/0022-0167.53.2.226

Tylka, T. L., & Hill, M. S. (2004). Objectification theory as it relates to disordered eating among college women. *Sex Roles, 51,* 719–730. doi:10.1007/s11199-004-0721-2

Unger, R. K. (1979). *Female and male.* New York, NY: Harper & Row.

Vandello, J. A., Bosson, J. K., Cohen, D., Burnaford, R. M., & Weaver, J. R. (2008). Precarious manhood. *Journal of Personality and Social Psychology, 95,* 1325–1339. doi:10.1037/a0012453

Yamamiya, Y., Cash, T. F., Melnyk, S. E., Posavac, H. D., & Posavac, S. S. (2005). Women's exposure to thin-and-beautiful media images: Body image effects of media-ideal internalization and impact-reduction interventions. *Body Image, 2,* 74–80. doi:10.1016/j.bodyim.2004.11.001

V

CONCLUDING REMARKS

10

FUTURE DIRECTIONS FOR RESEARCH AND PRACTICE

RACHEL M. CALOGERO, STACEY TANTLEFF-DUNN,
AND J. KEVIN THOMPSON

This volume has showcased the vast interest in self-objectification as a topic of scientific inquiry and social action from scholars across perspectives. Objectification theory has emerged as an important systematic framework for investigating the effects of sexual and self-objectification among women. Multiple perspectives on the underlying causal forces that bring about self-objectification were described, and a common theme across these perspectives is that the sexual objectification of women's bodies offers the most direct link to women's self-objectification. There is clear evidence that self-objectification is associated with a wide variety of negative consequences, threatening the healthy development and well-being of girls and women across multiple domains of living. Less is known about how to counteract self-objectification, but we hope that the ideas put forth in these chapters will inspire more empirical work in this direction. We conclude this volume with several further perspectives on the topic of self-objectification with the hope of informing scholarly and applied pursuits in this critical area of women's lived experience.

To advance research in this area, we must continue to refine the conceptual and operational meaning of self-objectification as a phenomenon. A key aspect of self-objectification is the *doubling* of women's attention that disrupts their flow of consciousness: "She becomes an object, and she sees herself as object . . . it seems to her that she has been doubled; instead of coinciding exactly with herself, she now begins to exist outside" (de Beauvoir, 1952/1989, p. 337). In this way, self-objectification involves taking a view of the self from one's own vantage point and from the perspective of another person simultaneously, thereby dividing women's attentional focus. This doubled or dual perspective on the self is not wholly captured by measures of self-objectification, yet this may be the process that is most critical to understanding the negative effects of self-objectification in women.

Another key aspect of the conceptualization of self-objectification is that women come to take a (heterosexual) male observer's perspective on their own bodies: They are watching themselves from the perspective of the internalized "panoptical male connoisseur" (Bartky, 1990, p. 72). This phenomenological experience of viewing oneself through the lens of the male gaze is not adequately captured with extant measures of self-objectification. Further, self-objectification involves a disconnection and distancing between the self and the body, which would seem to be an important aspect of the phenomenon to measure.

In summary, self-objectification in women appears to have multiple components in need of conceptual and operational development. In addition, there are other conceptually overlapping constructs that should be clarified. Further consideration should be given to whether self-objectification (as measured by the Self-Objectification Questionnaire) and self-surveillance (as measured by the Objectified Body Consciousness Scale) should be conceptualized as independent constructs or subdimensions of the same construct. We need more psychometric analyses, including exploratory and confirmatory analyses, to help discern the overlap and distinctiveness of possible subdimensions of self-objectification. Consideration of other appearance attributes that may constitute sexually objectified attributes or body parts (e.g., skin color, lips) would broaden our assessment of self-objectification and possibly improve the applicability of these measures to more diverse groups of women.

To understand the similarities and differences between different types of cultural objectification, we need greater clarity in the operationalization and measurement of the different types, such as sexual objectification, social objectification, or racial objectification. Finally, we need better assessment tools of state self-objectification that would be sensitive to shifts in self-objectification across a variety of contexts, especially real-world settings in which more research on sexual and self-objectification is needed. Perhaps the most important call to scholars for future research in this area is to further clarify operational definitions of self-objectification and refine the measurement tools to study it in diverse groups of women.

CAUSES

Taking as our starting point that sexual objectification plays a significant etiological role in women's self-objectification, we would ask for a wider formulation of how the power of the objectified gaze is sustained. In particular, we would invite consideration of the following topics that focus on wider causes and conceptual issues that need empirical clarification: (a) the fast and thorough proliferation of sexualized images, (b) the internalization of the anonymous other, (c) the harm and violence against women, and (d) socially sanctioned sexist ideology in patriarchal societies.

Fast and Thorough

A premise of objectification theory is that "the mass media's proliferation of sexualized images of the female body is fast and thorough" (Fredrickson & Roberts, 1997, p. 177). The pervasive sexualization and sexual objectification of girls and women in American culture (and similarly situated Westernized societies) is undeniably linked to the socialization of girls and women as sex objects (see Chapter 3, this volume). We would argue that the magnitude of this effect has increased due to the sheer scope and accessibility of explicitly sexualized depictions of girls and women with one click of the mouse or cell phone application. Because of the Internet, the objectification of women is even faster and more thorough—and more extreme. According to Paul (2005), the number of pornographic pages on the Internet increased by 1,800% between 1998 and 2004. Sexually explicit content that objectifies women includes frequent full-screen genitalia shots (Cowan, Lee, Levy, & Snyder, 1988); male ejaculation on the body, on the face, or in the mouth of a woman (Brosius, Weaver, & Staab, 1993); and the depiction of women in a passive role (Ertel, 1990). Moreover, people do not have to intentionally look for sex online to view it, as unsolicited pop-up advertisements and e-mail browser sidebars regularly expose women's breasts and buttocks. Given the harmful effects of sexual and self-objectification on women's performance (Chapter 6), mental health (Chapter 7), and a variety of other subjective experiences (Moradi & Huang, 2008), the systematic investigation of the effects of these increasingly mainstream pornographic images and objectifying advertisements, especially when they occur in educational or occupational contexts, is imperative.

These web images are not confined to Internet use in the privacy of one's home. The availability of cell phones with Internet capability brings a wide variety of sexual content into the public arena: Anywhere that cell phones are used there is the potential for sexual content to be displayed and dispersed. This means that there are more spontaneous opportunities for women to encounter sexual objectification in their daily environments—an interaction between media and interpersonal encounters of sexual objectification. A recent phenomenon that has caught the attention of the media is *sexting*—the text messaging of pornographic or nude pictures—because this activity was linked recently to two teenage suicides (Meacham, 2009). In one of these cases, a 13-year-old girl sent a picture of her breasts to a young boy she liked, and the picture was circulated widely within and outside her school. She was severely bullied and ridiculed by peers who frequently called her a "whore" and a "slut." She eventually hung herself. Objectification theory is well positioned to offer some explanation for this tragedy.

In Westernized societies, women's bodies continue to function as their primary social and economic currency (Henley, 1977; Hesse-Biber, Leavy, Quinn, & Zoino, 2006; Unger & Crawford, 1996). In responding to pressures to "be sexy" and messages on "how to get or keep your guy" (see any issue of *Cosmopolitan*), girls and women sexualize and objectify themselves to attract men (Manning, Longmore, & Giordano, 2005). Yet, just as often, they are punished for partaking in these behaviors (Abrams, Viki, Masser, & Bohner, 2003; Aubrey, 2004; Pollard, 1992; Tavris & Wade, 1984)—the classic double-edged sword that arguably may be linked to the 13-year-old girl's life described previously. As the opportunity for sexual objectification expands, younger girls and women have increasingly fewer contexts in which they are ensured protection from this exposure, and thus may come to engage in self-objectification more regularly. If this logic holds, we should expect self-objectification to be increasing in younger and younger cohorts of girls. We must also continue to question why women are sexualized and objectified to such a greater extent than men and identify the deeper psychic processes that may be contributing to this phenomenon (see Chapter 4, this volume).

Another medium that warrants more attention with regard to self-objectification is music videos, which are overflowing with sexualized content (Baxter, De Riemer, Landini, Leslie, & Singletary, 1985; Gow, 1990; Sommers-Flanagan, Sommers-Flanagan, & Davis, 1993) and rely heavily on provocative clothing, sexual innuendos, and light physical contact to portray the women as sexually attractive and appealing to men (Arnett, 2002; Gow, 1996; Hansen & Hansen, 2000; Smith, 2005). Popular music videos and songs feature extremely graphic sexual images, content, and behavior with striking themes of violence and sexual coercion more closely resembling pornographic videos than music videos. Moreover, the men in these videos are often depicted as the dominant sexual actors, whereas the women are positioned as the sexual objects, often with themes of sexual violence and female degradation (Oliver & Hyde, 1993).

A recent study provided some preliminary evidence indicating that heavier consumption of music television predicts higher self-objectification among a community sample of adolescent girls, which, in turn, predicts a host of negative consequences, including lower body esteem, more anxiety and depressive symptoms, more dieting, and less confidence in math ability (Grabe & Hyde, 2009). Like other forms of media, the more often that people are exposed to music videos, the more tolerant they are of sexual harassment and the more likely they are to endorse sex role stereotypes and to view women as sex objects (Ward, 2002, 2003; Zhang, Miller, & Harrison, 2008). In addition to music videos, an analysis of the content of popular television shows, movies, magazines, newspapers, and music among adolescents found that sexual content is much more prevalent in popular music lyrics than in any other medium (Pardun, L'Engle, & Brown, 2005). It is important to note that recent longitudinal research among a large sample of ethnically diverse adolescents demonstrated that it is exposure to sexually degrading lyrics specifically (woman = sex object, man = insatiable sexual appetite), and not sexual lyrics in general, that predicts earlier initiation of advanced sexual behavior among both girls and boys (Martino et al., 2006). In summary, theory-driven research that incorporates longitudinal designs into real-world settings is needed to guide investigations into the extent and scope of the sexual objectification of girls and women, and the extent and scope of its impact on women and men.

Anonymous Other

Self-objectification is broadly conceptualized as the phenomenological experience of taking the self-perspective of an anonymous external other. Research on self-objectification rarely identifies or operationalizes the anonymous other, the proposed "generalized male witness" (Bartky, 1990) or the "eyes of the indeterminate observer" (Kaschak, 1992). Who constitutes the observer, and which gaze is internalized? Clarifying these theoretical and phenomenological components is important to advance research in this area. Anecdotally, some women report that they feel objectified by other women (not just by men) and that they focus on appearance in response to pressures from other women. This is very likely true to some extent. Yet, Bartky (1990) called this account of "feeling objectified" by other women into question, noting that "women know for whom this game is played" (p. 72). That is, women view other women, and not only themselves, through the lens of the male gaze. Some cross-sectional research has demonstrated that women do objectify other women, although it is not to the same degree that men objectify women. This is partially due to women's own self-objectification: Women who reported higher self-objectification were more likely to objectify other women (Strelan & Hargreaves, 2005). Because both men and women are socialized to view women as objects, it is also likely that heterosexual women's objectification of other women stems from competition and comparison between women on the basis of their attractiveness to men (Cowan & Ullman, 2006; Loya, Cowan, & Walters, 2006). Additional research is needed to better understand the internalization of cultural practices of sexual objectification, as well as its promotion and perpetuation of self-objectification.

The anonymity of the perpetrators of sexual objectification is also important to qualify in research on self-objectification. Sexual objectification by anonymous and impersonal others—sometimes referred to as stranger harassment—is more common than by nonstrangers (Gardner, 1995; Macmillan, Nierobisz, & Welsh, 2000), yet receives considerably less research and practical attention. An exception to this is research by Fairchild and Rudman (2008), which offered new evidence directly linking stranger harassment and self-objectification to women's greater fear and perceived risk of rape and indirectly to more restricted voluntary movement (e.g., walking alone, avoiding certain places). These researchers also demonstrated that if women responded actively to the harassment (e.g., confronted the harasser), then they were less likely to report higher self-objectification, suggesting that active coping strategies may protect some women against self-objectification. However, in this study the majority of the women endorsed passive coping strategies in response to stranger harassment. Notably, the fact that self-objectification was linked to women's fear of rape, which in turn was associated with their actual decisions about where to walk or what places to avoid, further informs the discussion about the perspective of this internalized other. Would women be afraid to walk in certain places alone because they anticipate the female gaze or being sexually objectified by women? This is certainly possible, and we would not argue that it never occurs; however, with respect to women's general attitudes and behavior around their personal safety, it is important to delineate the predominant source of these constraints.

Additional evidence for the constraints engaged by the anonymous other comes from a program of study on swimming participation among adolescent girls. In a series of focused interviews, adolescent girls reported embarrassment as a major determinant of the frequency and quality of their swimming participation (James, 2000). Although perhaps not uncommon among teenagers, it was the source of this embarrassment that warrants our attention. It was not uncommon for the girls to report the feeling of being watched and talked about while at the pool: "You can feel them looking at you" (James, 2000, p. 270). Beyond the fear of negative body evaluations, some girls reported limiting their actual swimming behavior to performing laps as opposed to more playful games to avoid negative commentary. A small subset of these girls reported no constraints on their swimming participation, but the majority of girls did limit their participation in some way. Many girls described different strategies for making themselves less visible, such as covering up their bodies, staying in groups, swimming at remote venues, and avoiding pools. James noted that a perceived constraint did not necessarily determine participation, and girls appeared to negotiate these barriers in creative and effective ways. Yet, this is another important context in which girls' bodies are subject to evaluative commentary that further undermines and limits their physical performance.

Although the specific audience that these girls referred to ranged from unfamiliar male peers to girlfriends or more popular girls, James (2000) argued that "all of these audiences are in a sense refracted through male eyes" (p. 275). Is it the male gaze that is internalized and the perspective from which women come to view themselves and others? Can this be distinguished from the female gaze, and if so, how? Are these "gazes" subsumed within in the wider cultural practices of sexually objectifying women's bodies, broadening the idea of the anonymous other to include any sexual objectification perpetuated by anyone? These are empirically testable questions that scholars in this area may endeavor to answer. We also know that there are individual differences in the extent to which women self-objectify (Fredrickson, Roberts, Noll, Quinn, & Twenge, 1998; McKinley & Hyde, 1996; Noll & Fredrickson, 1998), which suggests that sexual objectification does not affect all women equally. We know very little about women who have intentionally opted out of the "objectification limelight," but more investigation into how the internalization of sexually objectifying practices are differentially negotiated by women would be a useful direction for further research.

Harm and Violence

Objectification theory also delineates the wider forms of sexual objectification in Westernized patriarchal cultures—sexual victimization, harassment, violence, incest, and rape–that harm girls and women. The global magnitude and scope of violence against women cannot be overstated (Watts & Zimmerman, 2002): One in five women has been physically or sexually abused by a man at some time in her life (World Health Organization, 1997). Violence against women is the extreme end of the sexual objectification continuum. There is a paucity of research on the conceptual and empirical links between these more extreme forms of sexual objectification and self-objectification. Hill and Fischer (2008) examined the associations between several cultural practices of sexual objectification and women's self-objectification and self-surveillance. They found that only sexualized gazing and harassment were related to how much women self-objectify, whereas experiences of sexual assault (perpetrated by men or women) were not, suggesting that only certain forms of sexual objectification may be directly linked to how much women self-objectify. These findings are not inconsistent with objectification theory, however, which asserts that more extreme forms of sexual objectification may bypass self-objectification and lead directly to negative psychological consequences. More research is needed to investigate the psychic links between the extreme forms of sexually objectifying practices and self-objectification.

Extreme forms of sexual objectification also harm women through the eroticization of artificially modified (mutilated) female body parts (for a review, see Jeffreys, 2005). For example, the Karen women of upland Burma are known in Europe as "giraffe-necked" women because they are required to wear brass rings fixed around the neck starting as early as the age of 5 years and increasing to a total of 24 rings. Brass rings are also put on the arms and legs so that a woman might carry between 50 to 60 pounds of brass while walking long distances and working in the fields. This custom stretches the cervical muscles in the neck and pulls apart the neck vertebrae to such a degree that women's necks cannot support their own heads if the rings are removed (A. Fallon, 1990). The practice of foot binding in China dates back to at least 900 A.D. and continued into the 20th century (A. Fallon, 1990; Jeffreys, 2005). From as early as age 2, girls were forced to bind their toes to the soles of their feet and large stones were used to crush the arch (Chang, 1991). Adult women are permanently crippled; unable to walk normally, they must be carried or crawl to move.

Some scholars have argued that there are parallel practices for women in the West. Jeffreys (2005) compared labiaplasty procedures among Western women to female genital mutilation in non-Western cultures. Brownmiller (1975) described how some Western women amputated their small toes to fit their feet into smaller, more pointed shoes—known to increase short- and long-term feet deformities due to twisted ankles, strained backs, shortened tendons, torn ligaments, and injuries from uneven paths, pavement cracks, elevator grids, and sidewalk gratings. More empirical inquiry is needed to understand the extent to which other forms of sexual objectification lead to taking a view of the self as an object, potentially perpetuating a cycle of sexual and self-objectification.

Sexist Ideology

Consistent with Mary Wollstonecraft's observation over 2 centuries ago, this volume integrates scientific evidence demonstrating that sexual objectification may operate in such a way to limit women's social roles and opportunities because it reminds and encourages women to police themselves, chronically self-monitoring and self-correcting to match accepted social norms and values. In line with this perspective, Bordo (1993) noted that the "social manipulation of the female body [has] emerged as an absolutely central strategy in the maintenance of power relations between the sexes over the past hundred years" (p. 143). Thus, self-objectification reflects a view of oneself through the veil of sexism (Fredrickson et al., 1998). A truly comprehensive theory of the objectification of women must identify and propose testable hypotheses about the origins of sexual and self-objectification.

Some empirical research has taken up this charge. In three social psychological experiments, Calogero and Jost (2010) found that subtle exposure to benevolently sexist stereotypes increased women's—but not men's—self-surveillance and body shame. Further, women's behavioral intentions, at least in the short term, involved more appearance-management behavior following exposure to benevolent sexism. Building on evidence that indicates a chronic appearance focus appropriates those physical, psychological, and financial resources necessary for achievement and healthy social interaction (Bordo, 1993; Breines, Crocker, & Garcia, 2008; P. Fallon, Katzman & Wooley, 1994; Fredrickson et al., 1998; Moradi & Huang, 2008; Tiggemann & Rothblum, 1997; Zones, 2000), these findings suggest that self-objectification serves to justify and maintain a system of gender inequality. Further, these findings implicate an imbalance of social power in women's self-objectification, which is consistent with prior scholarship in the area of women's objectification (Chapter 1, this volume). Experimental designs that vary the degree to which women feel powerful or powerless would be one way to test directly the effect of power on self-objectification (see Galinsky, Magee, Inesi, & Gruenfeld, 2006; Gruenfeld, Inesi, Magee, & Galinsky, 2008) and would seem to be an important direction for future research.

Situating self-objectification as a function of broader sexist ideology that subsumes particular incidents of sexual objectification widens the scope of prevention and intervention strategies and targets. More research is needed that integrates objectification theory with other social psychological frameworks, particularly within the social psychology of gender (Rudman & Glick, 2008), to investigate how structural and group-level dynamics and processes influence and perpetuate self-objectification. Assessing the direct impact of sexist ideology on self-objectification will be important for understanding the full range of adverse outcomes for women.

CONSEQUENCES

Self-objectification has been linked to other subjective experiences in women: more negative attitudes toward the body's reproductive functioning, such as breastfeeding (Johnston-Robledo & Fred, 2008; Johnston-Robledo,

Sheffield, Voigt, & Wilcox-Constantine, 2007) and menstruation (Roberts, 2004); more appearance-based and extreme exercise attitudes and behaviors (Hallsworth, Wade, & Tiggemann, 2005; Melbye, Tenenbaum, & Eklund, 2007; Prichard & Tiggemann, 2005); smoking (Harrell, Fredrickson, Pomerleau, & Nolen-Hoeksema, 2006); greater hostility toward other women (Loya et al., 2006); and self-harming behavior (Muehlenkamp, Swanson, & Brausch, 2005). All of these consequences represent critical aspects of women's health and well-being and warrant more research to replicate and clarify the effects.

Self-Harm

In particular, the role of self-objectification in women's self-harming behavior warrants deeper consideration. The definition of self-harming behavior includes cutting, burning, hitting or biting, head banging, excessive scratching, hair pulling, interfering with wound care, breaking bones, chewing (lips, cheeks, tongue, fingers), ingestion or insertion of toxic or sharp objects, excessive sun burning, and unnecessary surgeries (McGilley, 2004). Self-objectification may indirectly contribute to self-harm as a result of negative regard for the body and body alienation. For some scholars, this association is not surprising. Pipher (1994) stated that "self-mutilation can be seen as a concrete interpretation of our culture's injunction to young women to carve themselves into culturally acceptable pieces" (p. 157). In a large sample of American college women, Muehlenkamp et al. (2005) found empirical support for an indirect link between self-surveillance and self-harm: Self-surveillance predicted negative body regard, which predicted depressive symptoms, which, in turn, predicted more self-harming behaviors (e.g., cutting, burning). Although only preliminary, these results implicate self-surveillance in women's emotional distress and physical harm toward their own bodies. More empirical tests of these links are imperative.

We also wish to emphasize the role of self-objectification in self-harming behavior as defined by unnecessary surgeries. The tremendous increase in elective cosmetic procedures (surgical and minimally invasive) over the past decade or so is primarily due to the disproportionately higher number of female patients who sought these treatments: 91% of these procedures are routinely performed on women, whereas 9% are performed on men (American Society of Plastic Surgeons, 2009). This high percentage of women undergoing cosmetic surgery is particularly troubling because of the numerous deleterious consequences associated with these procedures, which are well known among cosmetic surgeons but virtually unknown among the general population, such as chronic pain, deadly infections, gangrene, nerve damage, loss of sensation, mutilated body parts, amputation, reoperation, cancer detection difficulty, suicide, and death (Haiken, 1997; Jeffreys, 2005; McLaughlin, Wise, & Lipworth, 2004;

Wolf, 1991; Zones, 2000). Arguably, chronic experiences of being viewed and treated as an object for the pleasure of others, and coming to view oneself as a measurable and malleable object for this use, might encourage women to support even further objectification of their bodies by electing to perform unnecessary surgical procedures on them. A recent study supported this reasoning: More interpersonal experiences of sexual objectification, self-surveillance, and body shame among women predicted greater psychological support for cosmetic surgery, even after accounting for general levels of self-esteem and self-presentation concerns (Calogero, Pina, Park, & Rahemtulla, 2010). In summary, the association between self-objectification and self-harm in women deserves much more scholarship and action.

Safety Anxiety

The earlier discussions on the role of stranger harassment and harm and violence against women in the perpetuation of self-objectification speak to an understudied component of objectification theory: the relationship between self-objectification and safety anxiety. Women's appearance focus includes concerns about safety and threats to the self because of the greater potential for women to experience sexual victimization and sexually motivated bodily harm (Brownmiller, 1975). When asked to describe what they do on any given day to maintain their personal safety, women list multiple strategies (e.g., checking backseat of car, holding keys between fingers in defensive position, pretending to talk on cell phone), whereas men list very few strategies for ensuring their personal safety on a daily basis (Fredrickson & Roberts, 1997). Thus, maintaining a chronic vigilance about both physical appearance and physical safety creates many more opportunities for women than men to experience anxiety.

To date, there has been virtually no examination of the proposition in objectification theory that women's experiences of self-objectification are linked to greater safety anxiety (Fredrickson & Roberts, 1997). A recent program of research has begun to address this gap by constructing and validating a new measure of personal safety anxiety for women (Calogero & Pina, 2010a) and examining the role of safety anxiety within an objectification theory framework (Calogero & Pina, 2010b). For example, Calogero and Pina (2010b) found that more frequent experiences of being viewed and treated as a collection of sexual parts predicted greater self-surveillance and worry about physical safety among women, and, in turn, physical safety anxiety predicted more sexual dysfunction, disordered eating, and depressive symptoms. Other research has shown that having more experiences of sexual objectification and the resultant safety anxiety is associated with women's greater use of personal safety strategies, but also greater endorsement of rape myths that cast women as responsible for (and therefore in control of) their own sexual harm (Calogero, Pina, & Sutton, 2010). Future research would advance objectification theory by examining safety anxiety and safety behavior in the context of women's sexual and self-objectification.

Opting Out

Self-objectification may also be linked to women physically opting out of a multitude of life experiences. Etcoff, Orbach, Scott, and D'Agostino (2006) reported that 67% of women ages 15 to 64 years across 10 countries actually withdraw from life-engaging, life-sustaining activities because they feel bad about their looks. Such activities include giving an opinion, meeting friends, exercising, going to work, going to school, dating, and going to the doctor. In a study of 52,677 heterosexual adult readers of *Elle* magazine ages 18 to 65, women reported greater dissatisfaction with their appearance and were more likely than men to avoid situations in which their bodies were on display (Frederick, Peplau, & Lever, 2006). Longitudinal research that traces the avoidance and opting out of life experiences, as well as thoughtfully constructed experimental designs, are essential for testing the effect of self-objectification on women's withdrawal from important life activities and domains.

COUNTERACTIONS

As researchers have begun to understand the specific consequences of sexual and self-objectification, questions have been raised about appropriate methods for addressing and changing these practices to reduce, and ultimately prevent, these negative consequences. Tylka and Augustus-Horvath (Chapter 9, this volume) offered an array of strategies and techniques for preventing self-objectification at the individual level and challenging cultural practices of sexual objectification. An important avenue for future research would be to subject these prevention and intervention approaches aimed at disrupting sexual and self-objectification to empirical testing. Menzel and Levine (Chapter 8, this volume) showcased one particular setting in which more research is needed: athletic environments and other physical contexts wherein women's bodies are the instrument and the vehicle through which they must perform. How might athletic involvement help or hinder women's experience of embodiment? Does embodiment protect girls and women against sexual and self-objectification, and if so, how?

Drawing from McKinley's work (Chapter 5, this volume), at what life stages would these proposed prevention and intervention approaches work most effectively? At what life stage must embodiment be experienced or internalized to effectively counter sexual and self-objectification? Critically, the targets of these counteractions must also include men. Indeed, an important focus for research in this area might be to investigate how men's sexual objectification of women can be reduced and disrupted. Changing men's views of women as sex objects would be beneficial to men's individual health and well-being, as well as enhancing the intimacy and quality of relationships with women (Chapter 9, this volume). In summary, there is a dearth of research on how to intervene and modify self-objectification in girls and women. This is another area in which empirical investigations are sorely needed.

DIVERSITY

Objectification theory is based on understanding the experiences of girls and women. This focus on girls and women does not deny that boys and men experience sexual and self-objectification. Indeed, those men who do self-objectify also report more body shame and disordered eating (Hebl, King, & Lin, 2004; Martins, Tiggemann, & Kirkbride, 2007; Tiggemann & Kuring, 2004), and the objectification of men in media is known to be on the rise (Luciano, 2007). We would argue, though, that the immediate application of current objectification theory to men's experiences is not warranted. Some scholars have applied objectification theory to men without fully considering the sexual objectification framework within which the experience of self-objectification is set to occur. Research with gay men supports this point: Gay men report markedly higher self-objectification than heterosexual men (Martins et al., 2007). Consistent with objectification theory, gay men are more likely to objectify in situations in which they experience sexual objectification by other men or anticipate the male gaze, and thus their higher self-objectification scores represent a striving to maintain a satisfying and pleasing appearance to men (Siever, 1994). Heterosexual men, generally speaking, do not feel sexually objectified by other men (Strelan & Hargreaves, 2005). When men feel sexually objectified by women, they do not seem to respond as negatively. In short, there are other psychological variables that are likely to be much more relevant to men's body-self relations. However, the nature of men's experiences of sexual objectification—or the lack thereof—represents an equally important way in which men experience their own bodies within a patriarchal system. Research is sorely needed to determine how the variability in the presence or absence of sexual objectification, and the attendant self-objectification, may lead men and women to take different perspectives on their bodies.

Objectification theory is largely based on the experiences of White heterosexual women and tested with samples composed predominantly of White, heterosexual, college-educated women, greatly limiting our understanding of the experience of self-objectification among women of color, lesbian women, and women over the age of 25. By virtue of sharing the biological reality of a female body, it is assumed that girls and women of all orientations and backgrounds will experience a shared set of psychological experiences from living within a sexually objectifying cultural milieu. We are lacking sufficient evidence for both the similarities and differences in self-objectification across diverse groups of women.

Some research suggests there are both similarities and differences in self-objectification between White women and women of color (Harrison & Fredrickson, 2003). In an experimental study of self-objectification among college students, women of color (Hispanic, Asian, and African American) reported levels of self-objectification similar to that of White women, but African American women reported significantly less state self-objectification when wearing a swimsuit compared with White women (Hebl et al., 2004), although the same pattern of relations between self-objectification, body shame, and disordered eating was observed. More recent research suggests that the objectification theory framework is applicable to African American women, but the patterns of relations between self-objectification and the proposed outcomes would be clarified by the use of more relevant assessment tools and constructs (Mitchell & Mazzeo, 2009). Investigating the applicability and utility of objectification theory for understanding the experiences of women of color in Westernized societies should be a high priority in the next decade of objectification research.

The evidence is also mixed for lesbian women (Hill & Fischer, 2008; Kozee & Tylka, 2006). For example, Hill and Fischer (2008) demonstrated that more frequent experiences of being gazed at, evaluated, and harassed were associated with higher self-objectification for both heterosexual and lesbian women, suggesting that living in a shared culture in which women are sexually objectified leaves all women open to experiences of sexual and self-objectification. They also found that heterosexual and lesbian women did not differ in frequency of being gazed at and harassed or in self-objectification as measured by the Self-Objectification Questionnaire, but lesbian women did report significantly less self-surveillance than heterosexual women.

Research on self-objectification in women who may depart further from the sexualized ideals of feminine beauty—due to disfigurement, disability, age, or social class—is even more limited (Augustus-Horvath & Tylka, 2009; Dillaway, 2005; Moradi & Rottenstein, 2007). Investigation of sexual and self-objectification across diverse groups of girls and women is sorely needed. In addition, empirical tests of objectification theory are largely based on the experiences of women in Westernized societies, primarily North American, British, and Australian women. More research is needed to fully understand the prevalence, type, and implications of sexual and self-objectification in other cultures, because these patterns should not be assumed to be the same (e.g., Crawford et al., 2009). In studies with nonnative English speakers, measures will need to be translated with care that the content of the items is not lost through misinterpretation, and new psychometric analyses will need to be conducted. Collection of such personal data may be difficult in some countries where the society is less open to women's rights and dominated by a more patriarchal political system. However, such studies are likely to yield essential and important findings that will expand our awareness of the importance of objectification and how it works in different societies.

CODA

A diverse range of scholars, with diverse perspectives, have offered integrative and innovative ideas about sexual and self-objectification throughout this volume. We look forward to reading future research that will further inform this area and effectively challenge the sexual objectification of women and the resultant self-objectification. We hope that this array of chapters will offer a call to arms to those interested in the areas of objectification of girls and women from a wide range of disciplines, including sociology, psychology, medicine, and public policy areas. There is no longer any doubt that many females, of diverse ages, ethnicities, and nationalities, are exposed to the psychologically harmful effects of being viewed as less than whole people. Our great hope is that this volume leads to many more conversations, research, and treatises on this issue.

REFERENCES

Abrams, D., Viki, G. T. N., Masser, B., & Bohner, G. (2003). Perceptions of stranger and acquaintance rape: The role of benevolent and hostile sexism in victim blame and rape proclivity. *Journal of Personality and Social Psychology, 84,* 111–125. doi:10.1037/0022-3514.84.1.111

Arnett, J. J. (2002). The sounds of sex: Sex in teens' music and music videos. In J. Brown, K. Walsh-Childers, & J. Steele (Eds.), *Sexual teens, sexual media* (pp. 253–264). Hillsdale, NJ: Erlbaum.

American Society of Plastic Surgeons. (2009). *2009 report of the 2008 statistics: National clearinghouse of plastic surgery statistics.* Retrieved from http://www.plasticsurgery. org/Media/stats/2008-US-cosmetic-reconstructive-plastic-surgery-minimally-invasive-statistics.pdf

Aubrey, J. S. (2004). Sex and punishment: An examination of sexual consequences and the sexual double standard in teen programming. *Sex Roles, 50*, 505–514. doi:10.1023/B:SERS.0000023070.87195.07

Augustus-Horvath, C. L., & Tylka, T. L. (2009). A test and extension of objectification theory as it predicts disordered eating: Does women's age matter? *Journal of Counseling Psychology, 56*, 253–265. doi:10.1037/a0014637

Bartky, S. (1990). *Femininity and domination: Studies in the phenomenology of oppression.* New York, NY: Routledge.

Baxter, L., De Riemer, C., Landini, A., Leslie, L., & Singletary, M. (1985). A content analysis of music videos. *Journal of Broadcasting & Electronic Media, 29*, 333–340.

Bordo, S. (1993). *Unbearable weight: Feminism, Western culture, and the body.* Berkeley, CA: University of California Press.

Breines, J. G., Crocker, J., & Garcia, J. A. (2008). Self-objectification and well-being in women's daily lives. *Personality and Social Psychology Bulletin, 34*, 583–598. doi:10.1177/0146167207313727

Brosius, H.-B., Weaver, J. B., & Staab, J. F. (1993). Exploring the social and sexual reality of contemporary pornography. *Journal of Sex Research, 30*, 161–170. doi:10.1080/00224499309551697

Brownmiller, S. (1975). *Against our will: Men, women, and rape.* New York, NY: Simon & Schuster.

Calogero, R. M., & Jost, J. T. (2010). *Exposure to sexist ideology, self-objectification, and the protective function of the need to avoid closure.* Manuscript submitted for publication.

Calogero, R. M., & Pina, A. (2010a). *Development and validation of the Physical Safety Anxiety Scale among university women.* Manuscript submitted for publication.

Calogero, R. M., & Pina, A. (2010b). *Physicality and safety as dual components of appearance anxiety in the objectification theory framework.* Manuscript submitted for publication.

Calogero, R. M., Pina, A., Park, L. E., & Rahemtulla, Z. (2010). Sexual and self-objectification predict college women's attitudes toward cosmetic surgery. *Sex Roles.* Advance online publication. doi:10.1007/s11199-010-9759-5

Calogero, R. M., Pina, A., & Sutton, R. M. (2010). *Extending the scope of objectification theory: Women's paradoxical reports of physical threat in the context of sexual objectification.* Manuscript in preparation.

Chang, J. (1991). *Wild swans: Three daughters of China.* New York, NY: Simon & Schuster.

Cowan, G., Lee, C., Levy, D., & Snyder, D. (1988). Dominance and inequality in X-rated videocassettes. *Psychology of Women Quarterly, 12*, 299–311.

Cowan, G., & Ullman, J. B. (2006). A structural model of women's hostility toward women. *Psychology of Women Quarterly, 30*, 399–409.

Crawford, M., Lee, I.-C., Portnoy, G., Gurung, A., Khati, D., Jha, P., & Regmi, A. C. (2009). Objectified body consciousness in a developing country: A comparison of mothers and daughters in the US and Nepal. *Sex Roles*, *60*, 174–185. doi:10. 1007/s11199-008-9521-4

de Beauvoir, S. (1989). *The second sex* (H. M. Parshley, Trans.). New York, NY: Vintage Books. (Original work published 1952)

Dillaway, H. (2005). (Un)changing menopausal bodies: How women think and act in the face of a reproductive transition and gendered beauty ideals. *Sex Roles*, *53*, 1–17. doi:10.1007/s11199-005-4269-6

Ertel, H. (1990). *Erotika und Pornographie: Repräsentative Befra-gung und psychophysi-ologische Langzeitstudie zu Konsum und Wirkung* [Erotica and pornography: Representative survey and psychophysiological longitudinal study on the consumption and effects of pornography]. Munich, Germany: PVU.

Etcoff, N., Orbach, S., Scott, J., & D'Agostino, H. (2006). *Beyond stereotypes: Rebuilding the foundation of beauty beliefs: Findings of the 2005 Dove Global Study*. Retrieved from http://www.campaignforrealbeauty.com/DoveBeyondStereo typesWhitePaper.pdf

Fairchild, K., & Rudman, L. A. (2008). Everyday stranger harassment and women's objectification. *Social Justice Research*, *21*, 338–357. doi:10.1007/s11211-008-0073-0

Fallon, A. (1990). Culture in the mirror: Sociocultural determinants of body image. In T. F. Cash & T. Pruzinsky (Eds.), *Body images: Development, deviance, and change* (pp. 80–109). New York, NY: Guilford Press.

Fallon, P., Katzman, M. A., & Wooley, S. (1994). *Feminist perspectives on eating disorders*. New York, NY: Guilford Press.

Frederick, D. A., Peplau, L. A., & Lever, J. (2006). The swimsuit issue: Correlates of body image in a sample of 52,677 heterosexual adults. *Body Image*, *3*, 413–419. doi:10.1016/j.bodyim.2006.08.002

Fredrickson, B. L., & Roberts, T. A. (1997). Objectification theory: Toward understanding women's lived experience and mental health risks. *Psychology of Women Quarterly*, *21*, 173–206. doi:10.1111/j.1471-6402.1997.tb00108.x

Fredrickson, B. L., Roberts, T. A., Noll, S. M., Quinn, D. M., & Twenge, J. M. (1998). That swimsuit becomes you: Sex differences in self-objectification, restrained eating, and math performance. *Journal of Personality and Social Psychology*, *75*, 269–284. doi:10.1037/0022-3514.75.1.269

Galinsky, A. D., Magee, J. C., Inesi, M. E., & Gruenfeld, D. H. (2006). Power and perspectives not taken. *Psychological Science*, *17*, 1068–1074. doi:10.1111/j.1467-9280.2006.01824.x

Gardner, C. B. (1995). *Passing by: Gender and public harassment*. Berkeley, CA: University of California Press.

Gow, J. (1990). The relationship between violent and sexual images and the popularity of music videos. *Popular Music and Society*, *14*, 1–10.

Gow, J. (1996). Reconsidering gender roles on MTV: Depictions in the most popular music videos of the early 1990s. *Communication Reports*, *9*, 151–161.

Grabe, S., & Hyde, J. S. (2009). Body objectification, MTV, and psychological outcomes among female adolescents. *Journal of Applied Social Psychology, 39,* 2840–2858. doi:10.1111/j.1559-1816.2009.00552.x

Gruenfeld, D. H., Inesi, M. E., Magee, J. C., & Galinsky, A. D. (2008). Power and the objectification of social targets. *Journal of Personality and Social Psychology, 95,* 111–127. doi:10.1037/0022-3514.95.1.111

Haiken, E. (1997). *Venus envy: A history of cosmetic surgery.* Baltimore, MD: Johns Hopkins University Press.

Hallsworth, L., Wade, T., & Tiggemann, M. (2005). Individual differences in male body image: An examination of self-objectification in recreational body builders. *British Journal of Health Psychology, 10,* 453–465. doi:10.1348/135910705X26966

Hansen, C. H., & Hansen, R. D. (2000). Music and music videos. In D. Zillman & P. Vorderer (Eds.), *Media entertainment: The psychology of its appeal* (pp. 175–196). Mahwah, NJ: Erlbaum.

Harrell, Z. A., Fredrickson, B. L., Pomerleau, C. S., & Nolen-Hoeksema, S. (2006). The role of trait self-objectification in smoking among college women. *Sex Roles, 54,* 735–743. doi:10.1007/s11199-006-9041-z

Harrison, K., & Fredrickson, B. L. (2003). Women's sports media, self-objectification, and mental health in Black and White adolescent females. *Journal of Communication, 53,* 216–232. doi:10.1111/j.1460-2466.2003.tb02587.x

Hebl, M. R., King, E. B., & Lin, J. (2004). The swimsuit becomes us all: Ethnicity, gender, and vulnerability to self-objectification. *Personality and Social Psychology Bulletin, 30,* 1322–1331. doi:10.1177/0146167204264052

Henley, N. (1977). *Body politics.* Englewood Cliffs, NJ: Prentice-Hall.

Hesse-Biber, S., Leavy, P., Quinn, C. E., & Zoino, J. (2006). The mass marketing of disordered eating and eating disorders: The social psychology of women, thinness, and culture. *Women's Studies International Forum, 29,* 208–224. doi:10.1016/j.wsif.2006.03.007

Hill, M. S., & Fischer, A. R. (2008). Examining objectification theory: Lesbian and heterosexual women's experiences with sexual and self-objectification. *Counseling Psychologist, 36,* 745–776. doi:10.1177/0011000007301669

James, K. (2000). "You can feel them looking at you": The experience of adolescent girls at swimming pools. *Journal of Leisure Research, 32,* 262–280.

Jeffreys, S. (2005). *Beauty and misogyny: Harmful cultural practices in the West.* New York, NY: Routledge.

Johnston-Robledo, I., & Fred, V. (2008). Self-objectification and lower income pregnant women's breastfeeding attitudes. *Journal of Applied Social Psychology, 38,* 1–21.

Johnston-Robledo, I., Sheffield, K., Voigt, J., & Wilcox-Constantine, J. (2007). Reproductive shame: Self-objectification and young women's attitudes toward their reproductive functioning. *Women & Health, 46,* 25–39. doi:10.1300/J013v46n01_03

Kaschak, E. (1992). *Engendered lives: A new psychology of women's experience*. New York, NY: Basic Books.

Kozee, H. B., & Tylka, T. L. (2006). A test of objectification theory with lesbian women. *Psychology of Women Quarterly, 30*, 348–357. doi:10.1111/j.1471-6402.2006.00310.x

Loya, B. N., Cowan, G., & Walters, C. (2006). The role of social comparison and body consciousness in women's hostility toward other women. *Sex Roles, 54*, 575–583. doi:10.1007/s11199-006-9024-0

Luciano, L. (2007). Muscularity and masculinity in the United States: A historical overview. In J. K. Thompson & G. Cafri (Eds.), *The muscular ideal: Psychological, social, and medical perspectives* (pp. 41–65). Washington, DC: American Psychological Association. doi:10.1037/11581-002

Macmillan, R., Nierobisz, A., & Welsh, S. (2000). Experiencing the streets: Harassment and perceptions of safety among women. *Journal of Research in Crime and Delinquency, 37*, 306–322. doi:10.1177/0022427800037003003

Manning, W. D., Longmore, M. A., & Giordano, P. C. (2005). Adolescents' involvement in non-romantic sexual activity. *Social Science Research, 34*, 384–407. doi:10.1016/j.ssresearch.2004.03.001

Martino, S. C., Collins, R. L., Elliot, M. N., Strachman, A., Kanouse, D. E., & Berry, S. H. (2006). Exposure to degrading versus nondegrading music lyrics and sexual behavior among youth. *Pediatrics, 118*, e430–e441. doi:10.1542/peds.2006-0131

Martins, Y., Tiggemann, M., & Kirkbride, A. (2007). Those Speedos become them: The role of self-objectification in gay and heterosexual men's body image. *Personality and Social Psychology Bulletin, 33*, 634–647. doi:10.1177/0146167206297403

McGilley, B. H. (2004). Feminist perspectives on self-harm behaviors and eating disorders. In J. Levitt, R. Sansone, & L. Cohn (Eds.), *Self-harm behavior and eating disorders: Dynamics, assessment and treatment* (pp. 75–92). New York, NY: Brunner-Routledge.

McKinley, N. M., & Hyde, J. S. (1996). The Objectified Body Consciousness Scale: Development and validation. *Psychology of Women Quarterly, 20*, 181–215. doi:10.1111/j.1471-6402.1996.tb00467.x

McLaughlin, J. K., Wise, T. N., & Lipworth, L. (2004). Increased risk of suicide among patients with breast implants: Do the epidemiologic data support psychiatric consultation? *Psychosomatics, 45*, 277–280. doi:10.1176/appi.psy.45.4.277

Meacham, A. (2009, November 29). Sexting-related bullying cited in Hillsborough teen's suicide. *St. Petersburg Times*. Retrieved from http://www.tampabay.com/news/humaninterest/article1054895.ece

Melbye, L., Tenenbaum, G., & Eklund, R. (2007). Self-objectification and exercise behaviors: The mediating role of social physique anxiety. *Journal of Applied Biobehavioral Research, 12*, 196–220. doi:10.1111/j.1751-9861.2008.00021.x

Mitchell, K. S., & Mazzeo, S. E. (2009). Evaluation of a structural model of objectification theory and eating disorder symptomatology among European American and African American undergraduate women. *Psychology of Women Quarterly, 33,* 384–395. doi:10.1111/j.1471-6402.2009.01516.x

Moradi, B., & Huang, Y.-P. (2008). Objectification theory and psychology of women: A decade of advances and future directions. *Psychology of Women Quarterly, 32,* 377–398. doi:10.1111/j.1471-6402.2008.00452.x

Moradi, B., & Rottenstein, A. (2007). Objectification theory and deaf cultural identity attitudes: Roles in deaf women's eating disorder symptomatology. *Journal of Counseling Psychology, 54,* 178–188.

Muehlenkamp, J. J., Swanson, J. D., & Brausch, A. M. (2005). Self-objectification, risk taking, and self-harm in college women. *Psychology of Women Quarterly, 29,* 24–32. doi:10.1111/j.1471-6402.2005.00164.x

Noll, S. M., & Fredrickson, B. L. (1998). A mediational model linking self-objectification, body shame, and disordered eating. *Psychology of Women Quarterly, 22,* 623–636. doi:10.1111/j.1471-6402.1998.tb00181.x

Oliver, M. B., & Hyde, J. S. (1993). Gender differences in sexuality: A meta-analysis. *Psychological Bulletin, 114,* 29–51. doi:10.1037/0033-2909.114.1.29

Pardun, C. J., L'Engle, K. L., & Brown, J. D. (2005). Linking exposure to outcomes: Early adolescents' consumption of sexual content in six media. *Mass Communication & Society, 8,* 75–91. doi:10.1207/s15327825mcs0802_1

Paul, P. (2005). *Pornified: How pornography is transforming our lives, our relationships, and our families.* New York, NY: Times Books.

Pipher, M. (1994). *Reviving Ophelia: Saving the selves of adolescent girls.* New York, NY: Ballantine Books.

Pollard, P. (1992). Judgments about victims and attackers in depicted rapes: A review. *British Journal of Social Psychology, 31,* 307–326.

Prichard, I., & Tiggemann, M. (2005). Objectification in fitness centers: Self-objectification, body dissatisfaction, and disordered eating in aerobic instructors and aerobic participants. *Sex Roles, 53,* 19–28. doi:10.1007/s11199-005-4270-0

Roberts, T. A. (2004). Female trouble: The menstrual self-evaluation scale and women's self-objectification. *Psychology of Women Quarterly, 28,* 22–26. doi:10.1111/j.1471-6402.2004.00119.x

Rudman, L. A., & Glick, P. (2008). *The social psychology of gender: How power and intimacy shape gender relations.* New York, NY: Guilford Press.

Siever, M. D. (1994). Sexual orientation and gender as factors in socioculturally acquired vulnerability to body dissatisfaction and eating disorders. *Journal of Consulting and Clinical Psychology, 62,* 252–260. doi:10.1037/0022-006X.62.2.252

Smith, S. L. (2005). From Dr. Dre to Dismissed: Assessing violence, sex, and substance use on MTV. *Critical Studies in Media Communication, 22,* 89–98. doi:10.1080/0739318042000333743

Sommers-Flanagan, R., Sommers-Flanagan, J., & Davis, B. (1993). What's happening on music television? A gender role content analysis. *Sex Roles, 28,* 745–753. doi:10.1007/BF00289991

Strelan, P., & Hargreaves, D. (2005). Women who objectify other women: The vicious circle of objectification? *Sex Roles, 52*, 707–712. doi:10.1007/s11199-005-3737-3

Tavris, C., & Wade, C. (1984). *The longest war* (2nd ed.). San Diego, CA: Harcourt Brace Jovanovich.

Tiggemann, M., & Kuring, J. K. (2004). The role of body objectification in disordered eating and depressed mood. *British Journal of Clinical Psychology, 43*, 299–311. doi:10.1348/0144665031752925

Tiggemann, M., & Rothblum, E. D. (1997). Gender differences in internal beliefs about weight and negative attitudes towards self and others. *Psychology of Women Quarterly, 21*, 581–593. doi:10.1111/j.1471-6402.1997.tb00132.x

Unger, R., & Crawford, M. (1996). *Women and gender: A feminist psychology* (2nd ed.). New York, NY: McGraw-Hill.

Ward, L. M. (2002). Does television exposure affect emerging adults' attitudes and assumptions about sexual relationships? Correlational and experimental confirmation. *Journal of Youth and Adolescence, 24*, 595–615. doi:10.1007/BF01537058

Ward, L. M. (2003). Understanding the role of entertainment media in the sexual socialization of American youth: A review of empirical research. *Developmental Review, 23*, 347–388. doi:10.1016/S0273-2297(03)00013-3

Watts, C., & Zimmerman, C. (2002). Violence against women: Global scope and magnitude. *Lancet, 359*, 1232–1237. doi:10.1016/S0140-6736(02)08221-1

Wolf, N. (1991). *The beauty myth.* New York, NY: Morrow.

World Health Organization, Department of Injuries and Violence Prevention. (1997). *WHO violence against women information pack.* Retrieved from http://www.who.int/violence_injury_prevention/vaw/infopack.htm

Zhang, Y., Miller, L. E., & Harrison, K. (2008). The relationship between exposure to sexual music videos and young adults' sexual attitudes. *Journal of Broadcasting & Electronic Media, 52*, 368–386. doi:10.1080/08838150802205462

Zones, J. S. (2000). Beauty myths and realities and their impacts on women's health. In M. B. Zinn, P. Hondagneu-Sotelo, & M. Messner (Eds.), *Gender through the prism of difference* (2nd ed., pp. 87–103). Boston, MA: Allyn & Bacon.

INDEX

United Nations, 11

Validity, 30
Vanity Fair, 83
Variables, temporal sequencing of,
    152–153
Victimization, sexual, 227–228
Videos, music, 220–221
Violence, 58, 223–224
Vulnerability, 57

Ward, L., 7
Ward, L. M., 86
Ward, M., 92
Waters, P. L., 90
Watson, N., 43, 131
Web pages, pornographic, 219–220
Weight class sports, 177n2
Weight-focused sports, 177n2
Weight gain, 107
Weightism, 204–207
Wesselink, P., 60
Westernized societies
    breast-feeding in, 83–84
    individual differences in self-
        objectification, 139–140
    mutilation/modification of women's
        bodies in, 224
    objectification in, 4, 7
    physical attractiveness in, 31
Wicklund, R. A., 129
Wiederman, M. W., 146
Williams, C. L., 67
Wolf, N., 6, 86, 109
Wollstonecraft, M., 3, 9
Women
    biological stages of, 107–108
    desexualization of, 108
    fear of rape in, 222
    Karen/Burmese, 224
    life-and-death giving "powers" of,
        78

objectification of, by other women,
    88, 221–222
of older age, 106–107
oppression of, 57
relationships with other women,
    193–194
safety anxiety in, 227–228
self-harm in, 226–227
sexual harassment of, 6
sexuality of, 56, 87
stereotypes about. *See* Stereotypes
    about women
strategies to fight self-objectification,
    188–190
violence against, 58, 223–224
vulnerability of, 57
young adult, 103–105, 110
Women's bodies
    acceptance of, 92–93
    activities of, 81–85
    attributes of, 24–26
    changing of, 132
    distancing from, 85–87
    dual reactions to, 77–78
    gendering of, 102–103
    honoring of, 196–197, 200–201
    ideals of beauty for, 8–9
    and mainstream media, 6–7
    monitoring appearance of. *See*
        Appearance monitoring
    mutilation/modification of, 224
    positive attitudes toward, 92–93
    respect for, 199–200
    self-objectification as solution to,
        88–89
    as social/economic currency, 88, 220
    social norms for, 53–54
    as target of male gaze, 6–7
Workplace, 65

Yoga, 92, 200
Young, I. M., 86

ABOUT THE EDITORS

Rachel M. Calogero, PhD, is an assistant professor of psychology at Virginia Wesleyan College in Norfolk. She completed her PhD in social psychology in 2007 at the University of Kent in Canterbury, England, where she subsequently held a postdoctoral research fellowship funded by the Economic and Social Research Council. Dr. Calogero has published and presented extensively on self-objectification in women, with particular interest in the environmental and sociocultural antecedents of self-objectification. Her research also includes investigations of sexist ideology, fat prejudice, disordered eating and exercise practices, and closed-mindedness. As a social psychologist, her interests include an analysis of the sociocultural, social–cognitive, and self-processes that contribute to the legitimization of oppressive social practices.

Stacey Tantleff-Dunn, PhD, is an associate professor of psychology at the University of Central Florida. She received her BA from George Washington University in 1989 and her PhD in clinical psychology from the University of South Florida in 1995. Dr. Tantleff-Dunn joined the faculty at the University of Central Florida in 1996 and founded the Laboratory for the Study of Eating, Appearance, and Health. Her research area is body image, particularly interpersonal and media influences on body image. Her research and clinical work include a focus on interpersonal psychotherapy, particularly as they relate to body image, eating disturbance, and obesity. Dr. Tantleff-Dunn is coauthor of *Exacting Beauty: Theory, Assessment and Treatment of Body Image Disturbance*, and she serves on the editorial boards of *Body Image: An International Journal of Research* and *Eating Disorders: The Journal of Treatment and Prevention*. She has over 15 years of clinical experience providing direct services and supervision of assessment and psychotherapy for individuals, couples, and families.

J. Kevin Thompson, PhD, is a professor of psychology at the University of South Florida in Tampa. His research interests include body image, eating disorders, and obesity. He has been an associate editor of *Body Image: An International Journal of Research* since 2003 and has been on the editorial board of the *International Journal of Eating Disorders* since 1990. He has authored, coauthored, edited, or coedited eight previous books in the areas of body image, eating disorders, and obesity.